Tae Kwon Do Pakistan

Volume I

The Martial Art of Tae Kwon Do and its Historical

Development in Pakistan

By

Saleem A. Jehangir

The man who brought it to Pakistan

Ranked among Pioneers in History of Martial Arts

Black Belt 1970

Tae Kwon Do Pakistan

by Saleem A. Jehangir
© All rights reserved
http://www.saleemjehangir.info/

1st Edition
May 2014

Layout & Formatting
Ahmed Grafics

Title Designed by
Uzma Shah

ISBN
978-0-9907362-2-6

Price:
Hard Copy $14.95
Ebook 5 $

Printer
AG Printing Services, Karachi
http://www.ahmedgraf.com/

-------- Available at: --------

Karachi:
FAZEEL BOOK SUPERMARKET
507/3, Temple Road, Urdu Bazar,
Karachi. Phone : 021-32212991

Lahore:
KITAB SARAI
Ghazni street, 1st Floor, Al-Hamd
Market, Urdu Bazar, Lahore.
Phone: 042-7320318

Islamabad:
SAEED BOOK BANK
A1-Rehman centre, F-7 Markaz, Jinnah
Super, Islamabad. Phone : 051-2651656~58

also available on **Amazon.com**

Dedication

This book is dedicated to all those who made it possible for me to learn and spread this essential martial art, and to all those who made this world a wonderful place for me to live in.

Table of Contents

Acknowledgements

If only man could be Grateful, he would be at Peace.

I am deeply grateful to God Almighty for His countless blessings and mercy, and to the following individuals and groups, because without their association my achievements in Tae Kwon Do would not have been possible:

- To The University of Michigan, for including Tae Kwon Do in its Physical Education Curriculum, thereby providing its students with a platform to learn the great martial art. The first training of Tae Kwon Do started at the establishment of the University of Michigan Tang Soo Do Club in 1962 by a Black Belt, Jim Young, who used to dedicate every evening to training us in the Racquet Ball courts of the Michigan Yost Field House Gymnasium building.

- To the Grand Master Hwa Chong, for leading the training of Tae Kwon Do at the University of Michigan from 1966 onwards, for organizing a multitude of tournaments in Michigan and Ohio, for organizing the First All Michigan Tae Kwon Do Championships, and then the First All American Inter-Collegiate Tae Kwon Do Championships, for working hard to have it included in the American Athletic Union and in the Olympics, for being my teacher, my coach, my trainer, my mentor for all times to come, for providing me with the philosophy that I have conducted my life with, and for giving me a code of honor to live by. Where ever he is, he is with me in his guidance and training. To Terry Goebel, Joe Lloyd, Jackie Adler, Patrick Harrigan, and others at the University of Michigan Tae Kwon Do Club, who supported every effort I made.

- To The Director of the National Sports Training and Coaching Center in Karachi, Khwaja Saleem Ahmed (marhoom) and his staff (including the security guard Saifu), for being exceptionally cooperative in providing facilities at the NSTCC in 1971, without which the prestigious beginning on a grand scale would not have been possible.

- To the numerous newspapers, magazines, Pakistan Television, and radio programs, for including Tae Kwon Do events in their media presentations, and specially to the Sportimes magazine for publishing my articles for two years.

- To Zia Moheyuddin, for including me in his Zia Moheyuddin Show in 1972 on Pakistan TV, a show that perhaps reached more people in the country than any single newspaper or magazine did, and which did the most in publicizing the good cause that we pioneered.

- To my dedicated batch of students who were with me all along, and who carried the banner after I left. Of significant mention are Asif Hussain, Musarrat Hussain, Wasim Akhtar, and Humayun Mirza.

- To all those who came after me and promoted the art to this day, who were instrumental in spreading the art in Pakistan to hundreds of thousands of students, and who are to be credited for making Tae Kwon Do the second most popular sport in Pakistan, after Cricket.

- To the club photographer, Mr. Aziz, whose dedication to our club was symbolic, who documented history by taking wonderful pictures of every occasion, some of which are included in this book.

- To Mohammed Umair for searching me out, establishing a website for me, and arranging for me to appear on Karachi Metro TV in a morning talk show in March 2012, thereby triggering a resurgence of Tae Kwon Do in me which resulted in writing this book.

- To all the parents and guardians who brought their children regularly to the NSTCC (despite scarcity of public transportation in those times) and showed equal dedication.

- To all my family members and friends who supported my efforts by joining NSTCC or to be just there with me in my endeavors.

- Lastly to my parents, especially my dearest mother who missed me dearly for the entire 40 years that I was away from her in the USA. She loved me very deeply and stayed sad, from the time I left her in 1965 to go to USA, till she died in 2005. Luckily for me, I came back to be by her side in the last 5 months of her life. May God grant her the highest place in the Hereafter.

Foreword

If I only hear, I forget

If I only see, I remember

But if I do, I understand

It's all about doing, if you really want to understand. I have thought of writing this book many times since 1988 when I returned to Pakistan as Director Production of HinoPak Motor Company in Karachi. But I had always said to myself and to others that I do what others write and talk about. I am a doer. Not a writer, or a speaker. But now as I turn 68 and see few years left in my life, I want to leave something behind that people will remember me with. As it is, they have already forgotten who started Tae Kwon Do in the sub-continent. I may have not been inspired to write this book if it were not for a young dedicated student of Tae Kwon Do in Karachi, Mohammed Umair, who researched the issue on the internet and contacted me in the USA in 2011, and developed a website in my name (saleemjehangir.info) to restore the credit due me. Hence I have included him exclusively in the Acknowledgements.

So, I have embarked on writing this book, the purpose of which is two-fold, first to document the historic development of martial arts in Pakistan, and second to bring back the traditional form of Tae Kwon Do which is getting almost extinct from public practice, especially in its mental and spiritual development aspects. Philosophy, which was the gist of the entire training of Tae Kwon Do, without which it merely stands as a sport, is totally non-existent today. I have mentioned it in many chapters and even included it in the chapters on forms and sparring, for without Philosophy the entire physical training is just exercise.

I had to reminisce many facts and incidents, stretching my memory all the way back 47 years to compile what I have included in this book. There are many memories here without which my motivation to write this book would remain without spirit. I get inspired with these memories and want my reader to do the same, for in these memoirs lay the secrets of the spirits of martial arts. One has to extract them piece by piece and assemble them like a puzzle, to make it into whatever they are searching for in life. That is why I have thanked so many people in my Acknowledgements chapter, for each one of them provided me with the impetus to move forward to the next step. And life is like that, for those who want to succeed, they will have to take every word of wisdom, hint, opportunity, vision, statement, to motivate themselves so they can keep progressing.

The best way I can express this is to give an example of one of my first students. Among them were many who succeeded in life and all of them credited their success to the philosophic training that I provided them. There was one, Shahid Mir, who now operates a successful software company that does business with the USA. In one of his presentations he was asked where did he learn to be so successful in his business. He answered: on the Tae Kwon Do floor. This is what the training of martial arts is all about, using it in every phase of your life. You have to live martial arts, for Martial Arts is the Way of the Warrior whose goal is to achieve perfection in life.

Although I have used simplified terms in English, I have also used the common terminology from both

Korean and Japanese languages, because the soul of this book is in the modern day warrior who comes from these countries which are credited for implementing the spirit of martial arts in most phases of the lives of their people.

I have also used the male gender in my sentences to avoid using he/she and his/her everywhere. This is only for ease of reading. No separation of gender is intended, although some specific techniques are identified separately for the girls. I have also used the first person in the narration, because I want the reader to feel as if I am talking to him.

I have called this book "Tae Kwon Do Pakistan", because Pakistan was the among the few countries which introduced Tae Kwon Do as soon as it came on the international scene in the 1960s. I was already training in it in 1965, and competing at US national levels as a Pakistani during the mid-1960s. This book authenticates the facts with pictures, certificates, and media coverage, further proving that we as Pakistanis can be among the pioneers who can learn, teach, be ranked among the best, and can do our share to make this world a better place.

I believe that, if you have properly grasped your philosophy of learning, you would not need to be taught everything. You will need only the first lesson, the lesson that points you in the right direction. I learned everything in life this way.

Introduction

Every soul is potentially divine. The goal is to manifest the divinity within by controlling nature, external and internal. Do this either by work, or worship, or psychic control, or philosophy, by one or more, or all of these, and be free. This is the whole of religion.

<u>Martial Arts is the Way of the Warrior</u>
<u>And this book is written to help you in becoming that Warrior</u>

From my childhood, if I saw something beautiful I would always want to share it with others. I have done this all my life, from the small things to the big things I experienced in life. Bringing Tae Kwon Do to Pakistan was one of those experiences, which I want to document by narrating the whole saga.

I have divided this book into three volumes due to the nature of its contents:

Volume I

- History of Tae Kwon Do

- Tae Kwon Do development in Pakistan

- Pioneers of Tae Kwon Do in Pakistan

Volume II

- Philosophy of Martial Arts, Tae Kwon Do in particular

- The method of converting philosophy into action and transforming into training

- The Basics of training

- The Basic defending and striking techniques

- Transforming the basic defending and striking techniques into one step and two step techniques

- Transforming the step techniques into sparring

- Transforming free sparring into unarmed combat

- Sport Tae Kwon Do rules and regulations

- Good health and eating habits

- Character building and reformation of the society

Volume III

- Forms (Hyungs) in Tae Kwon Do up to 1st Dan Black Belt level

- Forms (Hyungs) in Tae Kwon Do up to 10th Dan Black Belt level

History of Tae Kwon Do

Man has always fought, still fights, and will always fight

Summary

Pakistan came into existence in 1947. Before that it was all India under the British for 150 years. Before the British, it was India under the Mughals. Before that it was India under the Muslim Sultans, before that it was India under Asoka, and before that......we can go back thousands of years to the earliest of the known settlements of Harappa and Moenjodaro. In all of India's history, the presence of martial arts is felt throughout, as skeletons with bows and arrows are found in the 6000 years old streets of the Indus Valley civilizations mentioned above, or as it was in the Hindu scripture Maha Bharata, or as it was the period of the Huns, the Rajputs, the Marathas, and the Mughals.

But these were all martial arts that used weapons. As we trace the source of the weaponless art, or the art of unarmed combat, we go back in time from Japan, Okinawa, to Korea, to Philippines, to China. In China we see the art taking its first root as an art form, which can be now traced to Kung Fu. Who brought it to China? The legend goes back to the Buddhist sage, Bodhidharma, who travelled from India to China in 520 AD to teach Buddhism. Travel in those days was dangerous and life threatening as bandits and dacoits looted caravans and travelers along the routes. In addition, travel was very demanding in terms of physical endurance and safety. Bodhidharma is credited for developing some exercises that, not only strengthened the body for the strenuous elements of travel, they also helped in defending oneself from physical attacks. Since we know that Buddhism preached Non-Violence and Peace, these were not designed to be offensive techniques, but intended to be defensive in nature. Bodhidharma is said to have trained his companion monks in the same. Little did Bodhidharma know that he was laying the seed of that which would one day bloom into a series of full-fledged weaponless martial arts.

Tae Kwon Do has a history stemming from the middle of the first millennium A.D. The original name was Tae-Kyon, and represented the un-armed combat form practiced in the ancient Silla Dynasty of Korea. Tae-Kyon originally consisted of foot techniques. Hand techniques were introduced under the Japanese occupation, and styles of unarmed combat bearing various names emerged. In 1955, Korean dignitaries, inside and outside of the art, gathered to select one name to represent the national activity. Tae Kwon Do (Tae meaning kick, and Kwon meaning fist, Do meaning the way, the whole name Tae Kwon Do meaning the way with the kick and the fist) was chosen to include many styles under its heading.

During the Japanese occupation of Korea in the Second World War, most of the martial arts training centers were closed. Later as the Japanese started to teach their version called Karate Do to the Koreans, the dojangs (clubs) opened up. After WWII, when Japan gave Korea independence, Korea evolved its own style to be later called Tae Kwon Do. Tae Kwon Do borrowed its roots from the Chinese Kung Fu, hence the more circular movements in kicks, forms, and blocks.

During the First and Second World Wars, Japan introduced the use of Karate as a form of weapon when confronted in hand to hand combat. It is in this period that the interest started to attract the eye. Then finally when the first James Bond movie, Dr. No, hit the screen, the world saw for the first time a glimpse of the "Karate Chop" and its power. Although the "chop" in the movie lacked speed, power and accuracy, it intrigued the world with its mystery. Everyone wanted to know how and where to learn this "chop". The use of the chop became more and more common in movies, and the interest in actually showing more of the art brought the masters of the art to Hollywood. As the migration of the masters to the USA proceeded, there were those who wanted to teach it to the serious learners, they went to the campus towns where they found the young, athletic, intellectual pursuer of the art ready to adapt to it. It is here that the grass roots development of the martial art of Karate, Tae Kwon Do, and other less popular styles took place. Soon it became a part of the universities' Physical Education curriculums. University of Michigan was one of the first colleges to adapt it in 1962. This is also the time that Bruce Lee and Chuck Norris, one of the earliest students of the art in the USA decided first to teach it to the actors (James Coburn being the first of them) and then became actors themselves. The first of the Bruce Lee movies, Enter the Dragon, hit the street like fire. The popularity of Karate soared like a rocket, both in the movies, among the movie goers, and the much larger group that wanted to learn the real art of self-defense. The fate of the martial art of Karate/Tae Kwon Do was sealed. And so were the names of its pioneers in history.

In the 1960s, its pioneers brought the art to the universities and the metropolitan cities in the USA. USA became the nurturing grounds for the martial arts. Judo, Jui Jit Su, Aikido, and others spread like wise. Martial Arts experts from Korea and Japan started to pour into the US as the demand grew. The first of the US black belts were still not ready to take over the movement. The masters kept the schools growing and took most of them under their association umbrellas. Many associations cropped up around the country. Soon the parent associations in Korea and Japan started to issue the Black Belts. The Japan Karate Association, the Okinawan Shotokan, the World Tae Kwon Do Association, International Tae Kwon Do Federation, etc., came into limelight.

Somewhere along the line, masters in Korea, specially belonging to the Korea Tae Kwon Do Association, began to address the unexpected phenomenal growth of Tae Kwon Do in the USA. Surely they were not going to give the controls of the art away. A sudden shift in the standardization of the art to be "exported" was noticed. Test requirements for Black Belt certificates were established, and the certificates were issued from the Korea TKD Association. The forms, known as Hyungs in Korean and Katas in Japanese, started to change. The original traditional art was to be preserved, and a lighter, sporty version was to be exported.

As the pioneers of the art focused on including it in the American Athletic Union of the USA, the need surfaced for scoring and refereeing. Up to now, free sparring was either with no contact or with light contact at best. Heavy contact led to disqualification of the attacker. How could you judge the power in a light strike, or the theoretical power behind a strike with no contact? Hence the rules of the game started to change. The use of protective gear was made, similar to that used in Olympic boxing. But the body was also to be guarded since there were powerful kicks involved. So the guards appeared for the body and the face. Gloves that allowed grabbing, and foot guards that allowed contact with feet, were employed. Now you could make full heavy contact, and it was easier to judge. AAU started to train referees, and certificates were issued to ones who passed the training. And furthermore, how could you judge a Kata or Hyung, when there was no set of judging criteria. Katas had to show power, agility, smoothness, focus, versatility, you name it; it had to have it because it is the gist of Karate &Tae Kwon Do. So the criteria was developed for the forms competition also. An additional category was introduced in competition, that of displaying power through the use of breaking boards or bricks. Tae Kwon Do was the first martial art after Judo to be included in America's sport control body, the American Athletic Union, and later in the Olympics.

Master Hwa Chong led this struggle with the AAU to recognize Tae Kwon Do as a popular American sport. He was the one who steered it into the Olympics and took the first team to the Olympics in 1988. He was the USA Tae Kwon Do team manager for the Olympics in Barcelona, Spain, in 1992, and was finally appointed as Chairman of the AAU Tae Kwon Do committee in 1993. He was also named as the President of the US Tae Kwon Do Union in the mid-1990s.

Recorded history of Tae Kwon Do in Pakistan begins in 1971 when a young engineer from the USA, Saleem Jehangir, returns to his homeland to teach to his people what he learned abroad.

Today, Tae Kwon Do is administered from Korea through the Kukki Won, which handles training and rank certification matters. The World Tae Kwon Do Federation and the International Tae Kwon Do Federation literally administrate 90% of the Tae Kwon Do activities around the world. The WTF concentrates on the sport version of Tae Kwon Do, and the ITF on Tae Kwon Do as a martial art. All Tae Kwon Do learners and instructors should be indebted to these organizations and the gentlemen who run them for giving such capable administration.

(Ancient History (50 BC-1900AD

The earliest records of some form of Tae Kwon Do practice date back to about 50 BC. At that time, Korea was divided into three kingdoms: Silla, which was founded on the Kyongju plain, lasted from 57 BC to 936 AD; Koguryo, founded in the Yalu River Valley, lasted from 37 BC to 668 AD; and Paekche, founded in the southwestern area of the Korean peninsula, lasted from18 BC to 600 AD. Silla, the smallest of these Kingdoms, was constantly under invasion and harassment by its two more powerful Northern and Western neighbors. Each time they invaded, they left their influences on the Korean martial arts communities.

Tae Kwon Do, which was known as Tae Kyon then, first appeared in the Koguryo kingdom, but it is the Silla's Hwarang warriors who are credited with the growth and spread of Tae Kyon throughout Korea. Silla received help from King Gwanggae and his soldiers from the Koguryo kingdom to drive out the invaders. During this time a few selected Sillan warriors were given training in Tae Kyon by the early masters from Koguryo. The Tae Kyon trained warriors became known as the Hwarang. The Hwarang set up a military academy for the sons of royalty in Silla called Hwarang-do, meaning "The way of flowering manhood." The Hwarang studied Tae Kyon, history, Confucian philosophy, ethics, Buddhist morality, and military tactics. The guiding principles of the Hwarang warriors were loyalty, filial duty, trustworthiness, valor, and justice. Tae Kyon was spread throughout Korea because the Hwarang traveled all around the peninsula to learn about the other regions and people.

During the Silla dynasty (A.D. 668 to A.D. 935) Tae Kyon was mostly used as a sport and recreational activity. Tae Kyon's name was changed to Soo Bakh and the focus of the art was changed during the Koryo dynasty (A.D. 935 to A.D. 1392). When King Uijong was on the throne from 1147 through 1170, he changed Soo Bakh from a system that promoted fitness to primarily a fighting art.

Somewhere along the line, the legendary Buddhist monk, Bodhiharma, appears on the scene in China in 520 AD. He taught Kung-Fu at the Shaolin monastery for nine years. A few years after this period, a form of Chinese art using hands and feet, called Kwon Bop (based on Shaolin Kung-Fu), entered Korea. Some believe that it entered Korea as Nei-chia (internal Kung-Fu) and Wai-chia (external Kung-Fu) during China's Sung and Ming dynasties.

Tae Kyon is considered the earliest known form of Tae Kwon Do. Paintings from this time period have been found on the ceiling of the Muyong-chong, a royal tomb from the Koguryo dynasty. The paintings show unarmed people using techniques that are very similar to the ones used by Tae Kwon Do today.

What followed was a time of peace. The Hwarang turned from a military organization to a group specialized in arts, poetry and music. It was in 936 A.D. when Wang Kon founded the Koryo dynasty, an abbreviation of Koguryo. The name Korea is derived from Koryo.

During the Koryo Dynasty the sport Soo Bakh Do, which was then used as a military training method, became popular. During the Joseon-dynasty (also known as the Yi-dynasty. 1392 A.D. - 1910 A.D.) this emphasis on military training disappeared. King Taejo, founder of the Joseon-dynasty, replaced Buddhism by Confucianism as the state religion. According to Confucianism, the higher class should study the poets, read poems and play music. So Martial arts became something for the common man.

The first widely distributed book on Tae Kyon was during the Yi dynasty (1397 to 1907). This was the first time that it was intended to be taught to the general public, in previous years the knowledge was limited to the military. During the second half of the Yi dynasty, political conflicts and the choice to use dialog instead of military action, almost led to the extinction of Tae Kyon. The emphasis of the art was changed back to that of recreational and physical fitness. The lack of interest in it as an art, caused it to become fragmented and scarcely practiced throughout the country.

(Recent History (1900s

Although its roots can be somewhat traced back to ancient Korea, it is a historic fact that modern Tae Kwon Do as we see it today is a recent development. In fact, the only documented history begins in the mid 1900's. Until the 1960s, Tae Kwon Do was essentially the same as Shotokan Karate. "The modern karate of Korea," according to Master Sihak Henry Cho, "with very little influence from Tae Kyon, was born with the turn of the 20th century when it was imported directly from China and also from Okinawa through Japan." "Tae Kwon Do," he claimed, "is identical to Japanese karate.... Some of the Korean public still use the word 'karate' in their conversation." This should not come as a surprise. By the time of the Japanese occupation, Koreans had lost interest in the martial arts. There were few native martial artists left and since they were forced to teach in secret after 1909, they had to restrict the number of students they could accept. At the same time, many Koreans probably went to Japan for an education (like Master Choi Hong Hi) and returned with some knowledge of either Judo or Shotokan Karate. Thus, by the end of the occupation, Korean martial arts were known by a minority while the Japanese arts were diffused throughout the populace, especially among those of the upper classes who had Japanese education.

In the early 1900's the art evolved with a combination of Chinese and Japanese techniques, which did not demonstrate the incredible kicking power of the art nor its traditional values or philosophy. In 1909 the Japanese invaded Korea and occupied the country for 36 years till 1945. To control Korea's patriotism, the Japanese banned the practice of all military arts, Korean language, and even burned all books written in Korea. This ban actually kindled the interest back in Soo Bakh. Many Koreans organized themselves into underground groups and practiced the martial arts in remote Buddhist temples. Other people left Korea to study the martial arts in other countries like China and Japan. In 1943 Judo, Karate and Kung-fu were officially introduced to the Korean residents, and the martial arts regained their popularity. In 1945, Korea was liberated and the Korean people began their struggle to re-establish their national identity. Various styles of Korean Martial Arts, called Kwans, that had survived by going underground during the Japanese occupation of Korea, began to re-emerge and be once again taught to the Korean people. Firmly dedicated to promoting a single Korean national identity, the Korean government endorsed a Martial Arts unification plan proposed by General Choi Hong Hi. After World War II, when Korea became independent, several Kwans emerged, like the Chung Do Kwan, Moo Duk Kwan, Yun Moo Kwan, Chang Moo Kwan, Oh Do Kwan, Ji Do Kwan, Chi Do Kwan, and the Song Moo Kwan.

The first Tae Kwon Do school (Kwan) was started in Yong Chun, Seoul, Korea in 1945. Many different schools were opened from 1945 through 1960. Each school claimed to teach the traditional Korean martial art, but each school emphasized a different aspect of Tae Kyon. This caused different names to emerge from each system, some of them were: Soo Bakh Do, Kwon Bop, Kong Soo Do, Tae Soo Do and Kang Soo Do. The Kwans united in 1955 as Tae Soo Do. In the beginning of 1957, the name Tae Kwon Do was adopted by several Korean martial arts masters, for its similarity to the name Tae Kyon.

The Korean Armed Forces were also formed in 1945 and in 1946, Second lieutenant Choi Hong Hi, began teaching Tae Kyon at a Korean military base called Kwang Ju. The greatest turning point for Korean martial arts started in 1952. During the height of the Korean War, President Syngman Rhee watched a 30 minute performance by Korean martial arts masters. He was especially impressed when Tae Hi Nam broke 13 roof tiles with a single punch. After the demonstration President Rhee talked with Choi Hong Hi about the martial arts, he then ordered his military chiefs of staff to require all Korean soldiers to receive training in the martial arts. This caused a tremendous surge in Tae Kyon schools and students. President Rhee also sent Tae Hi Nam to Ft. Benning, Georgia, for radio communications training where he gave many martial arts demonstrations and received considerable media publicity.

During this same time period in Korea, special commando groups of martial arts-trained soldiers were formed to fight against the communist forces of North Korea. One of the most famous special forces was known as the Black Tigers. The Korean war ended in 1953. In 1954, General Choi Hong Hi organized the 29th Infantry on CheJu Island, off the Korean Coast, as a spearhead and center for Tae Kyon training in the military.

The actual name Tae Kwon Do wasn't made official until 1955. At that time General Choi Hong Hi organized a movement to unify Korea's various martial arts styles (Kwans) into one art and presented the name "Tae Kwon Do" to a committee specially formed to select the new name. On April 11, 1955, at a conference of Kwan masters, historians, and Tae Kyon promoters, most of the Kwan masters decided to merge their various styles for mutual benefit of all schools. The name "Tae Soo Do" was accepted by a majority of the Kwan masters. Two years later the name was changed again, this time to "Tae Kwon Do" The name was suggested by General Choi Hong Hi because of its resemblance to Tae Kyon. In consequence, it provided continuity and maintained tradition. Further, it described both hand and foot techniques. Tae Kwon Do was recognized as the name for the newly unified and officially recognized Korean martial art. General Choi Hong Hi is also credited for developing most of the original Tae Kwon Do forms which are now practiced by the ITF, and is considered the Father of Tae Kwon Do.

Dissension among the various Kwans that did not unify carried on until September 14, 1961. Then by official decree of the new military government, the Kwans were ordered to unify into one organization called the Korea Tae Kwon Do Association (KTA), with General Choi Hong Hi elected as its first president. In 1962, the KTA re-examined all the black belt ranks to determine national standards, and in 1962 Tae Kwon Do became one of the official events in the annual National Athletic Meet in Korea. Subsequently, the KTA sent instructors and demonstrations teams all over the world.

In Korea, the study of Tae Kwon Do spread rapidly from the army into high schools and colleges. In March of 1966 General Choi Hong Hi founded the International Tae Kwon Do Federation (ITF), which he also served as president. General Choi Hong Hi went to the communist North Korea where he attempted to introduce Taekwondo to the North Korean people. Because this visit was unauthorized, he fell into disfavor with the South Korean government. His International Taekwondo Federation (ITF) was displaced by the new World Taekwondo Federation (WTF) under the leadership of Mr. Un Yong Kim. Mr. Kim later became the Vice President of the International Olympic Tae Kwon Do Committee, and a full contact sport version of Taekwondo became popular to a point that it became an official Olympic sport.

General Choi Hong Hi later resigned as the KTA president and moved his ITF headquarters to Montreal, Canada, from where he concentrated on organizing Tae Kwon Do internationally. His emphasis on Tae Kwon Do was as a martial art and not as a sport. By 1974, General Choi announced that some 600 qualified ITF instructors were spread throughout the world.

With the resignation of General Choi Hong Hi from the Korea Tae Kwon Do Association, Un Yong Kim was elected the new KTA president. Feeling that Korea was the mother country of Tae Kwon Do and that the world headquarters should be located there, he dissolved the ITF's connection with the KTA and on May 28, 1973 created a new international governing body called the World Tae Kwon Do Federation (WTF), which coincided with the first World Tae Kwon Do Championships that were held in Seoul, Korea. At the first inaugural meeting, Un Yong Kim was elected as president of the WTF and drafted a charter for the federation. The WTF is the only official organization recognized by the Korean government as an international regulating body for Tae Kwon Do.

General Choi Hong Hee required the army to train Tae Kwon Do, so the very first Tae Kwon Do students were Korean soldiers. The police and air force had to learn Tae Kwon Do as well. At that time, Tae Kwon Do was merely a Korean version of Shotokan Karate. In 1961 the Korean Tae Kwon Do Union arose from the Soo Bakh Do Association and the Tae Soo Do Association. In 1962 the Korean Amateur Sports Association acknowledged the Korean Tae Kwon Do Union and in 1965 the name was changed to Korean Tae Kwon Do Association (KTA). General Choi was president of the KTA at that time and was asked to start the ITF as the international branch of the KTA. The southern government was overthrown in 1961. General Choi Hong Hi left for Canada and established ITF (International Tae Kwon Do Federation), as a separate entity, two years later.

Demonstrations were given all over the world. It took a while before real progress was made, but eventually, in 1973, the World Tae Kwon Do Federation (WTF) was founded. The First World Tae Kwon Do Championships were also held in 1973. In 1980, WTF Tae Kwon Do was recognized by the International Olympic Committee (IOC) and became a demonstration sport at the Olympics in 1988. In the year 2000 Tae Kwon Do made its debut as an official Olympic sport. There were several attempts to unify ITF and WTF but unfortunately these failed.

The World Tae Kwon Do Federation has since made a major effort to standardize tournament rules and organize world class competitions. After the 2nd World TKD Championship in Seoul, the WTF became an affiliate of the General Assembly of International Sports Federation (GAISF), which has ties to the International Olympic Committee (IOC). The IOC recognized and admitted the WTF in July 1980. In 1982 the General Session of the IOC designated Tae Kwon Do as an official Demonstration Sport for the 1988 Olympic Games in Seoul, Korea.

ITF practices a more traditional form of Tae Kwon Do, while WTF has a strong emphasis on sparring. ITF started concentrating on the forms developed by General Choi, while the KTA (which later, on May 28, 1973, became the WTF) concentrated on the Palgwe's. Later the WTF abandoned the Palgwe's and started concentrating on Taegeuks. Slowly, the WTF emphasis turned to sparring. This is also the reason why a lot of people would rather call WTF Tae Kwon Do a martial sport than a martial art.

ITF practices the so-called light-contact part of Tae Kwon Do, while WTF practices the so-called full-contact part. ITF focuses more on the traditional way of Tae Kwon Do.

Since Modern-day Tae Kwon Do's official birth on April 11, 1955, its development as a sport has been rapid. Over 30 million people practice Tae Kwon Do in more than 156 countries.

Pioneers of Tae Kwon Do in History

The pioneers of the Kang Duk Won Tae Kwon Do Association:

Kang Duk Won Martial Arts Association

Home • History • Promotions • Schedule • Instructors • Location • Links • Cale

History and Lineage

| Great Grandmaster Byung In Yoon 1920 - 1983 | Great Grandmaster Chul Hee Park 1933 - | Great Grandmaster Hwa Chong 1939 - |

Great Grandmaster Byung In Yoon

Mr. Yoon learned Chuan Fa in Manchuria, China in the 1930's. In 1937 he went to Japan to be educated at Nihon University. While at the University he participated in an exchange with Toyama Kanken where Mr. Yoon received rank in Shudokon. After World War II, Mr. Yoon taught Kwon Bup in Korea until the Korean War. It was during the Korean war that Mr. Yoon became a POW. He was unable to return to South Korea and remained in North Korea until his death in 1983.

Great Grandmaster Chul Hee Park

As a youth Mr. Park became a student of Byung In Yoon in Korea in 1946. After Mr. Yoon disappeared during the Korean War, Mr. Park continued to teach Kwon Bup along with Jung Pyo Hong. About 1954, Mr. Park and Mr. Hong founded a new Kwan, which Mr. Park named Kang Duk Won (School of Virtue). Mr. Park continues to teach Kang Duk Won Kwon Bup to this day. During one of his visits to the United States in November of 2001, Mr. Park was an honored visitor to the Kang Duk Won dojang in Muskegon.

Great Grandmaster Hwa Chong

Mr. Chong became a student of Mr. Park in the mid 1950's. Through Mr. Park's correspondence with Mr. Stolberg, Mr. Chong was able to get help from Mr. Stolberg to come to the United States in 1967. Mr.

Manchuria, China

chuan fa

↓

Byung In Yoon

kwonbop

↓

Chul Hee Park kwonbup Kang Duk Won

Great Grandmaster Byung In Yoon 1920 - 1983

Grand Master Park Chull Hee, Senior student of the Great Grandmaster Byung In Yoon, co-founded Kang Duk Won "Academy of Moral Teaching" with Grandmaster Jong Pyo Hong in 1954. Teacher of Grand Master Hwa Chong.

Grand Master Hwa Chong, President of World Kang Duk Won Tae Kwon Do Federation, ex-President of US Tae Kwon Do Union, pupil of Grand Master Park Chull Hee.

Master Saleem Jehangir, Vice-President World Kang Duk Won Tae Kwon Do Federation, President Pakistan Kang Duk Won Tae Kwon Do Federation, Founder-President Pakistan Tae Kwon Do Association, pupil of Grand Master Hwa Chong.

General Choi Hong Hi, Four Star General in the Republic of Korea Army, later Defense Minister, Founder of Oh Do Kwan & the International Tae Kwon Do Federation (ITF)

Korea Tae Kwon Do Association

The Korea Tae Kwon Do Association (KTA) is the National Governing Body (NGB) for Tae Kwon Do in the Republic of Korea (ROK), just like the United States Tae Kwon Do Union (USTU) is the National Governing Body for Tae Kwon Do in the United States of America. The World Tae Kwon Do Federation (WTF), which was formed in 1973, is made up of Tae Kwon Do NGBs. These NGBs, and not individuals, are members of the WTF. Individuals may be affiliated to the WTF through their NGB, but individuals cannot join the WTF directly.

Dr. Un Yong Kim became the 5th President of the KTA in 1971. Dr. Kim subsequently became the 1st President of the WTF in 1973 and around 1990 he gave up the post of KTA President.

The KTA is alive and well and probably is the largest, most active NGB for Tae Kwon Do in the world. KTA is at the following address:

The Korea Tae Kwon Do Association
#607, Olympic Center, 88 Oryoon-dong, Songpa-ku, Seoul, Korea

For my reader who is interested in more details on the chronological development of Tae Kwon Do organizations, I have included here a synopsis collected from various websites on the internet. It is important to read this history to understand how a martial art can spread to become the main theme of character building in a country.

A commonly believed chronological history of development of Tae Kwon Do in the 1900s is as follows:

1905 : Occupation of Korea by Japan. Japanese educational curriculum was imposed on all Korean schools, and Korean students were taught Judo and Kendo at the schools.

1906 : Tae Kyon was secretly practice and passed on to a few students, like Han IL Dong and Duk Ki Song

1909 : The Japanese forbade the practice of any kind of fighting Arts in Korea. However it did not stop totally the practice of Martial Arts. The follower of martial arts found a place to learn and practice it in the Buddhist temples of Korea and Japan.

1930 : Around the 1930s Mr. Choi Hong Hi (Founder of Tae Kwon Do), began his Martial Arts learning under Master Han IL Dong, who was his calligraphy instructor. He began teaching Tae Kyon to Mr. Choi Hong Hi who was in his youth and quite frail in physical built.

1936 : Hwang Kee (founder of Tang Soo Do), another student of the outlawed Martial Arts, was only 22 years old when he mastered the Art of Tae Kyon and SooBak Do. Master Hwang Kee then traveled to Northern China where he studied the T'ang Method. It is there that he worked to combine the two styles until 1945.

1937 : Mr. Choi Hong Hi was sent to Japan (Kyoto) to further his education. Here he met a fellow Korean Mr. Un Yong Kim, who was engaged in teaching Shotokan, a Japanese Okinawan

Martial Art. After two years of concentrated training, Mr. Choi earned his first degree black belt in Shotokan. Then he went to the University of Tokyo where he continued his training and attained his second degree black belt, at this time he began teaching at the YMCA. When the World War II began, Mr. Choi was forced to enlist in the Japanese Army.

1941 : Because of the pressure of the World War II and in order to fulfill military requirements, the Japanese lifted the ban on Martial Arts in Korea. From this year, Judo and Juken-jutsu (bayonet art) also began to be taught in Korea.

1943: Karate and Kung-fu were officially introduced to Koreans, and ended up getting popular with the masses.

1945 : Korea was liberated and the native Arts of Tae Kyon and SooBak resurfaced. Other Martial Arts that also surfaced were: Bang Soo Do, Kong Soo Do, Kwon Bop, Tae Soo Do, and Tang Soo Do. The Japanese occupation of Korea brought to the Korean people a renewed interest in Martial Arts, as a result several schools (Kwans) opened in Seoul. Below are the five Kwans in chronological order:

- Chung Do Kwan or Chong Do Kwan (Gym of the Blue Wave) : Founded by Lee Won-Kuk in 1945, in Yong Chun, Seoul.
- Moo DukKwan : Founded by Hwang Kee, at the end of 1945. Hwang Kee taught an art he eventually named Tang Soo Do.
- Yun Moo Kwan : Founded by Sup Chun Sang (Sup Jun Sang; Chun Sang-Seop).
- Chang Moo Kwan or Kwon BeopDojang : Founded by Yun Pyung (In Yoon Byung; Yun Byung-In), at the YMCA in 1946.
- Chi Do Kwan : Founded by Yon KuePyang.

After the Korean War (1953-1954), three more Kwans appeared:

- Kang Duk Won Academy of Moral Teaching: Founded by Master Park Chull Hee with Grandmaster Hong Jong- pyo   in 1954
- Ji Do Kwan: Founded by GaeByang Yun.
- Sang Moo Kwan: Founded by ByungChik Ro (Ro ByungJik; No Byong-Jik).
- Oh Do Kwan (Gym of My Way) : Founded by General Choi Hong Hi, with the help of Tae Hi Nam.

1945: The Korean and the Japanese Martial Arts gained a lot of popularity. So in this year the Korean Judo Association was formed.

1946: The Tae Kyon instructors began teaching the military troops in KwangJu, Korea.

1946-1947: Mr. Choi Hong Hi (at time he was first Lieutenant of the Korean Army's 2nd Infantry Regiment), taught Martial Arts to Korean and Americans stationed at Tae-Jon. This was the first time that Americans were introduced to what eventually become known as Tae Kwon Do.

1947-1948: 1947 was a year where Mr. Choi Hong Hi rose rapidly through the ranks. He was promoted to captain and then Major. In 1948 he was posted to Seoul as the head of logistics and become Taekwondo instructor for the American Military police School in Seoul. In late 1948, Mr. Choi become the Lieutenant Colonel

1949: Mr. Choi Hong Hi was promoted to full colonel and visited the United States for the first time, attending the Fort Riley Ground General School located in Kansas. While there this art was introduced to the American public.

1952: President Seung Man Rhee of Korea observed a 30 minute demonstration of martial arts by the Korean Masters and was so impressed with Mr. Nam Tae Hi's breaking demonstration, that he asked Mr. Choi Hong Hi about the art. President Rhee then ordered all soldiers to receive training in this art. The 29th Infantry Division of the Korean army was organized and activated by Mr. Choi Hong Hi at the Cheju Island in 1953. This unit was responsible for all Tae Kyon training of the Korean Army and the Black Tigers, an elite unit involved in espionage missions behind enemy lines.

1953: By the end of this year, Mr. Choi Hong Hi commanded the largest civilian gym in Korea, the Chong Do Kwan.

1953-1954: After the Korean War, three more Kwans appeared. The Ji Do Kwan, Song Moo Kwan, and the Oh Do Kwan.

1955: Technically this year was the beginning of Taekwondo as a formally recognized art in Korea. During this year, a special board was formed which included leading master instructors, historians, and prominent leaders of society. Several names were submitted for this new Martial art. Finally on April 11, 1955, the board decided on the name of Tae Kwon Do, submitted by Mr. Choi Hong Hi. The name of Tae Kwon Do replaced the different and confusing names used before, such as Dang Soo, Gong Soo, Tae Kyon, Kwon Bup, and others. During this year Mr. Choi Hong Hi spread Taekwondo to the universities and military posts across Korea. The third District Command in Tae Jon become one of the main centers for this new art.

1959: Taekwondo spread beyond its national boundaries. Mr. Choi Hong Hi and nineteen of his top black belts toured the Far Eastern countries. The tour was a major success. Also in this year Mr. Choi Hong Hi was elected President of the Korea Taekwondo Association, and published his first Korean text on Taekwondo entitled "Tae Kwon-Do Guidelines ". During this year, Mr. Choi Hong Hi attended the modern weapon familiarization course in Texas, USA. He used this opportunity to visit several Tae Kwon Do schools, one of them was the Joon Rhee school, who was one of the pioneers of Taekwondo in the USA, and who later on became the Secretary General of United States Taekwondo Association in Washington D.C.

1961: The Korean Tae Kwon Do Association (KTA) was founded on September 14, 1961, with Mr. Choi Hong Hi as the President. At this time the Chi Do Kwan left the organization. The Chung Do Kwan, the largest civilian school in Korea, remained distant from the KTA and develop their own organization called the Korean Soo Bakh Do Association which become the rival of the KTA. In 1962, the Korean government stepped into the dispute when they recognized all the black belts certified by the KTA, as a consequence many Martial Artists who had left, returned to the KTA.

1962 : South Vietnamese troops requested to be taught Tae Kwon Do, so Mr. Nam Tae Hi, known as the right hand man of Mr. Choi, and three other instructors were sent from the Oh Do Kwan to teach fifty soldier from various branches of the Vietnamese Armed Forces. Two instructors returned to Korea after six months, but Mr. Nam Tae Hi and SeungKyu Kim stayed a full year returning on December 24, 1963.

1962-1963: Taekwondo entered Thailand. Malaysia and Hong Kong.

1963 : Mr. Choi Hong Hi hosted a famous demonstration at the United Nations headquarters in New York.

1964 : On February the Tae Kwon Do Association was formed in Singapore.Also on this year Mr. Chong Lee introduce Tae Kwon Do in Canada.
1965 : Mr. Choi Hong Hi led a goodwill mission of Tae Kwon Do to West Germany, Italy, Turkey, United Arab Republic, Malaysia, and Singapore. This was the basis for not only establishing Tae Kwon Do Associations in these countries but also the formation of the "International Tae Kwon Do Federation" (ITF.).

1966 : Mr. Park Jong Soo introduced Tae Kwon Do to the Netherlands. Also on this year Mr. Hong Hi Choi, lost his leadership of the KTA (Korean Tae Kwon Do Association), because the South Korean government did not like a goodwill trip to North Korea by a Tae Kwon Do demonstration team lead by Mr. Choi Hong Hi. Mr. Choi Hong Hi resigned in this year as a president of the KTA, and on March 22, 1966, he founded the International Tae Kwon Do Federation (ITF.) in association with Vietnam, Malaysia, Singapore, West Germany, the United States, Turkey, Italy, the United Arab Republic, and Korea. The headquarter of the ITF eventually moved to Canada.

1967: The Hong Kong Tae Kwon Do Association was formed. also in this year Mr. Choi Hong Hi visited the All American Tae Kwon Do Tournament held in Chicago, Illinois, where he discussed expansion, unification, and policy of the United States Tae Kwon Do Association with leading instructors. This visit led to the formal establishment of the U.S. Tae Kwon Do Association (USTA) in Washington, D.C., on November 26, 1967. The USTA was superseded in 1974 by the U.S. Tae Kwon Do Federation (USTF).

In 1977, the kwan names were replaced by serial numbers. The kwans, in order from 1st kwan to 9th kwan, are: Songmookwan, Hanmookwan, Changmookwan, Moodukkwan, Odokwan, Kangdukwan, Jungdokwan, Jidokwan, and Chungdokwan.
1971: Tae Kwon Do was established in Pakistan by Master Saleem Jehangir, who returned from the USA as an engineer, and opened the first school of formalized training at the very reputable National Sports and Training Center, Karachi, Pakistan.

The Development of Tae Kwon Do in USA

Americans were first introduced to Tae Kyon in 1946 when General Choi Hong Hi instructed Korean Army troops and some American soldiers stationed with the 2nd Infantry Regiment. Later in 1949 Gen. Choi Hong Hi attended Ground General School at Ft. Riely near Topeka, Kansas in the United States. While in the U.S., Gen. Choi Hong Hi gave public demonstrations of Tae Kyon to the US troops. This was the first display of Tae Kyon in America.

In 1956, Master Jhoon Rhee arrived in Texas for military training by the USAF. While at the USAF, he taught what was possibly the first American class in Tae Kwon Do. He was called back almost immediately to complete a year of active duty in the Korean Army, but he then returned to Texas in late 1957 to attend Southwest Texas State College in San Marcos, Texas. Later, he taught Tae Kwon Do as a physical education course at the college and opened the first Tae Kwon Do club for the public.

Master Rhee later transferred to the University of Texas at Austin and taught in an even larger club. Then in 1962, he moved to Washington, D.C. to become a professional instructor.

Master Jhoon Rhee has remained a major contributor to American karate. In 1966, he hosted his First National Karate Championships in Washington, D.C. (these competitions lasted until 1970). He also hosted publicity events such as giving free instruction in Tae Kwon Do to US congressmen in 1973, and having his students march in Washington Fourth-of-July parades. It was he who first introduced padded sparring gear in the early 1970s. He still teaches at his Washington Dojang.

A Tae Kwon Do demonstration, at the United Nations headquarters in New York City in 1963, resulted in the formation of the U.S. Tae Kwon Do Association in 1967, which later was superseded in 1974 by the U.S. Tae Kwon Do Federation.

When Karate was first introduced into the United States, few people noticed a distinction between Japanese Karate and Korean Tae Kwon Do. As a result, Korean Tae Kwon Do was often taught in the US as Karate. For example, Ernest Lieb, USAF, studied karate under Chun Il Sup while stationed in Korea and became the first karate chairman of the AAU and later the President of the American Karate Association. Atlee Chittim is another example. In 1948, he returned from Korea where he had studied Tae Kwon Do, and became affiliated with the USKA. He gave limited instructions at various YMCA's in San Antonio, Texas, and in 1955, he began teaching at San Antonio College, as a brown belt. Some say it was Chittim who sponsored master Jhoon Rhee's entry into the United States in 1956. In any event, it was Master Rhee who later promoted Chittim to black belt. A third example is Allen Steen, karate pioneer in the American Southwest, who started karate under Master Jhoon Rhee in 1959 at the University of Texas. He earned his black belt in 1962. In 1966, he was a member of the victorious U.S. National Karate Team in Hawaii. That same year, he won the International Karate Championships in Long Beach, beating Chuck Norris and Joe Lewis.

In 1961, Master Sihak Henry Cho opened what is believed to be the first permanent commercial Tae Kwon Do school in the U.S.. It was located on Twenty-seventh Street in New York City and had about four dozen people working out at it. He later opened a larger school on Twenty-third Street in Manhattan. Master Cho was still teaching in 1983. Like Master Rhee, he originally came to the U.S. as a student to work on his MBA.

While in New York, Master Cho visited a Judo school and gave a demonstration of Tae Kwon Do. He writes:

"The people who were there were amazed to see the kicks and the different things they had never seen before. The only thing that we had in New York, like the rest of the States, of course was Judo which was popular at the time."

Master Henry Cho decided to stay and became one of the early pioneers of American Tae Kwon Do. Other masters who arrived from Korea during the early 1960s were: Masters Richard Chun (1962),

Chong Lee (1964), and Heell Cho (1969).

In 1965, Master Hwa Chong also arrived from Korea to pursue his MA in Economics at the Michigan State University in East Lansing. Before coming to the USA, he was a student of Master Park Chull Hee, and the Tae Kwon Do instructor to the US Army stationed in South Korea from 1964-67. He was also the instructor for the presidential police for the late President Sigman Rhee. Master Hwa Chong started the first Tae Kwon Do classes at the University of Michigan in 1966. He later formed the Michigan Tae Kwon Do Association in 1968, organized the first Michigan Tae Kwon Do championships in 1969, and the first All American Tae Kwon Do Collegiate Championships in 1975. He later took the team for a first time demonstration in the Olympics in 1984, and was appointed as manager of the first team to the Olympics competition in 1988. He was elected as President of the AAU National committee for Tae Kwon Do from 1993 to 1996. Michigan AAU Tae Kwon Do was established in 1975 under the leadership of Master Hwa Chong. It organized its first tournament on Nov. 2, 1975, at the Huron High School in Ann Arbor, Michigan. Admission was only $1. Several hundred competitors from all over Michigan took part in it, including Master Saleem Jehangir from Pakistan. Winners from this tournament went to the US National Championships from where the winners were sent to the World Championships.

Due to the efforts of the US AAU TKD Committee, Tae Kwon Do was represented in the World Games held in Manila in 1977, and in 1978 US hosted the Third World Tae Kwon Do Championships.

Tae Kwon Do was included in the Olympics for the first time in 1988. Master Chong took the first team from USA into the Olympics, one of his students, Lynette Love, also won a gold medal.

The American Tae Kwon Do Association (ATA) is a smaller organization, and has many similarities to the ITF. The ATA has a copyright on the forms of the organization, so these forms cannot be used on competitions by non-members. There are many organizations, but the three mentioned above have the most members.

Americans contributed to changes in both Karate and Tae Kwon Do, primarily as a result of American tournament experience. In the early 1960s, fighters generally fought from a stationary position, using 80% hand techniques and 20% foot techniques. Kicks were usually stomach level or lower, and few fighters would kick with their lead leg. The standard kicks were front kicks or roundhouse kicks off the back leg. The counter reverse punch and the step-through lunge punch were the standard hand techniques. Open tournament competitors in the same period (1962-1964) were better kickers, but their hand techniques were primitive (overhead knife-hand strike, etc.) and they also fought from a stationary stance, with no footwork. Counter techniques and combinations were unknown. Kicks included roundhouses off both lead and trailing leg and spinning back kicks. Most of these kicks came from the Southwest (possibly due to Master Jhoon Rhee's influence there), as did kicks to the head and jump side kicks. East Coast fighters introduced the jumping double front kick, and used the lead leg roundhouse more than other early stylists. West Coast fighters stuck to the older Japanese styles. In 1965, Mike Stone was released from the Army and won nine consecutive tournaments without being defeated, primarily using a lead leg roundhouse and double knife hands.

In the late 1960s, Chuck Norris became a champion by combining Korean kicks (including lead leg side kick) with Japanese hand techniques. He was also the first fighter to successfully introduce combination techniques. Joe Lewis also came to fame at this time by the use of the lead leg side kick and the crossing back kick, demonstrating the effectiveness of single technique specialization. Lewis also proved the effectiveness of a lead punch. As a result, lead techniques began to gain recognition, although they would not become widely popular until the 1970s. Footwork in this period became the standard back and forward movement still prevalent today. Later on, point fighters would establish the basis of American Kickboxing. After the emphasis by WTF on the sport form of Tae Kwon Do, Korean instructors began emphasizing competition rather than self-defense. As an example, touch blocks have long since replaced formal blocks in sparring.

As a sport, Tae Kwon Do progressed quite slowly. In 1962, Tae Kwon Do was included as one of the official events in the 43rd Annual National Athletic Meet. In May, 1973, the first bi-annual World Tae Kwon Do Championships were held in Seoul, Korea, with more than thirty countries participating. Tae Kwon Do's big break came when the International Olympic Committee (IOC) recognized and admitted the WTF in July, 1980. In May 1982, Tae Kwon Do was named an official Demonstration Sport for the 1988 Olympics in Seoul.

Bibliography :

A History of Tae Kwon Do by Dakin Burdick.
Tae Kwon Do by Gen. Choi Hong Hi.
The Official Hall of Fame Tae Kwon Do website: lacancha.com

History of Tae Kwon Do in Pakistan

We are a fighting nation, our history proves it

Ancient

Although the real roots of martial arts lie buried in the archaeological artifacts of history, the source of the current traditional martial arts is most commonly traced to a Buddhist monk from India, Bodhidharma, who traveled to China to teach Buddhism. He had developed exercises to strengthen his body and mind against the natural elements, and also developed a weaponless art to defend himself against attacks and physical abuse. Bodhidharma traveled to the eastern parts of China bordering India, and along with teaching Buddhism, he must have also taught what he had developed as an art for self-defense.

In time, this art shaped into the early forms of Tai Chi and Kung Fu. Many books have been written on this search into the ancient to find the roots of development of the current martial art forms.

Indian Sub- Continent

In India's thousands of years of history, various forms of combat arts took birth as invaders invaded and plundered the riches of India. The famous epic poem, Mahabharata, which was written thousands of years ago, speaks of the various forms of weaponry used in the wars that could equate to today's guns, missiles, and even something similar to today's laser guns.

But from the time of recorded history which could date back to the times of Buddha, 2500 years ago, various forms of martial arts and combative sports propped up like the stick fighting (now known as Gudka or Lathi), sword fighting (Talwar), dagger fighting (Khanjar), wrestling (Kushti, Kabaddi, Malakhra), bow and arrow (Teer Kaman), Spear (Bullum/Neza), etc.. In the modern day India, the only names that became internationally known were in wrestling, they were Gama and now Khali.

Although boxing was introduced during the British rule, there was no other known weaponless combat art existent in the Indian sub-continent. It wasn't until the James Bond movie, Dr. No, came on screen in the early 1960s that all of a sudden the empty handed "karate chop" caught the intrigue of millions in the sub-continent. Subsequent to the 007 movie, a series of movies featuring Bruce Lee and his contemporaries just added fuel to the fire. It was also the time that Cassius Clay, now Mohammed Ali, the boxer shot into prominence in the sub-continent especially after beating Sonny Liston and converting to Islam. The urge to learn the mystical martial art then commonly known as Karate caught fire, but there were no teachers who could teach.

1971

Recorded history of Tae Kwon Do in Pakistan begins in 1971 when I, Saleem Jehangir, returned as a young engineer from the USA to settle in Pakistan. During my student life in the USA, I had learned this art in its original Korean form of Tae Kwon Do in the mid-1960s. I was the first official Black Belt from the Indo-Pak subcontinent, and the first to establish an official school of martial arts in Pakistan and form the first Tae Kwon Do Association of Pakistan.

The story goes like this. I graduated in Mechanical Engineering from the University of Michigan in 1968, started my professional career with Ford Motor Company, but returned to Pakistan in 1971. My plan was to serve Pakistan auto industry as an engineer. I was interviewed at the then Ghandara Industries, now National Motors, who perhaps did not like my outspokenness, and did not find a need for me. It is ironical because in 1988, a major auto company in Pakistan, HinoPak Motor, offered me the position of Director Production, and later in 1992, when General Habibullah repurchased National Motors from the Government of Pakistan, he wanted to hire me as Director Production.

But back in 1971, I did receive offers from AmericanTyre Company and Esso Eastern. Since Esso was a larger concern and offered more potential for growth, I joined Esso as Operations Engineer and managed the bulk product operations at the oil storage terminal at Keamari in Karachi.

The James Bond and the Bruce Lee movies had been here, so the interest was already there. All it needed was a Black Belt. Luckily for me, the would-be learners of the art were already gathering at the Japanese Cultural Center, where the Cultural Attaché of Japan, Teratani San, who was a Black Belt in Judo, was training them in Judo. So the ground was ready.

I had an old friend from my days at NED Engineering College, Irshad Usmani, who used to train in Judo at the Japanese Cultural Center in Karachi. When Irshad found out that I knew Karate (Tae Kwon Do name was not known in Pakistan at that time), he invited me to the Japanese center one evening. I went over just to observe. It was summer time and the class was just starting on the lawns of the center. I was introduced to Teratani San and the students of Judo. The students gathered around me and listened to me talk of Tae Kwon Do. They did not believe that I could be genuine. It was too good to be true, a karate black belt in Karachi? So they asked me for a demonstration. I showed them a couple of forms and some one step techniques. I could tell that they were impressed with the power they saw in my demonstration and my simultaneous explanation of the source of power. The rest, as they say, is history.

National Sports
Training & Coaching Centre
KARACHI.
BUILT BY THE PAKISTAN SPORTS CONTROL BOARD
(MINISTRY OF EDUCATION)
GOVERNMENT OF PAKISTAN.

The National Sports Training & Coaching Center in 1971 (now Pakistan Sports Board)

DAWN

QUAID-I-AZAM
MOHAMMAD ALI JINNAH

K A R A C H I
22 Sha'ban, 1391
Wednesday, Oct. 13, 1971
Vol. XXX   No. 277
10 PAGES 25 PAISA
By Air 30 Paisa

Judo training at Coaching Centre

THE National Sports Training and Coaching Centre will hold coaching and training classes in judo and karate from October 15 at its premises.

Mr. S.A. Jehangir who learnt these Japanese arts also known as "art of self defence" in USA will supervise the classes. He also won the competent rank of black belt."

The centre has already received 15 applications including three girls to join the classes.

Following its inclusion as sport in Olympics in Tokyo in 1964 both judo and karate gained tremendous popularity all over the world but they are more popular in Europe and in particular in Scandinavian countries where many training schools have sprung up in recent years.

In Pakistan, Lahore took the lead in introducing the game. Coaching classes in these games were started in Karachi about couple of years ago but due to poor response they were later discontinued .—APP

Judo and karate training

The National Sports Training and Coaching Centre will hold coaching and training classes in judo and karate from October 15 at its premises.

Mr. S. A. Jehangir, who learnt these Japanese arts also known as "art of self defence" in USA, will supervise the classes. He also won the competent rank of black belt."

The centre has already received 15 applications including three girls to join the classes.

Following its inclusion as sport in Olympics in Tokyo in 1964 both judo and karate gained tremendous popularity all over the world but they are more popular in Europe and in particular in Scandanavian countries where many training schools have sprung up in recent years.

Both judo and karate are liked and learnt more by girls who take up these sports because it provides them with the art of self defence.

In Pakistan, Lahore took the lead in introducing the game. Coaching classes in these games were started in Karachi a couple of years ago but due to poor response they were later discontinued.

But the present scheme by the NSTCC has received response both from the boys and the girls.

The centre officials feel that a sizeable number of enthusiasts are likely to join the classes.

All desirous to join the classes can contact National Sports Training and Coaching Director Khawaja Saleem Ahmed.—APP.

Clipping of the first news announcement in Dawn newspaper, dated Oct.13, 1971

First Batch of Junior and Senior Belts 1972

Junior and Senior Belts 1973

Senior Belts 1973

Group Photograph 1972

One of my first students-to-be who recognized my genuineness and who immediately showed interested in learning, was a fellow Darius Khan. He contacted me if I would be interested in teaching. I asked him where? He arranged for a place in a vacant home in Bahadurabad. The house had a small courtyard where we assembled. I had brought my uniform and my black belt with me from the USA. I started the training with a prayer and the same enthusiasm with which I had established the Rochester Institute of Technology. The training lasted a few days when one of the students, who was on the national boxing team, Zia Butt, suggested that we go and talk to the Director of the National Sports Training And Coaching Center, Karachi, Khwaja Saleem Ahmad, who was also a degree holder in Physical Education from the USA. Khwaja Saleem was delighted to meet me and immediately agreed to facilitate the commencement of a Tae Kwon Do training program at the NSTCC. He was so receptive of my vision of promoting martial arts in Pakistan that he immediately said yes. The formalized training classes started in late 1971.

At that time the huge NSTCC was used only for occasional training camps of national caliber athletes and basketball teams. The NSTCC was closed for all other activities during the times that we trained there, with some 200 students, using the main hall and every available space on the premises. It had a huge hall with a wooden floor, a massive outdoor field, large changing / locker rooms, an athletic field, and a few acres for future development. Moreover it was located on top of a hill with overlooking views of entire North Karachi. Back then in 1971, there were no high rise developments in between the NSTCC and Nazimabad. It used to be a favorite activity after the training sessions, which ended at 8 pm, to sit on the lawns of the NSTCC, sip coke, and enjoy the glimmering views in the dark nights of Karachi. There was no traffic at night, no bus service or taxi, so only people with cars or motorcycles would come for training. Training was conducted in English, which further limited the learners to a particular category... English speaking, with transportation. They came in all ages, from 5 years to 50 years old, and from all

Saleem Jehangir on the Zia Moheyuddin Show in 1972

Saleem Jehangir singing on the Zia Moheyuddin Show

Zia Is Back Again

WHAT is rather remarkable about the Zia Moheyuddin Show is that it gets away with a lot of absurdity and even simplicity as engaging entertainment. This is the credit that Zia Moheyuddin gets, and he gets it again for the first show that goes on air on Tuesday night.

The recording of the ZM show was done at the Fleet club on Wednesday night. And for a resumption of the show from Karachi after a laps of year, I feel that it is a poor reopening of the popular programme.

Participants in the first show were Runa Laila, Qavi, Karate teacher Saleem Jahangir, and a few minor role players who walk in and out to suit the convenience of the overall pointlessness of the programme. And as always there is "philosophy" and poetry reading by the pivot of the show—Zia Moheyuddin himself.

What strikes the viewer in the show is the casual considerable role that the main guest singer Runa Laila plays. She plays a second fiddle in the programme and plays it exceedingly well. And adds to the interest of the show.

What however is the novel attraction in the 50 minute show is the performance of versatile Saleem Jehangir. He knows and teaches Karate, sings reasonably well (he sang two old numbers) and has an engineering background.

A trifle stunning was the Karate exhibited by sisters young Salma and Asma Ashraf. They are among the 22 girls acquiring the self-defence art of Karate—and according to Zia possibly to counter male aggression in our society!

A word about Runa Laila's appearance. It was far from impressive and equally far from being "mod" in outlook.

And Zia was rather vagabondish that evening, it that is a plausible definition of the man.

Zia has come to Karachi with his programme after exhausting his men, women and ideas in Lahore.

It should be interesting to see how he takes up the challenge of sustaining interest in what has now become a somewhat cliche ridden format of the TV.

Article in Dawn on the Zia Show

walks of life. One of the oldest students in the group was Nawab Khair Bukhsh Murrie of Baluchistan. An athletically inclined man in his mid-forties, who used to come to play squash at the NSTCC. Later on, he was the one who facilitated the Tae Kwon Do training camps in Quetta.

The Khwaja agreed on one condition that I can run the operation my way as long as the NSTCC takes credit for it. In addition we used to pay Rs 10 per student per month for use of the facility. This was all very agreeable to us. What a perfect start. NSTCC was a place of the highest repute and prestige, a place where only national sports stars were trained by visiting international coaches. And we were using it at the prime time in the evening. We had the whole place reserved for us. The hall, the lawns, the grounds, the lockers, you name it. The administrative staff was gone at 5 pm, and there was only Saifu, the security guard, who would be there for us. And he was there for us a hundred percent. He served us, took care of us, and did all this with love. He saw the NSTCC come to life from an occasional use to a full time use, 7 days a week. With scores of people coming to watch the TKD training sessions, they would enquire about other programs, and the Khwaja was able to start Badminton and Table Tennis subsequently. Saifu is still

Article about the Quetta training camp in the Daily Mashriq

کھیلوں سے نظم وضبط اور خوداعتمادی پیدا ہوتی ہے

کوئٹہ میں جوڈو اور کراٹے کے تربیتی انتظام پر وزیراعلیٰ اور وزیر خزانہ کا بیان

Group picture with Chief Minister, Sardar Ataullah Mengal, and Sardar Khair Bux Murree

31

Daily MASHRIQ THURSDAY

صوبائی وزیر اعلیٰ مسٹر عطا اللہ مینگل اور وزیر خزانہ میر احمد نواز بگٹی کراٹے اور جوڈو کی تقریب تقسیم انعامات میں ایک طرف میر خیر بخش مری جوڈو سیکھنے والے نوجوانوں کے ساتھ بیٹھے ہیں

کراٹے اور جوڈو کی تقریب تقسیم انعامات میں شریک ہونے والی خواتین

سردار مینگل کراٹے اور جوڈو کی تقریب تقسیم انعامات میں کانونٹ سینٹ جوزف سکول کی مس ایوان کو انعام دے رہے ہیں

زندگی کے ہر شعبے میں کامیابی کے لئے نظم وضبط کو برقرار رکھنا ضروری ہے

کوئٹہ کلب میں جوڈو کراٹے کی تربیت حاصل کرنے والے افراد سے زیر اعلیٰ بلوچستان کا خطاب

کوئٹہ (14 روز مبر دشافت رپورٹ) بلوچستان کے وزیر اعلیٰ سردار عطا اللہ مینگل نے کہا ہے کہ کراٹے اور جوڈو کو کھیلا چلنے میں بہت کارآمد ثابت ہوتے ہیں میرا خیال ہے کہ زندگی کے ہر شعبے میں کام آتے ہیں۔ انہوں نے توقع ظاہر ...

کراٹے اور جوڈو کی تقریب تقسیم انعامات کے موقع پر ایک بچی اور نوجوان جوڈو کا مظاہرہ کر رہے ہیں۔

News coverage of the certificate distribution ceremony with Chief Minister, Sardar Ataullah Mengal as Chief Guest

Karate Catches Quetta

NELSON HARRIS—Quetta

The oldest form of hand to hand fighting call it **Judo, Jujutsu, Okinawa-te** or **Karate** has over the years spread like wild fire around the world and now even in Pakistan countless number of institutions teaching the martial arts in different cities have sprung.

The young men and women of our country no longer desire to be left behind in any field in comparision with the rest of the world and have taken on a much more impregnated task than their predecessors. I can quite confidently say this because anyone seeing the determined and set attitude of the youth of our country will agree that today's posterity will achieve much more in the years to come in every sphere of life.

Take for example sports. Gone are the days when only a few form of games could be classified under the title of "SPORTS". Tod y the field is extensive and open to all and even the fairer sex have been given their due share in the field of sport

Karate an ever colourful form of sport has gripped **Quetta** like the severe Khandari winds which clutch at the heart of the Quetta-ites when it blows in the bitter winter season. Just over a couple of months three different institutions have taken over the responsibility of training the youth of this city in the now ever increasing and infectious fever of Karate and even the Movie houses seem to be doing a thriving business by running movies on Karate every week.

Let us take a close look at a class in session in the **YMCA Quetta**. The instructor here is Ibrahim Ismail who underwent his training of TAE - KWOON-DO at the **National Coaching Centre Karachi**, which was the very first institution of its kind in Pakistan. The students taking training from him compromise about forty in number and regularly without fail they attend classes form 6 pm to 8 pm. Discipline is strictly adhered to and the young men of Quetta who also love to be known as the **"Youth of Rock"** follow the directions of their Instructor to the letter.

Being an art foreign to our heritage and also bearing in mind its deadly significance these young men work with their heart and soul toiling to absorb as much as they

can in a short period of time to better their body coordination and improve upon their health.

Therefore in conclusion it can be said being an indoor sport, Karate is on the UP UP in our city and admissions in these institutions are being speeded up, not only by the young and energetic alone, but a large group of the elders have also started to move towards this beacon of light showing yet another means of losing weight.

25

Article about the Quetta YMCA Tae Kwon Do Club in Sun Magazine

there and remembers us all, and reminisces every moment he spent in those evenings. He even prays for us. Whenever I go there I become sad for leaving it. The sadness can be seen even in the eyes of Saifu who is always so delighted to see anyone from that time.

We used to charge Rs 100 per student, which included an admission fee of Rs 25, and Rs 75 for three months training. The uniform was sold separately for Rs 100. All the money we gathered would go into organizing and holding training sessions at other locations, holding tournaments, association functions like belt distribution ceremonies with chief guests, parents, and refreshments, and occasional treats for the senior students. Finally, we gathered enough money to buy a plot of land in Gulshan Iqbal to build our own Martial Arts Academy.

The training classes were held six days a week, from 6 pm to 8 pm, but each section group would come on alternate days only. This way we could handle the demand we had. In the best of the times, there were close to 200 students training at any one time. Every three months we would hold belt tests and students will be awarded certificates and belts if they passed.
The Khwaja expired in the 1990s. I pray for the blessing of his soul.

1972

The Zia Moheyuddin Show
The most popular show in those days on TV was the Zia Moheyuddin Show. Zia had already achieved his fame in Pakistan from the movie Lawrence of Arabia, and now he was host of the leading show in the nation. He personally came to see me at the NSTCC and offered me to be in his show. I was honored, and agreed. We worked out the details at the Karachi Television station. He learnt of my interests in singing and music and included two songs in the show also. The show was a hit and I became an instant celebrity in Pakistan. The club membership jumped to over 200. The show brought us extreme popularity in the nation, perhaps more than all the other newspapers and magazines put together. It was seen by the whole nation. And, from then on, Tae Kwon Do became a household name.

I would like to offer special thanks and appreciation to Zia Moheyuddin in this book for his contribution to the growth of martial arts in Pakistan.
Quetta Training Session

Nawab Khair Bukhsh Murree requested us to hold a training session in Quetta, Baluchisan. Since winters are very cold, and summers are very pleasant there, we agreed to do it at the end of the summer of 1972. Asif, Musarrat, Irshad Usmani went there first to start the classes, I joined them later for a weekend for the belt tests and distribution of certificates. Training sessions were organized at the convent schools for both boys and girls, separately. We were received with the full hospitality that Baluchistan is well known for. Another aspect that helped was the fact that many students, aside from the convent school students, were the children of the political hierarchy of Baluchistan. The entire elite of the province, including the Mazaris, the Mengals, the Murries, the sons of Khan of Qalat, all were there. The training sessions for them were held at the YMCA. Since I was working with Esso, I could not be there for the whole two weeks and went over there for the belt tests only. I was received with full fervor and hospitality. We were even invited to the residence of the legendary Khan of Qalat, where we spent a day and a night with his sons. The weather of Baluchistan was dry and cool, a big change from Karachi, so we all enjoyed it thoroughly. But good times don't last long, and we came back to manage our own Dojang at the NSTCC.

Pictures of Test in Progress at the NSTCC in 1972

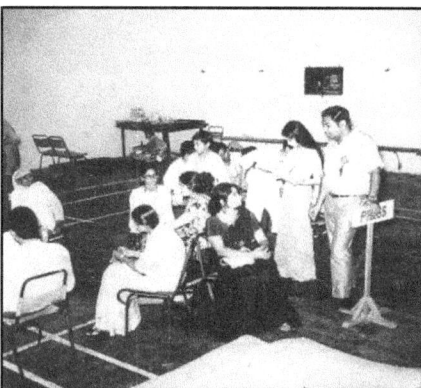

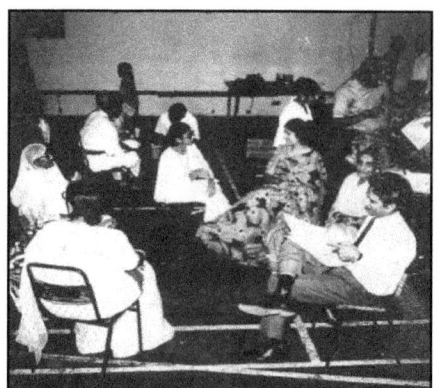

Pictures of Test in Progress at the NSTCC in 1972

Pictures of Test in Progress in 1972

Master Saleem Jehangir with Family Members at the NSTCC in 1972

This trip not only brought us closer to the political and educational hierarchy of Baluchistan, it laid the seed for the growth of Tae Kwon Do in Baluchistan. Today the province can boast about its talents in the martial art.

Other Training Sessions

Other training sessions were held for the Police, Navy, Saint Patrick and other schools. The news spread like wild fire and so did the interest in martial arts. News media, television and magazines played an extremely crucial role in popularizing the art in Pakistan. Demonstrations and training classes were organized in various cities of Pakistan including Quetta and Lahore (Punjab University), and more clubs propped up in Hyderabad, Thatta, Rahimyarkhan. The trend in teaching in schools grew with increasing number of schools including Tae Kwon Do in their Physical Education Curriculums. Today, Tae Kwon Do is all over the schools, colleges and universities, the account of which will be very hard to gather. The popularity of the art has grown to an extent over the last 40 years that Pakistan is now sending teams to compete in international championships, and recently even won medals in the female category in the Commonwealth games.

Although, in retrospect, I wish I had been here to witness and administer this phenomenal growth in Pakistan, but it is still very gratifying to think that we laid its seeds in history.

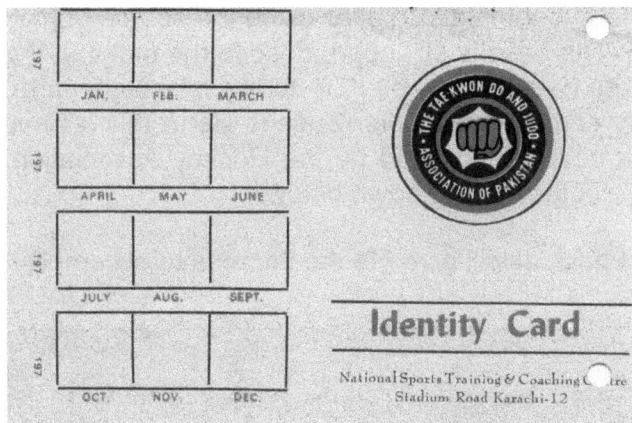

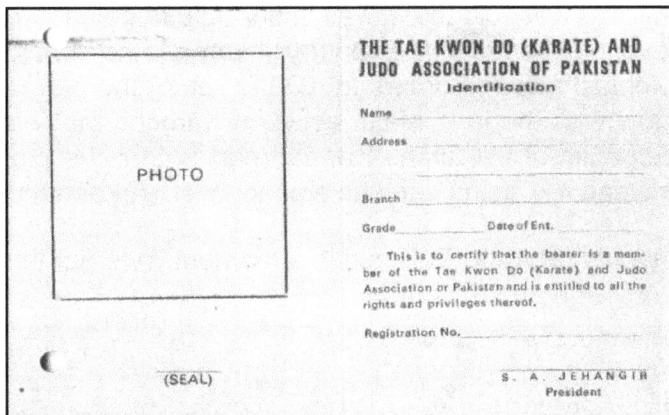

Association Badge and Membership ID Card

Formation of the Tae Kwon Do-Karate Association of Pakistan

Once we established ourselves at NSTCC, and the Khwaja gave us an office with an adjacent room for storage, we decided to form and register the association. We named it The Tae Kwon Do-Karate Association of Pakistan. Since the people in Pakistan were only familiar with the word Karate, we thought we would include it in, and at the same time educate the people with the word Tae Kwon Do. One of the students helped us have it registered quickly with the Registrar of Associations. We then decided on the insignia, which was the traditional fist, and had it printed on letter heads, ID cards, stationery, and the sticker to be put on your cars. This was a time when nobody carried guns, and if you were wearing a gee or had a sticker on your car, people took you seriously. I remember when the American School in Karachi had an annual carnival, they invited us to maintain order inside the school premises, and our club students dressed in gees did just the same. The days of the TT and the Klashnikovs were not in yet. *Application forms for the students were printed in a hurry, ID cards were issued, records were kept on every student. Since this was a troubled time with martial law, breaking up of East Pakistan, then Z.A. Bhutto coming into power, we asked for police certificates for every student. Or character affidavits signed by a first class gazette officer were also accepted. A bank account was opened and the money started to deposit into it. The money was used for all purposes to promote the art in Pakistan. There was an unfortunate incident that happened in the first year, the students who we trusted with the money took off with Rs 50,000, which was a large sum in those days, considering that a bungalow in Gulshan Iqbal on 400 sq. yds. sold for only Rs 100,000. From then on I implemented a check and balance system for the collection and deposit of money.*

The Vision of having our own place called the Martial Arts Academy

I always used to dream of having a place like they do in Korea and Japan, which is dedicated just for the teaching of the martial arts. It is headed by the Grand Master of the style of the art being taught. Most of us have seen it in the movies by now. I had that dream. I still do.

In order to fulfill that vision we decided to purchase an amenity plot in Gulshan Iqbal, which we did through KDA, Karachi Development Authority. We had saved enough money and made 50% of the payment, which was Rs 20,000, and demanded possession of the lot. But like fate would have it, General Zia toppled Bhutto in 1975, and took over as martial law dictator. He ordered all plots of land issued out in Bhutto's times to be withdrawn and re-issued. Our plot was issued out to the Karachi Hockey Association. This happened in 1976 soon after Gen. Zia took over. I flew back to Pakistan and filed a case with the Mohtasib (Ombudsman) in Karachi for the recovery of the plot. I have fought that case for 36 years now, with no avail. In those days, KDA was known to be the most corrupt land organization in the country. It still is. I was told that it was impossible to get land out of KDA again. Even after using the source of high level dignitaries in the country, it came to no conclusion. The case is still open, despite the fact that the Mohtasib issued orders to KDA to return the plot to us, no heed is paid by KDA to the executive order. Now with the land mafia active in Karachi, the recovery seems impossible. Such is life in this Islamic Republic of Pakistan. The sad part is that the plot has never been used by the Hockey Association, instead it is being used as a parking lot. An aerial picture of the site is shown below.

I would return to Pakistan in a moment if we get this plot back. It will give me the impetus to accomplish my vision and my dream.

Aerial View of the Plot allotted to the TKD Association

Offer from the chowdhuries of Boxing and Wrestling

As soon as the news spread that there is a genuine teacher of the martial arts in the country, I was approached by the then Secretaries of the Boxing and Wrestling Associations belonging to the Pakistan Sports Board (PSB). I don't want to publish their names because I don't want to malign anyone in this book, I just want to present the facts as they took place. They offered me to join them in opening a PSB association for Judo and Karate. They wanted to be a part of it also. I told them I already have a registered association but let me think about it. I discussed this with one of our well-wishers, a newspaper reporter for Daily Evening News, Ali Kabir. Ali Kabir had supported us with publishing articles in the evening paper every week. He knew we were genuine and warned me not to join PSB as it is a very corrupt board of the Government of Pakistan. Associating with PSB will malign my name with it, and then no newspaper of magazine will support us. He openly said that the interest of those secretaries was to fleece money from the government and use it for their personal purposes. When the Secretary of Boxing contacted me I told him that I am not interested in their offer. Soon after my rejection of their proposal, PSB announced in the papers that a Judo Association has been formed, and some one from Lahore was appointed as its Secretary. A grant of Rs 50,000 was made to it for the promotion of Judo. I prefer not to write any more on this issue.

My goal was to have my Association recognized by the Korea Tae Kwon Do Association (KTA) for which I had already contacted Master Chong. We were approached by ITF's General Choi Hong Hee who wanted us to join ITF. Neither KTA nor WTF contacted us and the matter was put on the back burner. At my request to the Consulate General of South Korea, the WTF did send us high dan black belts to train our students at the NSTCC for a couple of years, for which we all are grateful.

Master Chong, who is now the president of the World Kang Duk Won Tae Kwon Do Federation, has appointed me as its vice-president, and as president of the Pakistan Kang Duk Won Tae Kwon Do Federation. This honor gratifies me more than any title by the Pakistan Sports Board.

Request to train from various celebrities

As the newspapers and magazines started to publish about us, the interest grew from all sectors of life in Karachi. A Pakistani film actress of those days, Rackhshanda Khattak, had acted as a karateka in a film, when she heard about us she wanted to learn the real thing. So she sent a messenger to me at the NSTCC if I can come to see her at her house. This was to be a start of a series of disappointments on the culture existing in Pakistan. I could have never fathomed sending a message to any Ustad of any art to come and see me at my house. So, politely, I sent a message back to her that if she wants to learn she has to come to the NSTCC where I teach it to the rest. That was the last I heard from her. And she was not even one of the fore runners among actresses. I still don't know what she looked like.

Then later, I received a request through my students from the famous wrestlers of Pakistan, the Bholu Brothers. They had signed a bout with Inoki, the famous Japanese all-in-one wrestler cum martial arts fighter. They wanted me to come over to teach them at their Akhara (Wrestling Dojo) somewhere in western part of old Karachi. They did not know what Karate was and wanted an introductory training in it. I sent the same message back to them that I did to Rakhshanda Khattak. But this time I felt a little guilty, because the nation's prestige was at stake. But I am a humble human being, and the type that expects humility from specially those who want to learn something from me. I considered training them, but then I thought they are so grossly overweight that I will be spending the rest of my life in getting them to just lose weight. Then I also know the Phunnay Khan (show-off) mentality that permeates the entire wrestlers' minds in Pakistan. And I just didn't have the stomach for it.

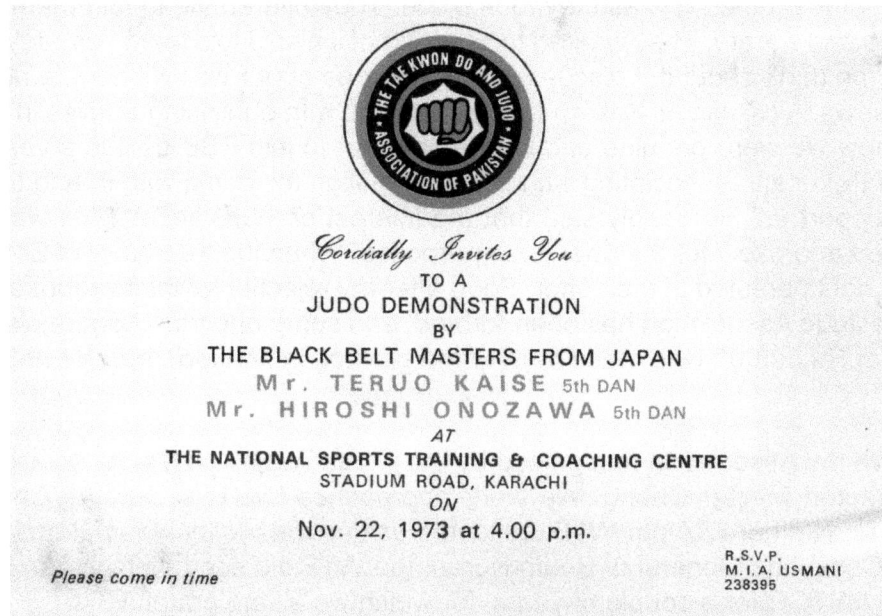

The Invitation Card issued by the Tae Kwon Do Association of Pakistan

The Consulate General of Japan speaking at the Judo Demonstration

The Judo Masters from Japan with Master Teratani San

Judo Masters displaying their skills

**Judo Masters with the Consulate General,
Master Teratani San and Doc at the Reception**

Tae Kwon Do student Darius Khan displaying throw in Tae Kwon Do

Yellow and Green Belts in 1973

White Belt group in 1973

Group Photo 1973

Group Photographs of 1973

1973

.The First Official Display of Judo organized by the TKD Association of Pakistan

My vision was not only to promote Tae Kwon Do, but to bring all martial arts to Pakistan, and even revive the old martial arts that were native to the sub-continent. Along this effort I requested Teratani San of the Japanese Consulate to arrange for some Judo masters to come to Pakistan. He agreed and obliged me with the visit of a few Judo masters, the best I had ever seen in person. These masters were 5th Dan Judo Black Belts, and were much larger in built compared to the average Japanese. Our association organized the display at the NSTCC and the invitations were issued from the Japanese Consulate to all the dignitaries of Karachi. In the demonstration, we started with a display of Tae Kwon Do forms, one step, two step techniques, sparring and board breaking. Then we turned the show over to the Japanese Judo masters. They displayed their skills using some of our students who had also learned Judo from Teratani San. One of the students was a huge man we called Doc (his name was Asad Ishaq). He was a veterinarian doctor and was built like a rock. He was some 6 feet 2 inches in height, very muscular, and hard like stone. I have never seen anyone built so strong like he was. Doc had taken a few months of Judo training before he joined the Tae Kwon Do classes. When he got up to wrestle with the Judo master, the near capacity crowd, which had filled the big hall at NSTCC, went into a roar with applause. I could see the concern on the Judo master's face as he entered the ring. I am convinced that he never encountered a stronger built opponent than Doc. So he took Doc seriously, and after a few minutes of struggling finally got him down.

The whole demonstration was like an extremely enjoyable show. Perhaps the most well attended among all martial arts events held in Pakistan at that time. The newspapers, magazines, and Pakistan Television covered this event. The Pakistan Sports Board Judo Association took the credit for arranging it. Such is the story in Pakistan. Sometimes I question why am I so different and then wonder which race I belong to. But, I am especially grateful to Teratani San for his contribution in bringing Judo to Pakistan.

Lahore

I got married to a beautiful girl from Lahore in the January of 1973. The Karachi Tae Kwon Do students hosted a demonstration and a gift giving ceremony for her (see pictures below). In the spring of 1973, I went back to Lahore with my wife, and used the opportunity to conduct short training sessions in Tae Kwon Do at the Punjab University campus on Canal Road. I found the students to be genuinely interested, so I gave them a taste of the art by sparring with them. My visit to Lahore was short for I had to return to my job at Esso.

Many years later, I went back to Lahore and was walking a park when I saw some students practicing Tae Kwon Do. I just stood there and watched them. They did not recognize me. There was a time when even people not studying Tae Kwon Do would see me and approach me. I was forgotten already? I didn't like the feeling, but such is life.

Saleem Jehangir with wife and other Family Members

Students presenting gifts to Mrs. Jehangir

The First All Pakistan Tae kwon Do Championships 1973

By the end of 1972 we were one year into the establishment of Tae Kwon Do in Pakistan, and thought that it was time to organize a nationwide championship. We did. There were not too many clubs operating then, only the ones we started. But, another style of martial art started in Karachi in 1972. This one was from Burma, called Bando, it was being taught by one Mr. Ashraf Tai. Although it had just started, and it was not Tae Kwon Do but had forms and sparring in it, we decided to invite his club. I am glad we asked them to participate, it brought another style for us to compete against, and also test them out for genuineness. It turned out that one of their performers was very good and he ended up winning trophies both in forms and sparring. The event was very well organized, and no mishap or any distasteful occurrence took place. As usual, newspapers and agazines covered this event well.

Spectators at the First All Pakistan Tae Kwon Do Championships in 1973

News Papers and Magazines that patronized Tae Kwon Do

Morning News, Daily Evening News, Evening Star, Dawn, Jang, Akhbar-e-Khwateen, Sun, Herald, and many others, all covered our events from time to time and we need to give them credit for doing their share in publicizing the art to the masses. I have included some cuttings from them in this book. There are many more, but I will save them for later editions.

Sportimes

Among the top and regular supporters was Pakistan's only sports magazine, Sportimes. Sportimes was a magazine of international repute whose editor, Mr. Sultan F. Hussain (marhoom), was also its founder. An extremely capable man in the journalism of sports, he was a wizard at remembering sports statistics, especially in Cricket. Sportimes was the only sports magazine of Pakistan, and a well-respected one with large circulation. It was available on every news stand throughout the country. Sultan F. Hussain personally supported my endeavors and for which I am forever grateful to him and pray for the blessing of his soul. Sportimes published my articles on TKD for almost 24 months, till I stopped writing them. Some of the pictures and articles published in it are included here.

Lathi (Long Stick) and Gadka (Short Stick) Training

To further my efforts in reviving the old native arts of the sub-continent, I arranged for an Ustad of Lathi and Gadka to teach us. He was the late Ustad Farrukh Mirza, who was from among the direct descendants of Bahadur Shah Zafar, the last Mughal king of India. He was also an Ustad of Indian classical music and an expert of hunting and fishing that I ever saw in person, a real Ustad in many arts. I had to invite him first to see what I am doing in the martial arts category. He was thoroughly impressed, and acknowledged that I do with my arms and legs what he does with a stick. Then he decided to accept me as his pupil and teach the art of lathi. He came with a kg of Mithai (Pakistani deserts) and performed Niaz (supplication) over it. Then he distribute d the sweets among us. This was the old custom of accepting you as a pupil. Then he taught us the moves. But like an Ustad, he taught us slow and gradually, till we showed that we really wanted to learn.

He was old, feeble, and with failing health and could not keep up with the training needs. So we decided not to pressurize him to teach us further. But I learned some of his secret moves, and also some of his secret recipes of making the feed for the fish. On our fishing trips together to Lake Haleji, he used to make that Chaara (feed) and throw it in the lake in the evening. Then he would wait a few hours. Then he would cast his hook, snag the fish, and pull one after another, keeping the ones he liked to eat and throwing back the ones he didn't. He would fish all night. And eat them all day. He said that the time to fish is the night. He did not use a fishing rod or any sophisticated bait, just a 10 lb. line with a hook and bait made out of white flour dough. He would cast it by hand and then wait, holding the line in his fingers and feeling the fish bite. He would then snag the fish and let the fish fight, pulling it in and then letting it go, as we watched the fish flap on the water and make that thrilling noise loved by all fishermen. The fight would take place as long as it took to tire the fish out. He did not care, he loved to fight the fish. Then when the fish was exhausted he would pull it in and slowly lift it from underneath with his bare hands as if it was dead. What an Ustad of fishing he was.

He was also an Ustad of music, having learnt it for decades. In another pursuit to gain from his musical genius, I urged him to include me in his sittings. He arranged musical sittings with some great Ustads of his times. My father told me that he was such a great critic of music during his times that he would not even listen to another Ustad if that Ustad didn't meet his minimum standard.

An Ustad of lathi and gudka, music, fishing, hunting, and god knows what else he was an expert at. O yes, I know…cooking. I have never tasted food like he used to cook on our hunting and fishing trips. His hunting style was very different too. He would search out the most remote corners of the world, somewhere where there is no road even. He would take the train to a small town in Sindh, then from there take a Tonga (horse carriage) to wherever the road took him, then he would get on a bullock cart to go the rest of the way in the forests to hunt.

His only advice to me was: if you really want to learn something, pursue it with it Junoon (obsession). We are so unfortunate in this respect not to have searched more like him and benefited from their

**Master Patrick Harrigan learning Lathi from (the late) Ustad
Farrukh Mirza**

knowledge and skills. People from the old school were like that. They did not even keep you in their company unless you showed dedication toward them. What a loss, so many of them died with the secret knowledge buried in their hearts.

He was a warrior in its truest sense, one who strove to achieve perfection in everything he did, and made his pursuit an obsession.

1974

This is the year I went back to the USA and spent the whole year training for my Second Dan under Master Chong in Michigan. I trained at Master Chong's club in Detroit metro area, and at the University of Michigan TKD Club in Ann Arbor. I also joined Ford Motor Company again, as a manufacturing engineer, this time in the Assembly Division. This was the year that Master Chong organized the First All American Inter-Collegiate Tae Kwon Do Championships in Ann Arbor. I helped him, along with the other students from his old batch, and also competed in the tournament. I lost in the free sparring category but was placed second in Forms competition.

When I left Pakistan I made Wasim Akhtar in charge of the Karachi TKD activities, he was not only the most dedicated student I had at that time, he was also the senior most and most trustworthy among my students.

I was tested in Michigan by Master Chong and was promoted to Second Dan in 1974.

Acknowledgment by Black Belt magazine

As I became active in the TKD circle, the news spread that I am back, old students came to reacquaint themselves and new ones got to know me for the first time. Somewhere along the line a reporter from Black Belt magazine found out about me and wanted to write an article. I asked Master Chong, he agreed. The reporter came to Master Chong's club and took pictures as well as interviewed both of us

1st AMERICAN INTERCOLLEGIATE AND OPEN TAE KWON DO-KARATE CHAMPIONSHIPS

MARCH 30, 1974	UNIVERSITY OF MICHIGAN	INTRAMURAL SPORTS BLDG.
Tournament President: **Dr. Rodney Grambeau** Director, Intramural and Recreational Sports Programs	Tournament Director: **Hwa Chong** Instructor, U. of Michigan Tae Kwon Do Club	Tournament Advisor: **Dayton Matlick** President A.M T.K.D.-K. Fed.

May 10, 1974

Dear Pupil,

I feel very happy to hear that the Pakistani youth organise and practice Tae Kwon Do diligently to cultivate the Body and the Mind for the Unification of the World. Your teacher, Mr. Saleem Jehangir, has been one of my best students at the University of Michigan Tae Kwon Do Club and has a fine personality. I believe that this Martial Art can become a tool of Unification of our divided world and shrink generation gap. We can then exchange differant ISMS and IDEALS, build a better world and live together. Your people have a rich goal and with efforts you are putting into it you will acheive it.

We had the First American Inter-Collegiate and Open Tae Kwon Do - Karate Championships last march; your teacher, Mr. Jehangir, won second place in the Black Belt Form competition. Much before this we had the First Michigan Inter-Collegiate and Open Tae Kwon Do - Karate Championships in November 1969; Mr. Jehangir was a Brown Belt then, he won the second place in the Brown Belt Sparring competition.

Next year we are planning to hold an International Tournament. I talk with Mr. Jehangir that there is a possibility of invitng a team from Pakistan. If everybody sacrifices and everybody works hard, the old saying" when there is a will, there is a way to acheive your goal " I can see your group at the International Tournament.

Always we should set the goal higher than we can reach. Therefore we should work hard and improve to acheive our goal. I am pleased that you have the fine leadership of Mr. Jehangir and in his guidance you will reach your goal someday.

I would like to hear from you about your progress more frequently.
I would like to help your group in any way I can.

Good Luck to you all,

Sincerely yours

Hwa Chong

Hwa Chong

Master Chong's letter to the Tae Kwon Do students in Pakistan (1974)

and published a very good article about me. I was going to be on the cover page, but an accident took place in a martial arts demonstration somewhere, and at the eleventh hour they decided to bring that incident on the cover because it involved safety of students. It was at a knife throwing demonstration in which the knife pierced the neck of the subject person, and the article brought out the unsafe elements of such displays of skill.

After my coverage in the Black Belt magazine, my popularity soared both in the USA and in Pakistan. The article became a testimonial to my efforts of pioneering the art in Pakistan. Later, many books and encyclopedias were published which also included me in them.

1975

The First All Pakistan Tae Kwon Do Championships

I returned to Pakistan for a few months to impart the training I had received from Master Chong. On this trip I held training sessions for the senior belts, and organized the first black belt test for the students in Pakistan. Wasim Akhtar was awarded the first Black Belt among students in Pakistan. Newspapers again wrote about us in good standing.

It was also the right time to organize and a country wide event, so we did. The First All Pakistan Tae Kwon Do Championships were held on 8th February of 1975. The event was a grand success and the media covered it with their usual enthusiasm as usual.

SPECIAL DONATION TICKETS

The Tae Kwon Do-Karate Association of Pakistan

*requests the pleasure of your company
on the occasion of the*

1st ALL PAKISTAN TAE KWON DO-KARATE CHAMPIONSHIPS

to be held on Saturday the 8th February, 1975 at
The National Sports Training & Coaching Centre
Opp. National Stadium, Karachi.

Programme :

Eliminations   :   10.00 a.m.
Finals & Demonstration :   5.00 p.m.

The Invitation Card to the First All Pakistan Tae Kwon Do Championships in 1975

FIRST ALL-PAKISTAN TAE KWON DO KARATE CHAMPIONSHIPS

1ST ALL PAKISTAN TAE KWON DO KARATE TOURNAMENT 1975.

It was all KI-YA inside the packed Sports Coaching Centre Karachi while the din of thunder and rain continued outside. The heavy downpour however did not stop the Karate enthusiasts from gathering for the first All Pakistan Karate tournament 1975. Over 3000 persons attended the occasion who also witnessed the exibition of the oriental fighting Arts.

The tournament was sponsored by the Tae Kwon Do Karate and Judo Association of Pakistan with the cooperation of the clubs in Karachi and Lahore where the Martial Arts are presently flourishing. Nearly 200 participants competed in the tournament which included the belt promotion test of the various affiliated clubs of The Tae Kwon Do Karate And Judo Association of Pakistan.

The elimination contest started around 10.30 in the morning which was jointly supervised by Mr Saleem Jahangir Black Belt 2nd Dan Chief Instructor of his Club and Mr Tai who is also a Black Belt 2nd Dan of Tai Karate Club Karachi. Initially there was Kata competition in Tae Kwon Do (KOREAN), Bando (BURMESE) and JU-Ka-Tuk (Japanese) styles of Karate, although the movements and styles were distinctly different but the basic sprit of the Kata were evident and appreciated by all present. The Katas performed in the Brown belt level were most complex and graceful and were applauded by the young spectators. There was keen competition between Asif Hussain and Wasim Akhtar both of The Tae Kwon Do Karate Association, but the latter won the tournament by beautifully demonstrating his favourite form known as "NOHAI".

For the 3000 spectators, who came to watch this first Karate Tournament the real excitement came when it was time for free sparring. The free sparring was conducted in two separate rings one for the senior Belts and one for the junior Belts, the senior being looked after by Mr Saleen Jehangir and the junior by Asif Hussain There was one Referee and four Judges for each ring and the scoring point was only given when all the four judges raised their flags. On the whole the decisions were fair and were appreciated by all present. Only those boys and girls took part in the free sparring who had earlier qualified for the finals in the morning session when the prelims were held. The participants were fighting for the best three positions in Pakistan. The contest was tough and could expect such things to happen in some times rules were also broken, but one sports of this kind as has been witnessed before in Boxing and Wrestling. In the Yellow Belt level there was a tie and all the Clubs did their best to go for the prizes. The results will be given at the end.

The most interesting fights were of the kids and the girls who were being cheered up all the time by their respective groups. The performance of the girl participants was quite good and it gave the male spec-

News Coverage on the Championship

55

tators a view of their ability to defend themselves. Comments of one of the spectators after seing the fair sex was "A time will come soon when we will be cooking and washing dishes" he was quite serious and did not like the idea of the girls being given this training. For the readers I am sure many of you are thinking of learning this art. Now coming back to the fight, in the green belt level it was a rough play but the students were doing their utmost to keep the tradition of the art and there was no misbehaviour. Scoring was mostly done with kicks as punches to the face was not allowed as this as well as other weak points were considered fouls so that there was no serious injury. The favourites in the green Belt were Ibrahim and Jabari of the Tae Kwon Do and Altaf of Tai Karate Club.

Few words about young Jabari, he has the sprit of a real karateka and fought very bravely against stronger opponents all his fights were clear and clean. I am sure if this boy is groomed well he will one day represnt Pakistan along with his other senior members. Altaf of Tai karate techniques, he is the only one who fought the highest number of fights and won them all until he lost to the unpredictable Ibrahim. Ibrahim with his formidable flying side kick keeps an opponent at a distance, a little opening there he is right in you and if the block does not come in time you are sure to break your ribs.

In the Blue and Brown belt level the fights were a demonstration of agile movements and smooth techniques, after seeing the fights the senior wing showed their best, there was not a single incident were a point was not being scored clearly and with precise control. Their movements were light smooth and full of power but the demonstration of control bought them big cheers from the on lookers. The favourite in the blue Belt was the strong built Mushtaq whose long and strong kicks can pass through any defence, he won the Blue Belt trophy. The other favourite for the Pakistan Grand Champion ship trophy was none but the unbeatable Asif Hussain of the Tae Kwon Do And Judo Association Of Pakistan. He was awarded a brown Belt recently, he is an expert with hand techniques coupled with his strong side and front kicks and when he attacks he is bound to score against any one. He fought the winners of all the belt level and won them all.

The free sparring contest was followed by demonstration of "Thai Boxing" by the Thai student of Karachi University. The Thai boxers entered the arena in colourful robes and head gears and commenced their ritual bowing motions. the boxers than danced to the beating of the drums in a rythmic motions and built up the tempo before actual Boxing. Following the Thai Boxing the Malaysian students demonstrated the art of Panjit Salad, they performed gracefully various Katas and then free sparing both the demonstrations were widely cheered by the spectators.

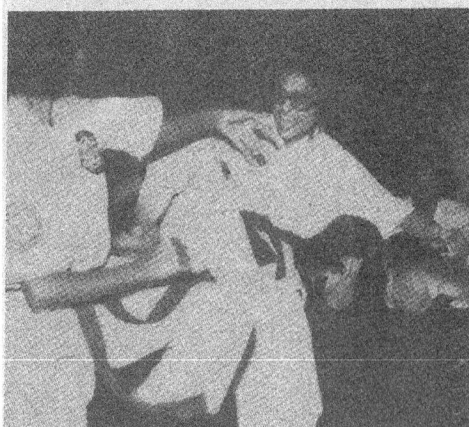

Master Saleem Jehangir with senior belts in 1975

Master Saleem Jehangir with senior belts at the NSTCC (photo in 1975 Jang newspaper)

Two Red Belts displaying high kicks

Article in Jang (Urdu news paper)

سلیم جہانگیرا پنے مخالف پر فلائنگ سائیڈ کک سے حملہ کر رہے ہیں

اس سینٹر تربیت وقتاً فوقتاً کرائے کے غیر ملکی ماہرین بھی تربیت دینے کے لئے آتے رہتے ہیں!

Article in Jang (Urdu news paper)

پاکستان میں کراٹے کا پہلا سنٹر

تحریر: مدثر مرزا

ابتدائیں پاکستان میں کراٹے کو متعارف کرانے میں بے پناہ دشواریاں اور رکاوٹیں حائل تھیں

ٹائی کانڈو کراٹے ایسوسی ایشن آف پاکستان کے نیشنل کوچنگ سنٹر کے انسٹرکٹرز تمر حسین مرزا، ہمایوں مرزا اور امتیاز حسین کلب کے بانی سلیم جہانگیر کے ساتھ

کراٹے کے ٹائپ کا انڈو اسٹائل کا تعلق کوریا سے ہے

Acknowledgment by the Encyclopedia of Marital Arts and History of Martial Arts

There are two books that I know wrote about me. But there are more out there, like Who's Who in Martial Arts, one will have to search.

Martial Arts Traditions, History, People by John Concoron & Emil Farkas

The Original Martial Arts Encyclopedia by John Concoron & Emil Farkas

Black Belt Magazine December 1975 issue

Website: Saleemjehangir.info

History of Tae Kwon Do after I left Pakistan in 1974

After I left Karachi in 1974, the club at NSTCC was still functional till 1976. First Master Waseem Akhtar, the first Black Belt from the TKD Association of Pakistan, managed the club and also acted as the Chief Instructor. I had requested the South Korean Consulate in Karachi for arranging instructors from Korea before I had left. This materialized and they sent more than one black be who trained at the NSTCC, Master Wasim and the other black belts trained under them. These instructors were more sport karate oriented and they concentrated on kicks that win points in tournaments. Hence more tournaments were organized at the NSTCC subsequently. They were there for two years and then returned to Korea.

Then Master Wasim too went to the USA in 1976, and his cousin Master Humayun Akhtar took over the management of the club. To our misfortune, Khwaja Saleem Ahmad who had supported us all along without a single incident of interference, retired. He was replaced by a new Director who was a political appointee of the PPP, much less qualified and a totally different type of a person. Things started to go sour and finally the club members were asked to find another place.

Some students, who had received their black belts, opened their own training centers. A professional manager got hold of Ashraf Tai and arranged a place for him at the Karachi Cricket Association grounds. This manager opened other places, and in the years that followed, Ashraf Tai became a known figure in the world of martial arts in Pakistan. Although he was not a Tae Kwon Do practitioner, he nevertheless served Tae Kwon Do by becoming a competitive force for the TKD students in Karachi. Hence I have included him here. He did serve the world of martial arts.

Among all who served the martial arts scene in Pakistan, I was the only one who did not take it professionally. Most of my students who stayed in it became professionals. My lead pupil Asif decided to go to Japan and learn under a master there. He came back and went to Saudi Arabia to train the king's guards. Everyone capitalized on it and financially gained from the art that I started in Pakistan. Today the uniforms used in karate and judo all over the world are exported from Pakistan, and so is the vast variety of protective gear used in martial arts. And the money made in all this is not small. I hope that all those who gain financially from it remember me as the man who brought the martial arts to Pakistan.

1976

I received my third Dan in 1976 and made a short visit to Pakistan to train the senior students once again

WELCOME

MR. SALEEM JEHANGIR
AND CONGRATULATIONS ON HIS
* 3RD DAN BLACK BELT.
* M.B.A. DEGREE.
* EXECUTIVE JOB IN FORD COMPANY
From: THE TAEKWONDO - KARATE
ASSOCIATION OF PAKISTAN
Take admission now at:-
THE NATIONAL SPORTS COACHING CENTRE
(Opposite: NATIONAL STADIUM)

Newspaper cutting from Dawn

1978

I made another visit to Pakistan again in 1978 and organized the second All Pakistan Tae Kwon Do Championships. This too was covered by the media and magazines.

In the years that followed numerous other championships were held. New martial arts magazines arrived on the scene and covered these tournaments. Tae Kwon Do is a household word now in Pakistan.

THE TAE KWON DO-KARATE
ASSOCIATION OF PAKISTAN

Cordially invites you to witness
The Tae Kwon Do-Karate
Championships-1978
on Friday the 21st of April, 1978
at 5-00 p.m.
to observe the Finals & Demonstrations,
& the giving away of prizes at The
National Sports Training & Coaching Centre:
Opp. National Stdium, Karachi-12.
(Please come in time and bring this card along).

N° 0018

Invitation card for the 1978 championships

Other Tae Kwon Do Clubs

Rahimyarkhan

In the subsequent years, a young man from Rahimyarkhan came to Karachi and trained at the NSTCC. His name was Shakeel Yousuf. He went back to Rahimyarkhan and opened up a training institute and actually ended up building one. It was the year 1988 that I visited him. This is the first dojang of martial arts that has been built in Pakistan and must be recorded as such. A dedicated student, he took upon himself to make his "solid" contribution. My brother who farms in RYK heard of it and took me there to see. Although he had never seen me before, Shakeel recognized me in an instant. As soon as I entered the training room he made the class come to attention and bow. I still remember that moment, as unexpected as it was, it was a pleasant surprise. I was impressed with the concrete facility he had built and congratulated him on it. Later I went back and trained them a bit. I gave him original copies of the Black Belt magazine that featured me, and all the Sportimes Magazines that carried my articles.

Eid card from the RYK Tae Kwon Do club

Association Outings

For team building and recreation at the same time, we often organized outings for the senior belts and used different places for the purpose.

Hawks Bay

This was our most frequent outing, going out to the beaches, Hawks Bay and Sands Pit. These places were close and had huts for rent. We would either arrange for somebody's hut or rent one. Only the senior students went on these outings, somehow the new ones stayed away themselves. These outings also gave a sort of a reprieve from the strict disciplined training that the students were made to go through at the NSTCC.

Haleji Lake

Once we organized an overnight trip to the Haleji Lake, approximately 40 miles away from Karachi into Sindh. One resourceful student booked a rest house in the area and just the senior boys, some 25 of them, went out and spent the night and day at Haleji lake. Everyone enjoyed the outing so much that no one slept the entire night. But some got rowdy and out of control with their pistols that they had brought with them. The "pistol culture" had started to creep into our students also, so I decided not to repeat this type of an outing again.

Chinese Restaurants

I used to treat the students once in a while at the Chinese restaurants. It used to cost us Rs. 5 per person on the average, so even if 20 of us ate it would amount to only Rs. 100. The rupee was still worth some amount. The Dollar was worth Rs.10. We did this especially with visiting trainers, I remember taking the Japanese Judo experts and the senior students after the very successful display at the NSTCC.

Desi Hangouts

Then of course there were the desi hangouts like the kabob walas, the nehari walas, and specially the fruit wala, Agha Juice at the Gole Market in Nazimabad, who made the best mango milk shake that you ever had in your life.

Respect and Reverence for the Teacher

As much as it cultivated friendships and camaraderie among the pupils, it sort of undermined my importance in their eyes. They started to feel friendlier with me and at times treated me like their trainer instead of a traditional martial arts teacher. Boys and girls with good family backgrounds still held the reverence they should have had, but on some of them the upbringing showed a little too obvious. Since learning goes along hand in hand with the reverence and respect for the teacher, I recommend for all teachers to maintain a necessary distance with their students. How much distance can be judged by how much respect you want and how much you want to teach.

The Story of the Russian

It is because of this reason, that I cited above, that kept me from teaching more than I had already taught. I am from the old school of learning who believes that the teacher, among all the people in your life, deserves the most respect. For if the teachers stop teaching you will go back toward Stone Age. There is a story that I heard on TV in Pakistan. The times were the 1980s when things had started to go downhill at a faster pace. The Afghanistan war with Russia had started. Arms and ammunition flowed into Pakistan at a severely unsafe rate. Armed crime started to spread rapidly. Politics of violence took birth and started to flourish. People couldn't sleep on the streets in the summer time anymore because someone would cut their throats while they slept. Armed robberies became common. Government got involved with the looters and protected them. Educational institutions, as well as all government institutions started to degenerate. People were worried what is going to happen. It is in these times that an interview with an old man sitting under a tree was shown on TV. The interview took place somewhere in the Punjab. The interviewer, a female, asked him what is going to happen to the country. And he said, nothing. Then he told her a story:

> He said that he was of Russian descent. There is a story that he heard in his childhood which is common among people of his heritage. And he painted a desperate picture of how the Tartars ravaged through a town and killed almost everyone, burned every place down, and literally destroyed everything. A man came running to his elder and shouted we are finished, we are destroyed. The old man looked at the bewildered man and asked him: is the teacher who teaches the children still sitting under the tree? The bewildered man said yes. The old man said then no harm has been done, we are not finished, we still have a future. As long as he is there and available to teach, we have hope.

Such is the importance of the Teacher. As for me, I am forever obligated to anyone and everyone who taught me even the most insignificant of things like tying a knot. I can never forget that individual and have the deepest regard for him.

Deteriorating Political and Ethical conditions of Karachi

As soon as I had reached Pakistan in July of 1971, the ouster of President Ayub Khan was in progress and General Yahya Khan had taken over as interim martial law administrator. The entire thing was orchestrated by the USA which gave $8 million to Z.A. Bhutto to come into power, so writes Nixon in his book. The nation broke into two and Bhutto took over as the most popular leader of the country ever. Before or after him no one has been as popular as he was. The country went into a democratic system, for which it was not used to. The first thing he did was to nationalize everything of any significance. This destroyed Pakistan's infrastructure and economy. Corruption went rampant. Police excesses became common. Although some good took place for the poor in the beginning, but the country was not ready for democracy, and couldn't handle it. Things started to go downhill, economically, socially, ethically,

Islamically, you name it, and degradation of values was everywhere.

Jealousy at Esso from my popularity

I was working with Esso then as Terminal Engineer in charge of bulk product operations at the Esso storage terminal in Karachi. The terminal manager had become very jealous of my popularity from the martial arts scene and embarked on a crusade against me. He and the maintenance engineer started to create problems for me while on job. I did not like that. I could have resigned and started earning from my Tae Kwon Do operations, but I chose not to do so. As much as I wanted to continue my goal in Tae kwon Do, I was very dissatisfied with my job at Esso, and the conditions in the country. So I decided to go back to the USA.

Decision to leave Pakistan

At that time we were living in a big house off of Jamshed Road and maintained a reasonably well-to-do life style. That and a flourishing Tae Kwon Do scenario, I could have done well if I stayed. Tae kwon Do was to me a philosophy of dedication, accomplishment, honor. If I started to make money from it all my deeper feelings for it would be gone. I did not want to do that. Plus my profession was engineering and I did not want to leave it. Lawlessness was increasing. Being an engineer I studied the trends, the graph of everything good was going down and the graph of everything bad was going up. I was faced with a dilemma, do I want my kids to grow up in this society? Or shall I leave for a better world and a better future, where personal safety, security, quality of life, practically everything is better? But if I leave I would have to leave my aging parents, brothers and sisters, the whole clan, plus my Tae Kwon Do set up. It was a decision that I hated to make, but a few things pushed me towards going back to the USA. One of them was the mentality of the management team at the Esso Terminal. The other was the deteriorating morality, ethics, economy, crime situation, and living conditions in Karachi.

Reluctantly I made the decision to go back. I told my father first. He became shocked and depressed. Then I told my mother, and she went into a depression. This is the part I regret the most. I left them in their old age. Esso raised my salary when I turned in my resignation, and also apologized for the ex-manager's behavior towards me. But I had already accepted my green card and I had to go to the USA in order to activate it, or lose it.

Sometimes events happen not necessarily for the better or worse, and you never get to know. All I know is that as soon as I came back and joined Ford Motor Company, I regretted why I came back. I went back to Karachi in 1975 with my newly born daughter and took over the TKD scene again, but not for too long. The fast deteriorating conditions in Pakistan again forced me to go back to the USA at the end of 1975 and join Ford again. I completed my MBA in 1977, and stayed with Ford through 1981.

There are only a few decisions I made that I regret. This was one of them. But I have also learnt that successful are those that take their destiny in their own hands and the whole universe orchestrates itself to make them successful.

Only God knows the Truth.

There is a lot I could write about that period, but I would rather have the pictures and articles tell the story.

Saleem Jahangir

(Black belt, 2nd Dan)

The flying side-kick. Saleem Jehangir.

He has the speed of a cougar, the deadliness of a rattler and the agility of a gazelle. He is man — replete with zeal and vigour. He is Saleem Jehangir, Pakistan's first Karate Black Belt.

It was a decade ago when Saleem stepped into the world of the martial art of Karate. It was in Michigan, USA, where Saleem was studying in those days, that he entered the school of Mr. Chang and began to learn under his dynamic guidance. Mr. Chang, who holds — a 7th Dan Black Black Belt — is also an All Korea Champion and the Korean Presidential Guard was trained under him.

Saleem had all along been, in his school and college days, a keen sportsman. The art of Karate had immediate attraction for him. Saleem had always been known to be a hot-tempered person and he himself was'nt very happy about this aspect of his personality. What impressed him most about the martial art of Karate were its qualities of discipline, patience, perseverance, courteousness, etc.

BEST STUDENT

But besides having a temper which was a bit on the hotter side, Saleem also happened to possess in his personality the desire for perfectionism. He worked hard and long. He learned patience. among other things and before he himself was aware of it, much to the pride of Mr. Chong, Saleem had become one of the best pupils he had taught.

But Saleem had still not achieved the coveted title of "Black Belt" and he dreamt about acquiring it. He would trudge everyday, about four miles to the gym, practise there for two hours and then walk back to his hostel room. This routine continued for five hard-fought years — until his dream was realised — the Black Belt!

COMING OF AGE

But Saleem Jehangir was not the kind of person to learn a martial art and keep it to himself. As soon as he returned home, he set up a small Karate training school, so as to acquaint the youth of Pakistan with this ancient yet novel physical art, which exercised and disciplined not only the body but also the mind. With rare devotion and considerable sacrifice on his own part, Saleem's school in Karachi made a niche for itself in Pakistan's sport world. The fact that Saleem Jehangir pioneered Karate in Pakistan must have been a source of personal satisfaction to this great sportsman in his moments of thought.

NOT EVERY BIT A SPORTSMAN

All of what comprises the personality of Saleem Jehangir is not all of it a sportsman and nothing much else. No doubt, today Saleem is where it must be the cherished dream of many a young Karataka to be. But Saleem has been a brilliant student too. Throughout his educational career, he has won several academic awards. After graduating from the NED Engineering College, Saleem left for the USA for his higher studies. At the University of Michigan, he was awarded a Scholarship. Not only is Saleem Jehangir a versatile sportsman, having led many of his school teams and having coached swimming and soccer to American school children at Summer camps in the USA. Saleem has also represented his school and college in Dramatics and in music competitions. In fact, he represented the Pakistan music squad at the United Nations. Among his other activities, Saleem has taught at Michigan Karate Club and the Michigan Self-Defence Academy. He is also founder of the Rochester Institute of Technology, Karate. Club at New York.

In the gym, Saleem Jehangir is a man possessed. He leaps eight feet up into the air, easily and effortlessly, and from that height produce every variety of flying kick there is in the book. But his attacks are not restricted to his feet alone. He can score with equal mastery with the help of projectile-like punches — forward and reverse.

He has fought the best and biggest names in the game and has beaten them all. He has faced other karate fighters of prominence beside the excellent tutorship he has received under the incomparable Mr. Chong.

One secret of Saleem Jehangir's tremendous physical form is that he keeps himself in good conditions through regular and demanding exercise. To Saleem, Kata is the most important ingredient of Karate. To him a Kata win is as important for a player as a match win because kata makes one practise all what karate teaches and trains the whole body. Saleem won second prize at a Kata competition held in Michigan recently.

HOME TO STAY

When Saleem came to Pakistan in 1971 on a holiday, he decided to introduce Karate to Pakistan. He was home on a very short visit but, , nevertheless, he studied the potential and interest for Karate in the youth of this country. He was no impressed that he decided to stay on.

July that year saw Saleem launching regular classes at the National Sport and Coaching Centre. There were 45 students already on the rolls for the first training group. He would train them six days of the week and at the same time, would continue

Article published in a local Sunday Magazine

Jehangir in a flying side-kick.

with his job at ESSO.

Very soon, Karate had become very popular among Karachi boys and girls. In a short span of two years, 700 boys and girls had been trained in this martial art. In 1971, Saleem Jehangir formally laid the foundations of the Pakistan Tae Kwon Do and Judo Association.

Married to a pretty girl from Lahore, Saleem is the father of a cute child. At present, he is in the USA, training for his higher Dan Black Belt and also working for the Ford Motor Company.

Asif Hussain in a fighting posture with Saleem

Articles Published in Sportimes

When the TKD activities had gained sufficient momentum, I talked with Mr. Sultan F. Hussain (marhoom), the editor and founder of the first and still the most reputable sports magazine of Pakistan, Sportimes, if he could write about us. He suggested that, instead of Sportimes writing, why not I write about TKD and he will publish it. I jumped on the idea and provided them with an article each month. This kept going for a couple of years till he retired, and I also stopped writing. I have included some of these articles on the following pages, which are self-explanatory.

INTRODUCING

an increasingly popular sport

KARATE

IT is believed that some 2,000 years ago a monk, called Bodhidharma, travelled to China to teach the secrets of Zen Budhism.

But the intense practices of the austerities of Zen led its disciples to weaken physically—and, in consequence, mentally.

So Bodhidharma devised exercises that would develop physical and mental control in his disciples.

Later, these exercises, together with the spiritual training of Zen, were picked up by the promoters of combative arts, and developed into what came to be known as the martial arts of Judo and Karate.

With the passage of more time, these arts spread from China to Korea and, recently, into the Western world.

And, today, the same are prominently listed as Olympic events.

INDEED, both Judo and Karate are designed to use human mechanism of motion to its optimum advantage, and the muscular movements to their greatest speed—the combined effect resulting in a tremendous momentum at the point of strike.

The physical training specialises in the sound and symmetrical development of the body, during which a student is supposed to let out all frustrations of physical endeavour, so that when he walks out of the class, he is a calm, contented and disciplined being.

But there is an upper "bound" to physical achievement, and to get there is no ordinary accomplishment. One has to put in years of hard practice for each fractional improvement beyond the barrier line.

At which stage, a student of these martial arts realises that there is another phase of development which knows no bounds and where the possibilities of improvement are unlimited—namely, the inner self.

After all, what good is one's body if the mind is left undeveloped, the student begins to think loudly ?

And so, he is given a code of ethics to follow—peaceful philosophies which help him to develop his inner self. He practises what he has learned and, at the same time, preaches them to others through the propagation of these martial arts.

THUS, the advantages of Judo and Karate can be listed under four different heads—namely, mental, physical, ethical and social.

On the mental side, these help build up poise, alertness, eagerness, courage, determination, fast thinking and split second decisions.

Physically, these generate health, agility, speed, strength, endurance, good posture and intelligent reactions.

Whereas, in terms of ethics, these foster the virtues of honesty, truth, honour and sportsmanship.

Socially, their exponents come to acquire forebearance, loyalty, civic sense and courtesy.

OVER the years, both Judo and Karate have been successfully used as excellent means of self defence by men, women and children in many countries of the world.

The Police and Armed Forces adopted and prescribed these in their training schedules. Not only did the knowledge increase their fighting potentials, it also helped them to reduce the incidence of crime and casualty.

A fighting stance

THE AUTHOR

SALEEM A. JEHANGIR, who will be 26 on November 16, has had a brilliant academic career. A mechanical engineer by profession, he has developed diversified extra-curricular interests—sports, dramatics and music. After his early education at St. Mary's Convent, Multan, and Sadiq Public School, Bahawalpur, he went over to Karachi, where he studied with distinction at Greenwood School, D. J. Science College and, finally, at NED Engineering College.

Between 1965 and 1968, Saleem was on the rolls of the University of Michigan in the United States. Besides securing an academic scholarship for his B. S. degree, he also coached swimming and soccer to children at summer camps. He even played soccer for the University, but it was his new-found love—karate—which held greater fascination for him.

Saleem's other sporting pursuits have included cricket—he captained Greenwood School—hockey, boxing, skiing, golf, badminton and athletics (400, 800 metres and Marathon). He had the good fortune to be trained by Hwa Chong, 6th degree Black Belt holder, All-Korean karate champion and coach of the Korean President's Guards. He was himself awarded a Black Belt in 1970.

Returning to Pakistan last year, Saleem joined Esso Eastern Inc. as Operations Engineer. He formed the Pakistan TAE KWON DO and the Pakistan Judo Association. For the past several months he has been conducting the highly-successful and widely-popular karate sessions at the National Sports Training and Coaching Centre, Karachi.

I am sure the teaching of Judo and Karate in schools and colleges—if introduced under expert supervision—cannot but generate martiality in our nation of tomorrow.

NEXT MONTH :
What does Karate offer you ?

WHAT

KARATE

OFFERS YOU

By SALEEM A. JAHANGIR

K ARATE owes its rapidly growing popularity to many reasons which only an exponent can fully realise and appreciate.

It offers optimum activity for the sound development of one's body and mind. It disciplines life, and its instructive value is great.

Karate has attraction also for those who watch its exposition which, to say the least, is a spectacle of human grace and agility.

Right :

The flying side-kick

The show business tycoons are interested no less in Karate, and they will not spare any money in sponsoring its cause and promotion.

Let us now examine at length as to what Karate really offers to different persons in its orbit.

To a student—I would say—Karate is a satisfying experience in his search for a discipline which he can use in all walks of life.

The physical achievement has a ceiling beyond which it is just not possible for a man to improve. Karate underlines this limitation, and undertakes to train the mind where the scope of attainment is unlimited.

In other words, a Karate student knows his physical strength, and has a highly sensitive mind. His reactions to danger are, therefore, never rash. Always sure of his movements, he will hit back with a telling force as often as necessary.

Which makes people think that Karate is an art aimed at developing super power in a man, to enable him to overpower his opponent in no time.

But nothing could be more misleading than this false impression about Karate. Because, the desire to conquer opposition emanates from fear, and the sooner it is accomplished the better for one's own survival.

Like other virtues, Karate is also the medium to reach fellow beings and an excellent means for a peaceful unification of the world. It teaches the philosophy of peace and non-violence—a concept associated with the brotherhood of mankind.

All this, I am sure, will sound vague to the readers. But ask one who practises Karate. Only he can realise the full impact of Karate on his life. And he would admit that Karate gave him the discipline which satisfied his longing for the perfection of his soul and body.

In fact, the urge to seek the refinement of the body and mind, is inherent in all. But it finds fulfilment through the sort of a discipline which only Karate training can foster.

SIMILARLY, a Karate demonstration is fascinating to an onlooker. I doubt if anyone from the non-Karate ranks and file can resist its overpowering force.

The Madison Square Garden in New York is the permanent venue of the World Karate Championship and—believe you me—a trip there is like going to a world of fantasy. Amazing acts of human strength performed with absolute concentrated force, fill the atmosphere with a sequence of marvel.

Spellbound with amazement, a Karate crowd is witness to a fantastic demonstration of human grace, speed and mobility. It witnesses, among other mar-

vels, fighting in self defence against more than one opponent.

The shattering of an ice block by an open hand strike—or, for that matter, the breaking of a pile of bricks with finger tips or the forehead—are common acts during a Karate demonstration.

Incredibly enough, a Karate exponent will knock off a cigarette from the lips of a person with a flying side kick, and he will use a flying front kick to break a pile of wooden planks held eight feet aloft in the air.

And the crowd will be entertained to a lightening "sudo"—the knife-hand strike—to slice off the neck of a bottle when it is not even held at the base.

TO promoters, a Karate billing is no less satisfying. Unlike other sports which are merely entertaining, Karate has also a philosophy of discipline behind it.

A Karate promotion is, thus, more than a magic show. It is also an organised effort at promoting discipline, brotherhood and peace in this world.

For, the institution of Karate turns out a set of people who walk the road confidently and are ready to fight for a right cause—as against injustice. They are the walking policemen—courteous and chivalrous.

NEXT MONTH : The Karate training

KARATE ▉▉▉▉▉▉▉▉ 3

THE TRAINING

By SALEEM A. JEHANGIR

NUMEROUS BOOKS have been written on the Karate technique, discipline and training. Yet the last word on the topic remains to be said. For, Karate is a science—and so vast in its scope that one simply cannot reduce it to a few chosen words and pictures.

So, it has been the endeavour of the promoters to give to the students just as much of Karate as their curiosity can take it. And I intend doing no different.

In fact, I would feel satisfied if I succeed in selling Karate's basic virtues which a student learns in his first few years with the institution—just a fraction of the total training.

Karate, I must repeat, has proved to be the ultimate in the arts of self defence, and its secret lies in having the full measure on one's faculty of self discipline, which is possible only after years of constant training.

And the route taken in the pursuit of Karate discipline and technique is not only very difficult but, also, different from other sports—something which holds out a unique challenge to the sportsmen joining the institution.

Usually, a Karate student starts from the **basic motions** and, after rehearsing the same thoroughly, learns the **basic forms** which are, again, practised until he is ready to grapple with the **basic techniques**. Finally, he is taught to pool his knowledge into a cohesive action through extensive free-sparring.

THE basic motions are the simplest form of Karate exercises and, hence, must be mastered first by a student. These include stances.

Now a stance is the posture of the body that has to be maintained throughout the training. The student is taught how to walk, turn or run in a stance—without of course, lifting his body up or down.

For example, in the front stance (*pix* 1) which the Koreans call *Chonggul Chaase*, one has to learn to move like a cat, maintaining one height.

Then he is taught how to punch (*pix* 2) in this stance. The punch is called *Chung Dan Konggyok* by the Koreans. In tournament bouts or exhibition matches, it carries one full point.

The student has to master this punching technique, and acquire speed and accuracy through continuous training. For, only then, does he get any further in his lessons.

Scientifically, a Karate punch has come to be considered as the most powerful of all. It is also the easiest motion, which explains as to why a student must learn it first.

Defensive blocks for the lower, middle and upper parts of the body follow next

KARATE

in Karate training. These are, respectively, called *Ha Dan Makki*, *Chung Dan Makk* and *Sang Dan Makki*.

In *Ha Dan Makki* (*pix* 3), the blocking hand is brought from the other shoulder, down, to deflect any strike aimed at the lower part of the body—such as, a kick to the groin.

Needless to say, this block, like others, becomes an effective defence shield during combat, once the necessary training has given it speed, accuracy and strength.

Similarly, the student is taught, to perfection, the defence against blows aimed at the stomach, face or head. In both *Chung Dan Makki* (*pix* 4) and *Sang Dan Makki* (*pix* 5), the motion of the blocking hand is intended to deflect—rather than stop—the blow.

It may also be of interest to the readers to note that the stance Chonggul Chasse has been maintained through all the three blocks.

I wish I could give here a complete breakdown of these motions, because it would take a series of action pictures to illustrate what I wish.

Not granted my wish, I would hasten to add that after a student has learnt and perfected the punch and the blocks, he is introduced to what are conveniently described as the offensive moves—such as the *Sudo*.

Now a Sudo (*pix* 6) is an open hand strike to the neck or the temple of an opponent.

A higher degree punch in a side stance—as illustrated in *pix* 7—is delivered by keeping the entire body away from the opponent. The side stance, it may be noted, is somewhat higher and, hence, it is called the Horse-Back stance.

All these motions are, basically, must for a Karate student. He must learn them, practise them and be able to execute the same with optimum power, accuracy and speed—before he can hope to proceed further.

Next month : "BASIC TECHNIQUES"

KARATE 4

THE BASIC TECHNIQUES

By SALEEM A. JEHANGIR

ONCE a student of Karate has mastered the basic motions, he is taught the technique of incorporating the same into actual combat.

Commonly known as one-step techniques—or **Dae Ryun** in Korean—these are, basically, the combinations of different motions.

In other words, a student is taught how to combine the basic motions into various arrangements for the purpose of combat.

To visualise what I mean, the readers will be well advised to study *pix* 8 carefully. They would note as to how a punch aimed at the face is blocked by **Sang Dan Makki** and, simultaneously, countered by a strike to the nearest pressure point of the opponent which, in this case, happens to be his solar plexus.

Pix 9 shows a different combat pose. Here a punch to the middle part of the body is, first, blocked by **Chung Dan Makki** and, then, followed through by a strike to the opponent's rib cage,

AND the only similarity in the two fight postures—which, I am sure, will impress the readers—lies in the simultaneous execution of the blocking and striking actions.

There are many other combinations of defensive and offensive motions, and each one of them has to be practised again and again—say, a thousand times—until it becomes a reflex action in a student.

The pre-condition of a reflex action is a must because, at a later stage, when a student is doing free-sparring—which is part of actual combat training—he has no time to think. His reflexes must answer all demands, and the action should be in keeping with the laid-out discipline.

Which prompts me to repeat the caution that the Karate discipline presupposes continuous training and, like the basic motions, each basic technique must be gone through until it becomes

part of one's reflexes.

TALKING of the basic motions and their subsequent arrangement into numerous combat actions, I may remind the readers that, purposefully, I have refrained from mentioning one too many. Indeed, the few motions so far discussed in these columns, implied the use of hands only.

But Karate believes in making use of each and every source of power available in a human body and—since legs are the stronger limbs—it bases its most powerful combat postures on kicks.

Which means that the major training on basic motions, is devoted to the learning of various kicking techniques.

The first thing in kicking that a student has to master is the **Front Snap Kick**, in which the leg is moved up from a front stance (**Chonggul Chaase**) and snapped forward with all force and speed—ending in the position shown in *pix* 10.

Next month :
ADVANCED BASIC
MOTIONS

Significantly, the contact is made with the ball of the foot.

Now a **Front Kick** is a good offensive as well as a defence weapon. It can stop an opponent wherever he is standing and, at the same time, damage him severely.

When combined with other motions—as in *pix* 11—the kick's utility becomes manifold and more vicious. The picture shows the simultaneous blocking of a punch by a **Chung Dan Makki** and the execution of the **Front Kick** to the opponent's solar plexus or rib-cage.

To perfect this kick—and, mind you, I am not exaggerating—it takes years of hard training and practice. By perfection I mean that it has to be so fast that it should be there wherever you

want it, without giving the opponent any chance to block it ; and it has to be power-packed to do any damage.

AND the same holds good for other kicks—including the **Side Kick**. But one must first perfect the **Front Snap** and its use in actual combat.

Because, a **Side Kick** reaches out higher up, means more power and, hence, is more difficult to learn.

In this action, as the leg moves up from a **Chonggul Chaase**, the body is suddenly turned into a side stance and the kick lashes out in a **Snap** or **Jerk**.

Pix 12 shows a **Side Kick** reaching out to an opponent's rib-cage whereas, in *pix* 13, it is aimed at his face.

In both the instances, one should observe that it is the edge of the foot which makes the contact—and for a good reason, too.

According to the experts, all power is concentrated at the edge of the striking

foot—thereby increasing the force per square inch.

Also, the sudden twist of the body and the hips in the direction of the kick, gives a **Side Kick** its tremendous power which has been demonstrated time and again at public exhibitions.

A single Side Kick has gone on record to have shattered multiple wooden planks. Such is the force it carries.

Once perfected—which means, again, years of hard training—a **Side Kick** is, then, practised as a combact technique such as the one illustrated in *pix* 14.

Here a punch is deflected by a **Sudo**, and a **Side Kick** delivered to the opponent's rib cage.

The beauty of the action lies in the positions of the legs and hands. While the legs (positioned as they are) provide the body with maximum balance and power, the hands placing is ideal for a counter attack.

KARATE 5

Advanced Basic Motions

By SALEEM A. JEHANGIR

AFTER a Karate student has learnt all basic motions and technique—and these include the ones not discussed hitherto—during the first three years of his training, he is introduced to a schedule comprising Advanced Basic Motions.

But the initial training—I repeat—must be thorough and faultless : so that, at the time of free sparring a student is able to perform with maximum effectiveness. And to ensure this, nobody is more responsible than the instructor in charge.

Therefore, it goes without saying that a Karate tutor would satisfy himself fully with the initial progress of his pupil before teaching him anything of an advanced and more complex nature—such as the **Back Kick.**

Now, as the name implies, a **Back Kick** is executed with one's back to the opponent. It shoots off—as illustrated in *pix* 15—from the ground to the face or midsection of the opponent, making a powerful contact with the heel. Note,

how the other foot is firmly positioned for balance.

The **Back Kick** is, particularly, useful in combact against more than one opponent. But, at the same time, it is a risky proposition also. For a striker, it is unsafe in the sense that, in the action, he has to have his back to the opponent. But once shot, it is something which cannot be blocked, and I would pity the opponent who is not fast enough to get out of its range.

Pix 16 shows another Advanced Basic Motion—a **punch** which comes handy in close-in fighting. But like a **Back Kick,** it also involves great risk for both sides and, hence, must be discouraged as far as possible during early sparring.

For, you cannot throw this sort of punch unless the opponent is precariously close to you—a situation in which your own safety is exposed to considerable risk.

Again, a close-in blow demands a much higher degree of Karate skill on one's part and until such time a student has learnt and perfected all that is classified as "advanced", he would do well by keeping his distance from an opponent in whatever he does—be that kicks or the punches.

In other words, his early sparring should be restricted to the need of keeping an opponent away and, also, of keeping away from the opponent.

THE "Flying" series of kicks is perhaps the most spectacular of all Karate motions and, at the same time, the most forceful also. It comprises a Front Kick, Side Kick, Fake Kick and Thrust Kick.

Pix 17 illustrates a **Flying Side Kick.** Like any other "flying" variety, it is aimed at the head of an opponent—the prime purpose being to gain height.

Observe the position of the legs, one

Next month :
ADVANCED
TECHNIQUES

completely extended ready to strike with the edge of foot and the other guarding the groin. Also note the double action by the hands, one at full stretch for the contact and the other covering defensively the solar plexus.

Comparatively, a **Flying Fake Kick** (see *pix* 18) packs more power, because the twisting motion of the body into the kick adds extra momentum and force to the strike.

In the illustrated action, notice how one leg is brought up faking a kick and the sudden twist of the body in the air as the other leg lashes out a side kick. Also observe carefully the defensive position of the two hands which are so placed that the vital points are not left unguraded.

But to master any of the flying kicks, one needs tremendous balance while he is airborne—and, on landing, a foolproof defensive stance against a possible counter blow by the opponent.

NOW what is exactly a stance ? Already, a casual mention of it has been made in these columns but, for the purpose of better appreciation, I would like to go a little deeper into what the expression actually means.

In Karate, a stance is the posture of the body that has to be maintained in relevance to the motion. Which implies that while one stance suits a motion or a combination of motions, it may not be applicable in a different circumstance.

That is to say that Karate has stances to suit all kinds of situations providing, in each case, the optimum stability to the body—called balance. At the same time, a correct stance gives a blocking or striking motion its maximum strength and speed.

The **Front Stance** is the strongest body posture in Karate—and most stable as well. One only has to recall the first illustration of this series to know what I mean.

Then there is the **Cat Stance** (*pix* 19)—or, for that matter, the **Horse Stance** called by the Koreans **Kima Chaasse** (*pix* 20). There is yet another which is known as the **Crane Stance** (*pix* 21)—in fact, many more.

All the stances are preciously useful and have to be practised over and over again as a pre-requisite to what follows.

In fact, the Karate training is a continuous process. It knows no end—not the fag end. It must continue for ever. Fancy my teacher calling himself a beginner after 18 years of association with the institution.

KARATE 6

Advanced Techniques

By SALEEM A. JEHANGIR

BEFORE a student is taught the advanced techniques of Karate— techniques which come handy in combat with an armed opponent—it is necessary that he should develop his reflexes to the highest degree, something that is achieved only through constant polishing of the basic fundamentals the institution has to teach.

During his basic training, a student—repeat—is kept constantly preoccupied with the thought and motions of fighting an opponent who is not armed.

Whereas, the advanced techniques equip him with the ability of combating an armed enemy.

Now the most common type of an armed enemy is the one who carries and brandishes a knife at you.

For, a Karate student will do well to know that of all weapons, a knife is easier to carry and—also—that it kills quietly.

And in dirty combat, I would say, a knife is the most popular weapon, and there is no knowing the damage a suddenly whipped out knife can cause to a person who does not know the advanced techniques of Karate.

Some of the knifing techniques are very common, and Karate teaches one not only to defend himself from a knife blow but, also, to retaliate with a counter punch or kick which would damage and incapacitate the striker.

I WOULD suggest the readers recall *pix* 9 of the series, substituting a knife in place of the punch aimed at the mid section of the Karate student. It would be noted that the defensive motion and the counter attack by the Karate student would hold good just the same. Only a defender would have to move much more faster against the knife.

Other knifing motions and their typical blocks are illustrated on these pages.

Pix 22 reveals how the knifing hand of the armed opponent is swept aside by the sweeping motion of the defender's foot—at the same time making all the vital points of the opponent vulnerable to a counter blow.

Pix 23 illustrates a more damaging technique, in which a Karate student blocks the enemy's knifing hand with **Chung Dan Makki**, simultaneously grabbing the striking hand and following with a side kick to the rib cage of the enemy as he is pulled forward.

Again, *Pix* 24 shows the climax of a technique which is even more damaging to the armed enemy. It may be noted as to how a knife blow to the head is blocked by **Sang Dan Makki**, while the other hand is moved under the knifing hand to effect a lock before the deadly twist which can cause a nasty fracture.

Indeed, the knifing techniques as well as their blocking motions have no end to them. The higher one goes in one's study of Karate, the more one learns—and is wiser by the day.

(To be continued)

Advanced Techniques (ii)

By SALEEM A. JEHANGIR

BY NOW, I am sure, the readers would have been worked up enough to appreciate the universal value of Karate. Some of the advanced techniques which the institution teaches its students for combat against an armed enemy, were discussed in my last column just to achieve such an impression.

Another object for the introductory piece on advanced techniques, was to prepare the ground for the more difficult, hence dangerous, Karate combinations which have to be executed extremely fast to be effective.

The illustrations on these pages are, therefore, aimed to re-affirm one's faith and confidence in the institution of Karate —being, as they are, the finer specimens of combat technique in self defence.

For instance, *Pix* 25 re-asserts as to what a Karate student can achieve through his hands and feet against a cunning and dangerous opponent in a tight situation. It may be noted that, apart from the speed factor, quick anticipation is the key to the success of the illustrated operation.

In the said action, the Karate student anticipates the opponent's intention of delivering a side kick and reacts with matching speed in his defence—more so, to the discomfort of his opponent.

It will be seen from the action that as soon as the Karate student sees the side kick coming, he ducks under it quickly— fast enough to reach the leg the opponent is standing on, to effect a neat topple with a kick.

But—God forbid—if the timings of the Karate student were to go off the beat in the illustrated operation, the opponent's side kick would strike his rib cage with a telling impact.

This technique comes particularly handy with short-statured persons who find it easier to duck and crawl under an opponent's kick which would logically appear to them to be long and high and—in consequence—offer them more time and space for a wider crawl.

Whereas, in *Pix* 26, the same student anticipates a front kick and quickly gets out of its range by sliding to one side,

before initiating a counter action in which he first goes for the opponent's "raised" leg to put him off his balance, and then turns him over for a nasty crash.

USUALLY, the advanced techniques are not meant for general consumption. An instructor would disclose these only to his most devoted pupils after years of faithful dedication. Hence it is not possible for any Karateka to say much about them.

Yet, there is no end to the process of learning in Karate. The advancement never stops. I learnt Karate for six years. My master had been at it for 18 years, while his tutor lived with it for nearly 25 years.

The two grand masters' display always left the onlookers spell bound. But they never revealed themselves fully on one single occasion. And it almost seemed that they had an endless store of knowledge to dish out to their fans. Every new occasion found them exhibiting something more fantastic.

(To be continued)

January, 1973

19

**BEST SPORTS
PHOTOGRAPHS
OF 1972**

**" Side Kick"
Photo: Ehtesham**

**" Over the bar"
Photo: IPS**

SPORTIMES

KARATE ▬▬▬ 8

ADVANCED TECHNIQUES
(III)

By SALEEM A. JEHANGIR

PICKING up the discussion from where I left it in my last column, I need not repeat that, in Karate, the advanced techniques become more and more sophisticated, as different combinations of kicks, punches and sudos are practised in combat against more than one person.

And that again reminds me of my master. He could take on a dozen of his best pupils simultaneously—and with such characteristic ease that one had to see the performance to believe it.

See pix 27. It shows a karateka in a striking posture against two unarmed opponents. Mind you, it is only a demonstration. In actual fight, the punch and the kick would not have stopped short of the aimed targets.

Another action to fight off multiple opposition is illustrated in pix 28. Note how the two opponents are forced to keep their distance from the karateka—apprehending, at the same time, danger to their own persons.

Now all opponents are not of one type. They differ from man to man. Some like to fight from a distance, while others go for close-in fighting.

Also, during combat, one confronts all sorts of situations, and it is not always possible for him to maintain his balance or fighting stance. Often a karateka has to do ground work to effect a throw which, I would say, is a technique by itself.

Pix 29 illustrates a typical throw of the

(Continued on page 49)

(from page 27)

opponent from a ground position. Another throwing technique—perhaps a more spectacular one—can be witnessed in pix 30.

In all Karate doings, it may be remembered, quick thinking and fast reflexes are a must. One has got to think of the right thing at the right instant, and move fast with it. Merely knowing the institution well is not enough for the purpose of achieving positive results.

Finally, I would say, Karate is dynamic —something that defies description in words and pictures. Like ballet, it has to be felt only.

(Concluded)

Next Month : THEORY OF POWER IN KARATE

KARATE

9

The Theory of Power

By SALEEM A. JEHANGIR

AN accomplished Karate exhibitionist excels in the mystic techniques the institution is renowned for. But the power factor which, I would say, is non-existent in other combative arts, takes the cake.

Now where does this unique power come from ?—in other words, how come that a Karate blow works up to a moment of tremendous impact ?

Continuous training is one explanation, of course. But there is also a scientific theory behind it, and to appreciate it fully one has to know his high school Physics well.

So it is the science of Physics that governs the theory of power in Karate.

Let's now see what it means in simple vocabulary.

A karateka achieves his moment of tremendous impact in four split-second acts which I propose to discuss somewhat in detail.

ACT ONE : In this, a karateka utilises the opponent's momentum to his own advantage. But how ?

Assume a mass travelling in a straight line at a certain velocity. If this mass collides with a stationary mass, it results in an impact : and if the constituents of both the masses are the same, the mass that was in motion, will shatter itself more than the stationary mass.

Similarly, assume a man running in a straight line at a certain velocity. If you just hold out a stick in his way, he collides with the stick and his own momentum hurts him.

Now assume the same man running towards you. If you hold out a fist in the direction of his motion, he collides with your fist and hurts himself.

Right :

This Jordanian student was able to perform the "brick breaking" act after only 11 weeks training in karate

Which means, that you can aim your fist at any of the charging person's pressure points, and his own momentum will be used against him.

ACT TWO : In this, a karateka adds his own momentum to that of the opponent, and is the gainer.

For the sake of an argument, assume two masses travelling towards each other in a straight line at a certain velocity. These will collide, and the resulting impact will be much greater and more forceful than in Act One.

Now assume an opponent rushing at you to beat you up. This time, you do not merely stick out a fist in his way, but put velocity in your fist to hit him. Result ?

You will discover that your fist, when given velocity, has done more damage to the opponent.

Which brings us to a scientific conclusion that you will hurt your opponent more when he charges at you, than if he were stationary.

Mind you, I use the fist as an example only. The kick, the sudo and other strikes can be fruitfully used in the same manner.

ACT THREE : In this, a karateka is careful not to waste any of his energy, which he accomplishes by keeping his muscles relaxed till the time and point of strike.

Which means that keeping the muscles of the body tense throughout a combat, leads to the wastage of energy—and that, by avoiding just that, a karateka manages to concentrate all his energy at one point which, incidentally, is the point he is striking at.

After all, what is power, as such ? According to theory it is the stored up energy in one's body. And if you lose energy, you lose power.

Using an analogy, I would say that just as the rays of light from all directions, when passed through a lens, converge to a point : in a Karate combat, the entire energy of one's body also collects to travel and converge at the point of strike.

The correct muscles play, therefore, increases a karateka's energy per square inch to a great extent.

ACT FOUR : In this, a karateka brings his force, momentum and kinetic energy into optimum play.

But to fully appreciate what it means, one must try to answer the following question:

If a man strikes your body, what is it that hurts you ?

Well, in Physics, it is described as the

(*Continued on page* 37)

Sportimes April 1973

MATCH-BY-MATCH

The MCC in Sri Lanka

TOUR RECORD

FIRST MATCH *vs.* CENTRAL PROVINCE at Kandy on February 14. Result : The MCC won by 166 runs.
Scores :
MCC : 273 for 8 (Greig 63, Amiss 55, Denness 53).
Central Province : 107.

After their vigorous ten-week sojourn in India, the MCC tourists played in a relaxed mood. Batting first on an awkward pitch, the visitors knocked up 273 for 8 in the stipulated 50 overs, thanks to half-century efforts from Greig, Amiss and Denness. The moderate opposition was then bowled out in 38.5 overs to give the tourists a facile victory in the one-day 'curtain-raiser".

SECOND MATCH *vs.* SRI LANKA at Colombo on February 16, 17, 18 and 19. Result : The MCC won by seven wickets with more than a day to spare.
Scores ;
Sri Lanka : 86 and 200.
MCC : 163 (Greig 61 ; De Silva 5 for 24) and 127 for 3 (Amiss 51 not out).

Although the MCC scored a convincing seven-wicket victory in the representative match against a Sri Lanka team, they had to labour hard for supremacy on a wicket which had been overwatered. As a result, fourteen wickets fell for only 168 runs on the first day. The home batsmen found survival difficult against the quick bowlers and scored only off the odd loose ball. The MCC batsmen also made heavy weather of their innings. Wood and Amiss failed again as an opening pair while Roope was clearly miscast as the No. 3 batsman.

The MCC managed to gain a 77-run lead on the second day which saw Greig make the top score of 61—his third knock of over half a century in three innings. With excellent figures of 5 for 24 in 14 overs, leg break bowler De Silva kept the visiting batsmen in check.

Arnold was involved in an unhappy incident with Tennekoon, blatantly obstructing him when he came through for a run and hindered him again when the batsman tried to take a second run. Both exchanged hot words but the umpires and the MCC skipper Mike Denness intervened to establish what was termed an "uneasy peace". Soon after the incident Arnold was "retired" to the outfield where he was heckled by the spectators whenever he attempted to stop the ball. Arnold was said to be annoyed by the umpires' refusal to uphold some of his LBW appeals and lost his temper. But there was little justification for his unsporting behaviour.

Sri Lanka's tail wagged briskly but they were finally all out for 200 which set the MCC a 124-run victory target. This was achieved for the loss of three wickets. Roope had a "pair" just as Mendis had for Sri Lanka. The MCC lost Wood, Roope and Denness for 58 before Amiss and Birkenshaw saw them home with an unfinished stand of 69 for the fourth wicket. And with more than a day to spare !

THIRD MATCH *vs.* PRESIDENT'S ELEVEN at Colombo on February 21. Result : The MCC lost by four wickets.
Scores :
MCC : 158 for 5 (Amiss 102 not out).
President's XI : 161 for 6 (Tennekoon 61).

Put in to bat after a heavy overnight storm had left the pitch damp and delayed the start, the MCC lost half the side in reaching 158 within the stipulated 45 overs. Amiss made a splendid 102 not out and laid strong claims for the opener's berth against Pakistan. In reply, the home team had eleven balls to spare when the visitors' total was passed. Tennekoon who had always done well against touring MCC teams again played a notable knock and was top scorer with 61. The large crowd was naturally overjoyed with the home team's victory.

(Concluded)

KARATE

(from page 12)

impact of the mass—an impact which is due to the force existent in that mass.

The science teaches us that Acceleration multiplied by Mass, makes Force ; and that Acceleration is the rate of change in Velocity.

Thus to increase Force, it is imperative that either you increase the Mass or/and the Velocity.

And in a human body, since it is not possible to increase the Mass, an increase in the Force can only be achieved through a corresponding increase in the Velocity.

Hence the speedier is your strike, the more will it have the force.

But what is kinetic energy ?

According to Physics, again, any mass travelling in a certain direction is supposed to possess kinetic energy ; and if this mass collides with another, it is the kinetic energy in it that produces the impact.

And if the formation formula of kinetic energy (which is half of the Mass multiplied by twice the Velocity) has any truth, then it is absolutely possible to achieve an increase in velocity by proportionately increasing the kinetic energy.

Similarly, by increasing the Velocity, once can achieve an increase in the momentum which, in Physics, is nothing but the product of Mass and Velocity.

Thus, it is proved, that by increasing his speed alone, a karateka can achieve improvement of the force, kinetic energy and momentum.

Which, in the implied sense, means that all Karate motions carry high speed, resulting in a tremendous impact at the point of strike.

The picture on page 12 demonstrates just what, in Karate, the concentrated power implies.

Next Month : **GRADING SYSTEM IN KARATE**

The Kingston Test

(from page 15)

separated. It was the highest first-wicket partnership for Australia in 56 Tests. Stackpole survived chances at 18, 71, 83 and 86 to reach 142—his first century against the Windies and his sixth in 35 Tests. Set to score 261 in 90 minutes plus 20 overs, the West Indies made no attempt to force the pace or go for the target. When the final over was bowled, she had lost Fredericks, Findlay and Rowe in reaching 67.

The Kingston Test was like the opening round of a heavyweight title fight in which the two opponents took time to size each other up and waited for an opening to land a telling punch. For the first time in 31 Test encounters between Australia and the West Indies, the opening Test had ended without a result. With more than three-and-a-half days consumed by the first innings of the two teams and more than two hours lost to the weather, a draw was the only result which could be achieved. And so to Bridgetown, Barbados, for the second round.—END.

10

THE GRADING SYSTEM

By SALEEM A. JEHANGIR

WHEN one joins the institution of Karate, little does one realise the enormity of the hard work one will have to put in. At the moment, one is only thinking learning the art of self defence. But with the passage of time, one comes to look into the depth of the plunge he has taken.

Because Karate, on the whole, is too vast a study to be attempted superfluously. It is a science, an organisation and, at the same time, action—seeking the development of one's mental and physical performance in a most systematic and thorough manner.

During training, there are, therefore, endless written and practical tests for a Karate student. And the institution awards degrees and belts to distinguish his various levels of attainment in skill and proficiency.

Periodically, he is tested in the basic forms of Karate—plus the self-defence and one-step techniques which he must use with hundred per cent positiveness during free sparring.

Now, as stated earlier, the basic forms constitute a study in mock fight against imaginary opponents ; the self-defence techniques involve real but limited action whereas, in the one-step techniques, one strives to hurt one's opponent also. The free sparring is actual combat in which both the self-defence and one-step techniques are judiciously used.

A Karate student is also required, from time to time, to write essays on the skeletal and muscular systems of human body, answer questions about the therapeutical working of human mind and, last but not the least, discuss the many physical therapies for muscular ailments.

Then there are many other topics for him to study—ranging from the technicalities of Karate to its philosophical and institutional aspects.

Obviously, a karateka is, thus, under constant pressure to know more and more about human body and human mind. More important, he develops his own in the process.

IN Karate, there are six belts—white, yellow, green, blue, brown and black —and these correspond with the degrees one receives while in training.

The first degree is the 8th KUP and, with it, goes the white belt. From there on, the climb-up reads as under :

7th KUP	.. yellow belt
6th-5th KUP	.. green belt
4th-3rd KUP	.. blue belt
2nd-1st KUP	.. brown belt
1st DAN-to-9th DAN	: black belt

Upto the brown belt, the examinations are every four months. But the promotions are difficult to get, particularly for the higher belts. Calculating the time a karateka is likely to take for his black belt, is roughly three years provided his progress has been excellent throughout.

For instance, a brown belt has to spend a full year in study and another six months revising his knowledge, before he can sit for a black belt test—easily, the most rigorous of its kind known to mankind.

The written test for a black belt lasts nearly two hours, at the end of which one has to fight multiple opponents simultaneously and, also, the Dans. Then follows a power display in which the breaking of a pile of bricks or wooden planks with a single blow, is undertaken. Finally, the test ends with 40 pushups and 80 situps.

I spent an extra year for my black belt—not of my own free will, but as a punishment. Fighting against a black belt Dan, I lost my temper and was, consequently, debarred. Such is the severity of discipline in Karate.

A karateka who attains the black belt, is also confirmed as a teacher. He has the authority then to have his own club for the purpose of passing on the knowledge to others.

HOWEVER, in the oriental countries, the conception of a black belt is that of a beginner. According to their definition, a black belt is one who has only finished learning the "fundamentals" of Karate, and is about to BEGIN his journey into the institutional refineries.

A black belt is, thus, supposed to advance his knowledge under the guidance of a Master Instructor (usually a 6th Dan) —sharing, at the same time, his acquired knowledge with others.

Then every two years, there are examinations for a black belt until he attains the position of a 5th Dan—a status with which he has to live for a minimum of 13 years. According to a theory, his physical advancement stops by the time he is a 5th Dan, and so he must devote his time and energy in the promotion of Karate and its philosophy.

In due course of time, the Master Instructor evaluates the accomplishments of the 5th Dan under his wings and, being satisfied, honours him with a promotion. And when a 5th Dan is elevated to be a 6th Dan, the stature of the Master Instructor is automatically raised to that of the 7th Dan.

As years go by and more institutions are established, the stature of a black belt rises higher and higher—finally halting at the 9th Dan.

These standards of promotion in Karate are adhered to strictly all over the world. Which means that a green belt in Pakistan will have the same standing in the institution as the green belts in Japan, Korea, China, the USA and, for that matter, anywhere in the world.

And in this unique uniformity, lies the untold story of Karate's popularity throughout the world.

Next Month : KARATE FOR WOMEN

SPORTIMES

Sportimes May 1973

11

FOR WOMEN

Right :
Piercing the eyes

By SALEEM A. JEHANGIR

BASICALLY, two types of women take to Karate. Among them are the thousands of females who, feeling insecure in the midst of hostile elements, join the institution, to learn what has come to be known as the art of self defence.

In other words, they seek in Karate the necessary safeguards against vulgarity, meanness and violence.

The second type of women which the institution attracts, can be described as the precious minority which is always on the lookout for adventure, excitement and thrill-packed action.

To this kind belong the athletes, scouts, detectives and the women in uniforms.

But in actual effect, Karate offers much more to its pupils than the mere techniques of self defence; and it is only when one gets to the depth of it that one is really wiser.

No wonder, then, every new recruit becomes, after some time, an ardent admirer of Karate. It is her canvassing, wholly uninspired, on which the institution thrives universally.

And the number in which women have been taking to Karate, is simply staggering.

Not because they are progressively advanced enough to go along men in all walks of life, but mainly due to the manifold advantages they stand to gain from the institution.

EXPERIENCE has shown that the Karate exercises tend to make the fair sex more beautiful by giving it extra grace.

Even the physicians and therapists have found these exercises highly useful in improving the texture and complexion of the skin.

According to the medical opinion, the Karate training also regulates the flow of blood in a human body, improves the digestion, prevents the formation of clots in the bold, cures asthama and forms an excellent remedy for muscular ailments—besides, relieving nervous tension.

SUMMING UP, I would say that the Karate women have confidence and, far from feeling weak and spastic, carry poise. They know no nervous tensions, but are always equal to a given situation—thanks to their competence in the art of self defence.

And yet, they lose none of their femininity. On the contrary, they look more feminine because of their improved chromosome content, slimmed figures and mellowed complexion.

They have friends, too—truly loyal and sound—friends belonging to the same order and institution.

Training session—Upper part block (Sang Dan Makki)

14

SPORTIMES

KARATE 12

The Cat Stance

By SALEEM A. JEHANGIR

SO FAR in my articles, I have covered a few basic motions, basic techniques and advanced techniques. Let us now go a little deeper into the art, for the art is vast and offers a host of techniques of offence and defence—the Strikes and Blocks, in Karate terminology.

Long Punches, like the front Stance Punch, are advantageous when the opponent is at a distance. But when the opponent is nearer, one of the better techniques is the Half Punch. The picture at right shows the **Half Punch in Cat Stance.**

This implies the lifting of the heel of the front foot so as to allow minimum weight on the front leg. Since the opponent would normally attack the portion of your body which is nearest him, the weight put on the front leg would cause it to be "swept" easily, resulting in imbalance.

The weight ratio between the front and hind legs in this stance is 30-70. It is advisable to use the half punch where the full extension of the arm is not possible due to the closeness of the opponent.

Choong Dan Sudo, that is blocking the middle part with a sudo, is the movement illustrated by the picture above. It entails the simultaneous blocking of the knife hand. One hand blocks the opponent's middle part and the other the solar plexus.

Application of Choong Dan Sudo is shown in the two photographs below, where the attacking hand is blocked differently. At left, the knife is blocked away, leaving the front section of the opponent's body open for attack. At right, the knife is blocked towards the opponent's inside leaving his side open for attack.

Some more blockings

By SALEEM A. JEHANGIR

PICKING UP from where we left off last month, just as "Choong" in the Korean stands for the middle part, "Ha" means the lower part. The picture at top left shows this move, known as Ha Dan Sudo, that is, blocking the lower part with sudo.

Similarly, **Sang Dan Sudo** implies an identical action in respect of the upper part. Thus, in the photograph at top right is blocked the opponent's knife—with a counterattack to his groin.

The two sequences below describe blocking with the arm (at left), follow by a counter-attack to the temple (righ

Yet another technique is seen in tl photograph above (middle), whil explains itself.

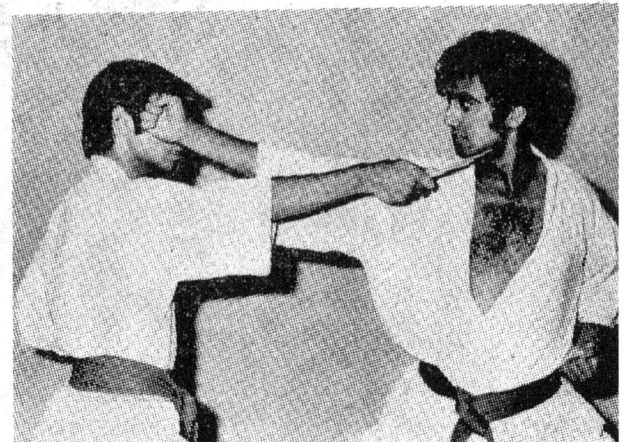

Choosing a Stance

KARATE 14

CHOOSING a fighting stance is a fighter's prerogative. He can switch stances during the fight, but it is more advisable to hold on strongly to a particular stance once you have made a decision to this effect.

The emphasis is necessary, because the fighting stance is the base from which every motion is executed.

At top right is seen an attack with knife-hand-sudo to the neck in the cat stance. The same stance is involved in the fighting posture shown by the photograph at right (middle). One hand guards the head and the other the middle part.

A **crane fighting stance** is illustrated below. In this case, the leg is also used

By

SALEEM A. JEHANGIR

—to guard the groin. The disadvantage of being unstable is countered by the availability of the lifted leg ready for executing a side kick.

NOW, here is a typical situation warranting the application of a self-defence technique. The opponent holds you by the hands (picture just below). The release is made by moving your wrists inwards and out in a circular motion, holding the opponent's wrists and kicking him in

the stomach (bottom photo).

And, this is just one of the techniques in Karate—quick release followed by instantaneous counter-attack.

Sportimes September 1973

KARATE 15

More of the Typical Situations

By SALEEM A. JEHANGIR

CONTINUING with typical situations, here is an instance (picture at top right), where you are held by the arm. There are two methods of release from this position as illustrated by the photographs in the middle of the page.

At left, you move your hand outside and bring it back in a circular motion, capturing the opponent's arm into an arm lock. A little twist from this position can break the opponent's arm.

At right, the hand is moved in the reverse direction, the effect being too apparent to describe.

* * *

IN case the opponent grabs you from behind (picture at left), the hold is opened by jerking your arms just like a chicken flapping its wings. This is instantaneously followed by a counter-attack as shown in the photograph at right.

Sportimes October 1973

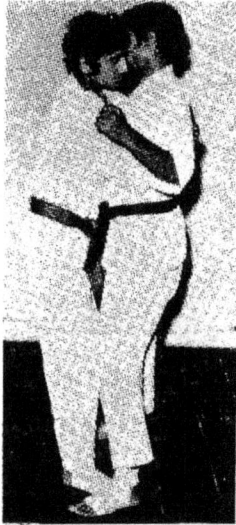

■ *By* SALEEM A. JEHANGIR ■

IN CASE one is confronted with a hold more commonly applied by wrestlers or peasant fashion fighters, as shown in the picture at left, the method of release is illustrated at right.

THE

CHOKE

THE CHOKE is the common type of a fatal attack. In the photographs just below is seen the opening mechanism of a choking hold (left) which is countered by an instantaneous double Sudo to the temples (right).

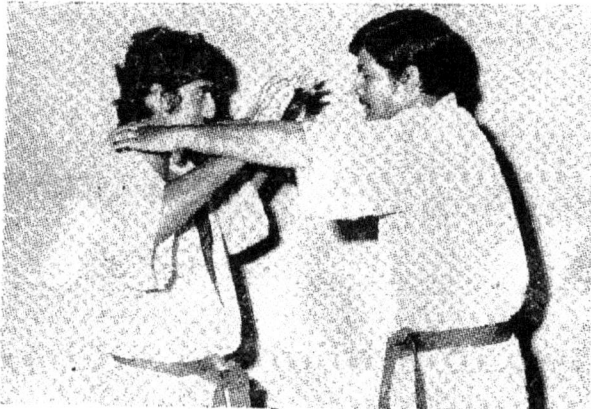

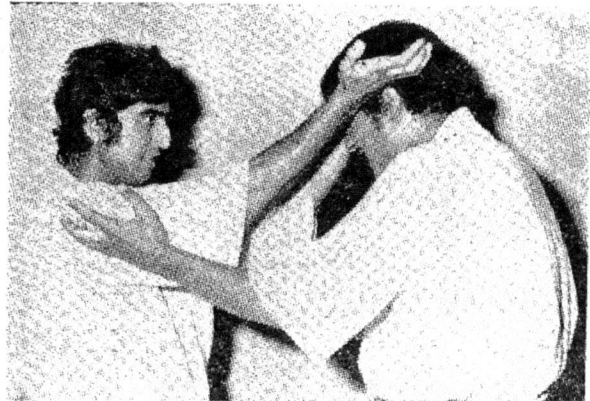

Another technique to defend oneself from the choke is shown at left. One of the opponent's arms is held and twisted to land in the position depicted by the photograph at right.

★

SPORTIMES

Sportimes November 1973

KARATE 17

More about the Kicks

By SALEEM A. JEHANGIR

KICKS are an important aspect of karate. I have already discussed the front and side kicks. But before concluding the present series, I must make a mention of the Round House Kick.

This is affected in a horizontal-circular motion and the contact is made with the "ball" of the foot. In the photograph above such a kick is being executed to the solar plexus.

Again, a round house kick can be of advantage while meeting difficult situations during combat. Below is seen this kick taking care of the head in a slapping fashion.

(Continued on page 31)

The pictures above and below illustrate two more techniques involving the choke and they speak for themselves.

SPORTIMES

RENDEZ-VOUS

Pakistan's Karate "Export"

The news concerning our Karate Expert, Saleem Ashraf Jehangir who had been writing a series of articles for this Magazine, reached us only a couple of weeks ago. Perhaps it was Saleem's modesty which kept him from informing us about his achievements or the packet containing some useful material pertaining to the First American Inter-Collegiate and Open Tae Kwon Do-Karate Championships got delayed in transit. Now we are pleased to publish the belated good news.

Saleem Jehangir (left), with his instructor, Mr. Hwa Chong and the trophy he won in Michigan

THE University of Michigan were the co-sponsors of a contest in which competitions were held last March at five different levels—inter-collegiate, open, high school, women and juniors (ages 12 to 15). Saleem A. Jehangir of Pakistan was placed second in the Black Belt form (KATA) competition. In this contest, one displays one's skills in the art through forms in which one fights with an imaginary opponent in all directions. KATA are known as the gist of Karate and only through these can one become a good fighter and a good Karateka. This exhibition is similar to the free floor exercises by a gymnast.

Points in the KATA competition are given on the strength, co-ordination, control, grace and complexity of movements exhibited. KATA, as different from Free Sparring, is one of the two types of competitions, and it is in this that Saleem Jehangir competed and won the second place in the All-American Cham-

pionships. As he himself put it, "I was out of shape and not upto my own standard. But it was an encouraging result which has launched me into a more vigorous training programme".

The tournament, one of the biggest events in Karate ever held in the United States of America, was a great success. More than 600 competitors in all Belt levels took part and were watched by thousands of spectators. For the Black Belts, there were over fifty contestants. Authorities of the Karate world—8th Dan and 7th Dan Black Belt holders—were present as organisers and judges of the tournament. These experts who organised the U.S. Karate Championships have written books on the subject and are internationally recognised as Masters of the Art. One of them, Mr. Hwa Chong, a 7th Dan Black Belter, has trained and coached Saleem Jehangir since 1966. At the announcement of the winners, the name of Pakistan was mentioned along

with that of Saleem Ashraf Jehangir whose services for the promotion of Karate in Pakistan were also given honourable mention.

Saleem Jehangir plans to take part in a host of other tournaments lined up for 1974. He says, "They are all worth participating in because you fight and compete against pupils of different styles—some Japanese, some Chinese and others from Okinawa and even Korea. The Korean style Karate is known as "Tae Kwon Do" and is by for the most popular form of Karate all over the world. This is the style my coach and mentor, Mr. Chong, is teaching me".

We wish Saleem Jehangir the best of luck in all his undertakings against all comers.

Sportimes March 1975

FIRST KARATE CONTEST

THE first All-Pakistan Karate Championships under the auspices of the Tae Kwon Do (Karate) Association of Pakistan were organised at the National Coaching Centre, Karachi. Even though the sport is still in its infancy in this country, the competition attracted about a hundred entries in the various belt divisions.

Apart from this indication of the growing popularity of karate, the sponsors

were also surprised by an almost unexpected number of spectators—more than 1500—despite the heavy rains that day. It was encouraging indeed to find that not a soul left the gymnasium until the four-hour demonstration of the Pakistani karatekas' skills was over.

Highlighting the proceedings was the green belt decider in which Mohammad Ibrahim defeated Altaf Sakhi. The skilful use of hand strikes and kicks in this fight brought the audience to their feet.

The Grand Championship trophy—donated by Saleem A. Jehangir, who is currently in Pakistan—was annexed by Asif Hussain. In all, some 45 prizes were awarded that evening.

A demonstration of Thai kick boxing by students from Thailand and a display of the Malaysian martial art of "Punchak Silhat" added to the variety of the occasion. Saleem Jehangir's feats—breaking wooden boards by hands and kicks and splitting a board in the air—were also appreciated by all.

Saleem A. Jehangir splitting a board in the air with a sudo-strike

Aqilur Rahman scoring with a kick to the head during the eliminations

April, 1975

Sportimes April 1975

Other Magazines and Newspapers

From The Publisher

He Started It All

In the labyrinth of different martial arts, practised on a large scale in Pakistan, one comes across many "masters", each claiming to be "the one and only" in the domain of excellence and credibility. Not all of them, though, are the "dans" they profess to be, and few, if any, have the credentials to occupy the centre stage, which they do with the connivance of the print and electric media.

And if we were to believe SALIM JAHANGIR, the man who started it all way back in 1971, each martial art club has become an economic unit for its promoter, and considers itself an association. He was sorry to say that all the good work he did to establish and popularise Tae Kwon Do in Pakistan, has been fragmented during his absence from the country. For one, who learnt this art for 17 long years from a senior most Korean master in the United States, and who still dreams of using his knowledge to develop traits of integrity, honesty, hard work, dedication, loyalty, brotherhood, chivalry, healthy body and sound mind among the young people through it, the present situation cannot but appear extremely distressing.

"Tae Kwon Do is a whole lot more than kicking and punching," he said while talking to Playtime. Look out for his interview, readers. We will give it to you soon. Meanwhile here is for your album his action photo of a flying side kick. Enjoy it and feel happy.

PIONEER – Salim Jahangir

02   PLAYTIME June 1990

Playtime Magazine

KARATE GAINING POPULARITY

IT is the stored energy in man, coupled with the inherent fear, that makes him lose his temper and indulge into physical violence Karate takes out the frustration and fear. A Karate student comes four times a week and trains for two hours each day. For two hours he expends his energy by training how to fight. When he walks out, he walks with confidence, for he has no fear and walks with no ambition to fight, for he has let his stored energy out.

By S. A. JEHANGIR

KARATE is getting very popular all over the world and there are sound reasons for it. Its philosophical and sociological advantages have been published earlier.

In this article I will discuss what attraction Karate has to the public and what does it offer to the student who practices it, to the spectator who enjoys it, and to the patroniser who works towards its flourishment

STUDENT

To the students it provides a means to develop a sound body and a sound mind. It provides in him a philosophy of peace and non-violence associated with brotherhood, and he works towards this noble cause using the institution of Karate as the medium to reach other fellow beings.

It is the inherent desire in man to reach perfection that keeps his soul frustrated and longing for some philosophy that can satisfy it. All the stu-

dents of Karate have felt this —that the philosophical and physical achievements through the training of Karate have satisfied their desire for search of a discipline that can cool their inherent desire for perfection of soul and the body.

PUBLIC

Often the public has a wrong impression of Karate. They think it is an art to develop super power through which you can over-power your opponent in no time. Never do they realise why and where does this desire to conquer your opponent comes from. It is this basic inherent fear in man that makes him desire all super natural forces to conquer over every man on earth. Karate builds up your physical achievements to let you know your limitations. And once you have learned that there is a limit that you can build your physical power. Karate then starts training your mind that has no limitation to its development. Hence the product is a man who knows the boundaries to his physical endeavours and has a mind trained to keep calm to use both the body and the mind to work towards a philosophy of a peaceful unification of the world.

This is the satisfaction that the training of Karate provides its students. I am sure this is vague to a reader but ask a student who continuously trains Karate of what and how much he has achieved. It is only him that can realise it.

To the spectator who comes to enjoy this sport, Karate provides a living spectacle of humane grace, agility, coordination and perfection in display.

strength and accuracy — like shattering of an ice block by an open hand, breaking of a pile of bricks by just one blow; slicing of the neck of a bottle, when it is not even held at the base, kicking off a cigarette from the lips of a person by a flying side kick, breaking a pile of wooden planks held 8 feet in the air by giving a front kick, breaking of a pile of bricks with finger tips or the forehead etc and other marvellous feats of speedy coordination as fighting multiple opponents simultaneously.

PATRONS

To the patrons it provides disciplined sport that has manifold advantages. Other sports are merely entertaining but this sport has a philosophy behind it.

This sport turns out a set of

people who walk confidently, ready to fight for right, ready to put end to injustice, fully equipped to solve problems through peaceful means. They work towards an evil free world, they world towards reforming a society—they are walking police-men ready to offer courtesy yet confident to defend right.

The patrons of Karate realise the noble aims the institution of Karate has and he has a dual satisfaction in patronising this institution. Its parton knows that by promoting the institution of Karate he is promoting peace, discipline and brotherhood in this world.

The readers can now have a slight idea why Karate is spreading so fast in the world as a sport—because it has given the sportsmen, the audience and its patrons what no other sports before has given.

THE STAR

GIRLS LINE UP FOR KARATE FINALS AT THE NATIONAL SPORTS TRAINING AND COACHING CENTRE.STAR PHOTO.

THE STAR

A group of the Karate students who are undergoing coaching at the National Training and Coaching Centre.

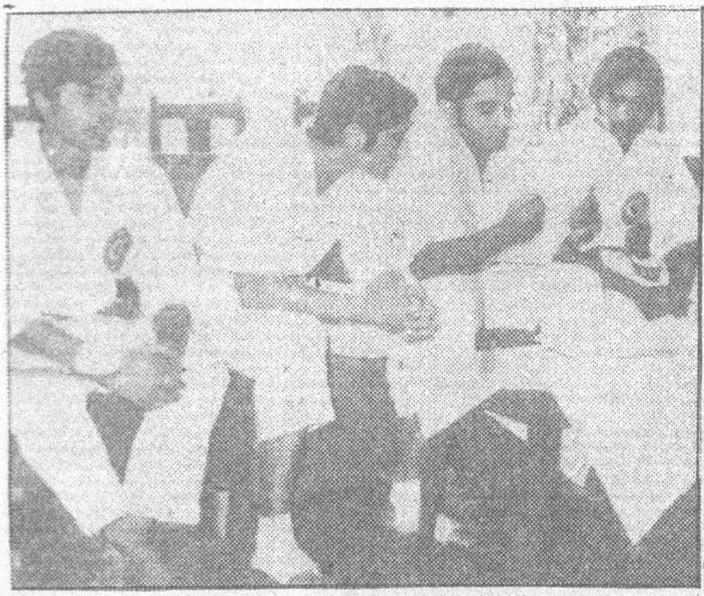

"کراٹے" کا کھیل مخالف پر حملہ آور ہونے کے علاوہ اپنے بچاؤ کی موثر تربیت بھی دیتا ہے

"کراٹے" کے کھلاڑی افتخار، پرویز، سلیم، مسرت اور آصف اپنے کوچ سلیم جہانگیر کے ساتھ ۔ (فوٹو مشرق)

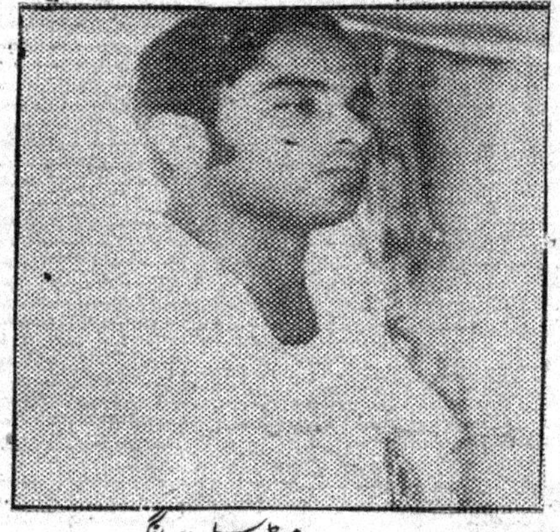

دنیا بھر میں کھیلے جانے والے اس کھیل کو نظم و ضبط کا بہترین نمونہ سمجھا جاتا ہے

رپورٹ : ابو نصر ملک

گزشتہ دنوں کوئٹہ کلب میں لڑکوں اور لڑکیوں کو کراٹے کی تربیت دی گئی اور تربیت کے اختتام پر بلوچستان کے وزیر اعلیٰ سردار عطاءاللہ مینگل نے انعامات تقسیم کئے وزیر اعلیٰ نے تقسیم انعامات کے موقع پر تقریر کرتے ہوئے اس کھیل کی تعریف کی اور کہا کہ ہر شخص کو کراٹے کا فن سیکھنا چاہیئے۔ کوئٹہ کلب میں کراٹے کی تربیت دینے والوں میں مسٹر سلیم جہانگیر اور ان کے چار شاگرد، مسرت، افتخار آصف، اور منیجر ارشاد عثمانی شامل تھے۔ مسٹر سلیم جہانگیر نے کراٹے کا اعلیٰ اعزاز بلیک بیلٹ حاصل کیا ہے۔

کوئٹہ کلب میں منعقد ہونے والی تقریب کے اختتام پر جناب سلیم جہانگیر نے نمائندہ مشرق کو بتایا کہ وہ ڈی جے سائنس کالج کراچی سے تعلیم مکمل کرنے کے بعد انجینئرنگ کی اعلیٰ تعلیم کے لئے امریکہ گئے اور وہاں انہوں نے اپنی تعلیم کے ساتھ ساتھ کراٹے کا فن بھی سیکھا اور ۱۹۷۰ء میں کراٹے کو اعلیٰ اعزاز بلیک بیلٹ حاصل کیا۔ اس کے بعد سلیم جہانگیر نے کراچی میں نیشنل کوچنگ سنٹر میں لڑکوں اور لڑکیوں کو کراٹے کے فن سے روشناس کرایا۔ اب تک انہوں نے پانچ سو سے زائد لڑکوں اور لڑکیوں کو کراٹے کی تربیت دی ہے ان کی خواہش ہے کہ یہ فن ملک کے گوشے گوشے میں فروغ حاصل کرے۔

کراٹے کی تاریخ اور فوائد کے بارے میں ایک سوال کا جواب دیتے ہوئے سلیم صاحب نے بتایا کہ یہ فن تقریباً دو ہزار سال پہلے چین میں شروع ہوا اور رفتہ رفتہ دوسرے ایشیائی ممالک اور جاپان تک پھیل گیا اور اب اس فن کو مغربی ممالک میں شہرت اور ترقی مل رہی ہے۔ انہوں نے کہا کہ یہ لڑائی کا ایک ایسا طریقہ ہے جس کے ذریعہ نہتا ہو کر حملہ کیا جاتا ہے اور مخالف کا حملہ بھی روکا جا سکتا ہے۔ کراٹے کا ایک حملہ اتنا موثر ثابت ہوتا ہے کہ مخالف کو جان سے بھی ہاتھ دھونا پڑتا ہے یا وہ شدید زخمی ہوتا ہے لیکن کراٹے کے ماہر ایسا نہیں

مسٹر سلیم جہانگیر

کرتے۔ وہ کراٹے کے اس فن سے اپنی حفاظت کرتے ہیں۔ کراٹے کی تربیت کی بنیاد نظم و ضبط پر قائم ہے۔ اس کے بارے میں کہا جاتا ہے کہ نظم پیدا کرنے کے لئے کراٹے کا فن سیکھنا چاہیئے اور یہی وجہ ہے کہ مغربی ممالک میں سکولوں اور کالجوں میں کراٹے کو نظم و ضبط اور صبر و تحمل پیدا کرنے کا ایک ذریعہ سمجھا جاتا ہے۔ اس کے ذریعہ یکسوئی حاصل کرنے، خطرے کو فوراً محسوس کرنے اور تنظیم پیدا کرنے میں اتنی کامیابی ہوئی ہے کہ مغربی ممالک اور بہت سے ایشیائی ممالک میں فوجوں کی تربیت کے لئے کراٹے کا فن ایک لازمی جزو بن گیا ہے۔

کراٹے کی تربیت کے دوران سخت قسم کی ورزش کرنا پڑتی ہے اور خیالی لڑائی میں مقابل کا تصور رکھنا پڑتا ہے اسلئے انسان کا غصہ اور خوامخواہ لڑنے کا جذبہ آہستہ آہستہ سرد پڑ جاتا ہے اور جب وہ تربیت گاہ سے نکلتا ہے تو وہ اس کا متمنی اور پر اعتماد ہوتا ہے کہ اسے اپنے دوسرے ساتھیوں کی مدد سے معاشرے میں ایک پرسکون اور عدم تشدد کی فضا قائم کرنا ہے مختصر یہ کہ ان لوگوں کے متعلق جنہوں نے اس فن کو حاصل کیا ہے اگر معلومات کی جائیں تو ان کے شب و روز میں یہ تمام خصوصیات واضح اور نمایاں نظر آئیں گی۔

پاکستان میں کراٹے کے فن کے فروغ حاصل کرنے کے بارے میں سلیم جہانگیر نے بتایا کہ پاکستان کی زمین اچھے کھلاڑی اور بہترین صلاحیتوں کے نوجوان پیدا کرنے کے لئے زرخیز ہے اگر صحیح طریقے سے نوجوانوں کی صلاحیتوں کو بروئے کار لایا جائے تو پاکستان بجا طور پر فخر کر سکتا ہے آخر میں انہوں نے کہا کہ ہماری یہ کوشش ہے کہ جس طرح کوئٹہ اور پشاور میں کراٹے کے کلب قائم کئے گئے ہیں۔ اسی طرح ملک کے دوسرے شہروں میں بھی اسی قسم کے کلب قائم کئے جائیں تاکہ اس فن کو مزید ترقی دی جا سکے۔

سلیم جہانگیر ایسو اسٹینڈرڈ کمپنی میں آپریشن انجینئر ہیں اور پاکستان کراٹے اور جوڈو ایسوسی ایشن کے بانی اور صدر ہیں وہ اپنے اسکولوں اور کالج کے زمانے میں کراٹے کے علاوہ ہاکی کرکٹ اور باکسنگ بھی کھیلتے رہے ہیں۔ اور کئی کھیلوں میں اپنے اسکولوں اور کالج ٹیم کے کیپٹن بھی رہے ہیں۔

KNOW KARATE

By S. A. Jehangir

Youth is a problem all over the world. The Karate experts feel that if this art is promoted it can solve the problem as the art gives a sense of discipline to the youth.

The need for such an art is more necessary for our country as we are passing through a new phase and the most important since our independence. We, therefore, are publishing a series of articles for those who may like to learn it.

History

Before we talk about the technicalities of Karate let's first understand how it came into existence. We all know that Karate is an art of self defence that developed hundreds of years ago in China when the need of unarmed combat was felt strongly during war times. And so it had

S. A. JEHANGIR

to be a MARTIAL ART that would involve building of sound bodies and sound minds through intense discipline. But no such science existed that would suffice the needs of such a disciplined art. Then one day a Budhist Monk called BODHIDHARMA travelled to China to teach the secrets of Zen Budhism. The intense practices of the austerities of Zen led its disciples to weaken physically and hence mentally. Bodhidharma then devised

exercises that would develop physical and mental control. These exercises with their disciplined physical and mental training were then picked up by the pioneers of the combative arts to develop into the art now known as Karate.

Now we can go ahead to realise what Karate is.

Karate

Karate literally translated would mean "The way with the hand". And so Karate utilises the hands, the legs, the head the fist the foot — in short, the human mechanism of motion to its optimum advantage, and, the muscular movements to their greatest speed, combined effect of which then resulting in tremendous momentum at the point strike.

spinal column throat and kidneys. Pressure points are those places where a hit would temporarily disable the human body. These places are the neck, nose, eyes, arm pit, and certain joints in the body. All strikes in Karate will be aimed at these points and no where else, since Karate practices concentration of energy and its emission only at the point of a strike. Through continuous training the mind is programme to utilise these vital points in the human body instantaneously during combat, hence no energy is lost in manouvering the opponent.

Knowing thus for the generalisation about Karate, lets now start on how to begin our training, (keep in mind this is an art, the learning process of which does not stop for years and years). Since all the Karate exercises involve intense strain on the muscles it becomes extremely necessary to tune up the muscular system before any Karate exercise is done, otherwise muscle ruptures would commonly result. This tuning up is done through the universal exercises such as stretching legs, arms and body, bending skipping, jogging, push ups, sit ups, rotational exercises of the neck and the waist, and other

Points of strike?

They are called the vital and the pressure points Vital points are those where a hit could cause permanent damage in the human body. These are the temple, solar-plexus, groin, and of

2

half to one hour.

"P.T." exercises.

Consider it like this — your muscles are asleep, you want to wake them up before you put them to work — this 'waking up' is done by these warm up exercises. Hence the reader, intending to pursue the training through these articles, should start tuning his muscular system. Every day these exercise should be performed for about

Now we can go ahead with the first Karate exercise — the FRONT SNAP KICK. But before this kick is executing make sure that all leg muscles are stretched. This can be done by swinging the leg in upward direction, with knee locked.

Stretch from ready position. Such leg 10 times every day before front kick exercise. Now from the ready position being the hind leg up, as shown in picture (1), and snap forward as in picture (2). Note the posture of the foot and the knee; the knee is locked and the foot is forward with toes curled up, and the contact is made through the 'ball' of the foot. The exercise should be repeated every day. 20 kicks, atleast with each leg. Going into a little detail of the mechanism of the front kick I may add that when the leg is brought up, as in picture (1), the muscle should be relaxed so no energy is lost, but when the kick is executed, from this position the, all muscles should tense at the time of contact. This sudden "locking" of the muscle and the joints should result in a "snapping" sound.

The power, contained in this kick, after continuous training for three months, can be imagined through picture (3), whence two wooden boards, each of one inch thickness, are broken by the sudden, impact.

(To be continued)

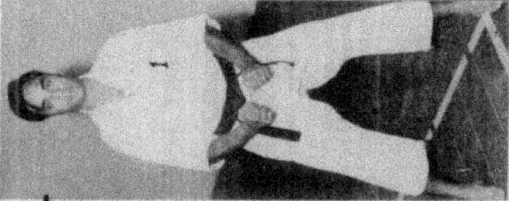

KNOW KARATE II
DISCIPLINE A MUST

By S.A. Jehangir

Discipline is a must for a Karate man. No discipline no Karate. Everything goes in a discipline manner. Youth has to forget what he is before he starts learning Karate. All that he knows when he walks out that he is a disciplined man.

In my last article I had emphasised on the warming up of muscles before beginning any Karate exercise. This practice is to be adhered to for all times, because he has trained much more than you, his kick is much more effective than yours.

Today we go on to our next exercise — the FRONT PUNCH. But before we go any further; lets clearly understand the term "Stance".

CHUNBEE

Stance is the posture of the body that has to be maintained in all exercise. In a stance, concentration should be given to the position of the head, shoulders, arms, legs, feet, eyes. The stance that we start all our exercises is the READY stance, which in Korean terminology is called the "CHUNBEE" stance. Picture (1) shows the "CHUNBEE" stance. Notice that the head is straight, eyes looking into the eyes of the opponent, shoulders are relaxed, hands are held with fists closed just below the belt, feet are placed a little wider than shoulders width and fist on the ground with toes turned inwards. This is an important stance because all Karate exercises start with the "Chunbee" stance.

CHONGUL CHAASE

From the Chunbee stance we go to execute our beginning exercises in the front stance, or in Korean the 'Chongul Chaase'. Picture (2) shows the Chongul Chaase. (about the punch we will talk later on), but notice the posture of the body — front leg is bent at right angles to the floor, hind leg is locked, weight is divided equally on both legs by keeping body straight, feet are flat on the ground, shoulders are held parallel to the wall directly opposite, the stance is wide and low. The student should practice this stance by keeping both hands on waiste and walking forward maintaining the Chongul Chaase with front, leg bent and hind leg locked, always. Repeat this exercise until you can easily, maintaining the front stance.

CHUNG DAN KONGGYOA

Now we can go ahead with the Front Punch, or in Korean "Chung Dan Konggyoa". But before we go ahead lets stop to realise the importance of Oriental terminology used during the training. This is so say that this has been nour-

ished and disciplined in the Orient. This art bases its success on the discipline involved — no discipline, no Karate — and it is a part of this discipline to learn all exercises by their Oriental names. Besides it makes it a lot easier to remember these exercises by their Oriental names, as experienced by students on the long run. Since the style of Karate we are learning is Korean, we will be using Korean terminology.

Now lets go back to our exercise for today — the front punch. Chung Dan Konggrok is executed from the Chunbee Stance as shown in picture (2). Notice that if it is the right hand punching, the right foot is in front, left foot is back, and left punch resting on side ready to execute another punch. From this position move forward with left foot and maintain the left front stance then execute the left punch, bring back the right punch to ready position simultaneously. Repeat this as you move forward.

Notice also that, the fist that is ready is in upright position and when is travers-es to punch it goes in a spiral to punch in the inverted fist position. From the laws of physics we know that a mass travelling in a spiral gathers more momentum than a mass travelling in a straight line. Similarly a punch travel-'ing in a spiral is more powerful than a punch that just shoots straight. The power contained in this punch can be imagined through picture (3), wherce two wooden boards, each 1 inch thick are broken by the sudden impact of the fist.

This exercise together with other exercises should be repeated everyday for good training. Important points to be remembered are; the front stance should be maintained, the punch should be aimed at the solar plexus or the nose, and all power should be concentrated at the point of strike. More clearly it means that no muscle should tense when you move forward, but when you strike all muscle should come to a sudden lock resulting in a snapping sound. Hence movements should be easy and graceful and strike should be harsh and tense.

Now, because you will be hitting with such force, your joints should be able to take the sudden shock, particularly the wrist, elbow and shoulder. To tune up these areas push ups on knuckles (with fists closed) and on fingers are recommended.

Remember all these exercise's are basic exercise only and not the actual technique. But before we teach the actual technique you have to learn these exercises because only through these exercises you would develop power, co-ordination and control.

The secret to all power is the right technique and continuous training.

(To be continued)

KNOW KARATE II

By S. A. JEHANGIR

IT is the stored energy in man, coupled with the inherent fear, that makes him lose his temper and indulge into physical violence. Karate takes out these frustrations and fear.

A Karate student comes four times a week and trains for two hours each time. For two hours he expends his energy by training him to fight. When he walks out, he walks with confidence, for he has no fear and as he walks with no ambition to fight, for he has let his stored energy out.

In the last two lessons we learned how to execute the front snap kick and the front punch. These were the offensive moves. To every offensive move there should be a defensive move. Lets go a little deeper into the terms offensive moves and defensive moves.

OFFENSIVE

Offensive moves, or in Korean —KONGGYOKKI, are strikes to the vital and pressure points to damage or cause temporary disability, Konggyokki can be very many depending on different techniques using the hands and feet. So far we have just learned the front kick and the front punch, Other Konggyokki we will learn later on. Konggyokki are very powerful and they are similar keeping right hand in front of groin guarding it. Then bring the left hand down to a little above the left knee, simultaneously pulling back the right hand to rest on the belt. The blocking hand should come down fast and with power ending in a lock resulting in a snapping sound. Now move forward with the right leg to maintain Chongul Chasse, take right hand over left shoulder keeping left hand guarding the groin, bring down, right hand to end in a jerk, simultaneously pulling back the left hand to rest on the belt ready for counter attack.

Keep moving forward to practise the exercise, you will realise that the other hand goes over the other shoulder and comes down crossing in front of your groin to lock suddenly just above the knee. You can see in picture (1) how your lower part is blocked by the piercing side kick. Remember, in this exercise, that you have to block your lower part, hence your blocking hand travels up to gain momentum to come down gathering speed to give it the maximum force at the point of strike, and your other hand simultaneously travels back to cock itself on your waist, ready for counter attack. This was the defensive move for the lower part. — HA DAN MAKKI.

GUARD

SANG DAN MAKKI: We learned the exercise to defend the lower part, now let us learn how to defend our upper part. The upper part block in Korean is called SANG DAN MAKKI.

Sang Dan Makki is meant to guard any strike travelling in the direction of the head e.g. a knife or a punch or a kick aimed at the face. Again, starting from Chumbee stance, move forward with the left foot to maintain Chongul Chasse, bring left hand down to guard groin and right hand in front of solar plexus, then pull the left hand up over the head, simultaneously pulling the right hand back to rest on belt. Again the blocking hand has to move fast and powerfully. Now move forward with right foot to maintain Chongul Chasse, keeping right hand to guard the groin and left hand over solar plexus, then pulling right hand over the head simultaneously retreating the left hand to rest on the belt. Repeat the exercise in forward direction. To visualise the use of this defensive move look at picture (2) which shows the right hand deflecting the opponents striking member, and left hand cocked on belt ready for counter attack. This block should be executed powerfully and fast as can be seen by the situation exhibited in picture (2); and remember you are not stopping the blow, instead you are deflecting it to the side.

COUNTER ATTACK

About counter attacks we will talk later on in our future lessons at present we have to concentrate only on the offensive and defensive moves. However, it should suffice to say, for the time being, that counter attacks are offensive strikes executed immediately after the defensive move is made; e.g. in picture (2) the knifing hand is blocked by one hand and the other hand is cocked ready to execute a counter attack, which could be a punch or a Sudo or finger pokes in the eyes. These are called counter attacks. Counter attacks could also be kicks. About all these we will talk later on.

ed to cause damage, hence it becomes extremely important to develop strong defensive moves. Defensive moves are again strikes but this time the strikes are not to the vital points but to the member used for offense. These defensive strikes are called MAKKI in Korean. Makki is aimed to "deflect" the striking member to break its momentum. We all know that it is much easier to deflect a mass travelling in a straight line than to stop it head on. Hence all our defensive moves will be to deflect the striking punch or the kick or the knife-hand (SUDO) etc.

DEFFENSIVE

HA DAN MAKKI: With this background let us go on to our first defensive move, the lower part block, or in Korean — HA DAN MAKKI From the Chumbee position move with left leg forward to maintain the front stance (Chongul Chasse, then take left hand over right shoulder keeping right hand in front of groin guarding it, Then bring

TO BE (CONTINUED)

KARATE FOR WOMEN

By S. A. JEHANGIR

The number of women learning Karate is increasing in fantastic proportions, day by day. No matter how distorted the world's conception of Karate as being effiminate is, this art is

increasing its female followers and there are very definite reasons for it.

Basically there are two types of women who join the institution of Karate. One is the type that feels insecure in today's world of violence and joins mainly to learn the art of self defence. The other is the athletic woman who likes to try different sports.

Both these types, they come and they stay, with time they discover the advantages of Karate training for women more and more and as they find out they convince other women to join the institution.

Here, it is not only self-defence that a woman learns, there are other advantages accompanying the training that particularly attract the female specie. Let us go a little deeper into these aspects, as we go let

us start with how it all started long ago, when Buddhist monks travelled far and wide to preach the secrets of Zen. They also taught physical and mental exercises that were very mystical in nature. Zen preaches strict self-defence and mental training and these exercise were designed to develop physical and mental strength in the human body so he can resist hunger, cold, heat and physical pains.

PHILOSOPHY

These exercises were so effective that the followers of Zen could live without food for days and still maintain freshness and serenity on their faces and could fight off opponents trying to rebuke their philosophy. The wisemen of those days saw the powers lying under these mystical exercises. And so the warrior class of those days took up these exercises and moulded them into the shape that prepared them as warriors strongest in the nation.

WARRIORS

Meanwhile Zen maintained its discipline in the form what we know as Yoga.

These exercises were sacred to the Orientals and the followers of Zen and were disclosed only to the most devoted pupils. Among the warriors such were the powers of this training that one warrior could manoeuvre many armed opponents single handed. The armed fighters used this training to evolve fantastic generals. And the pioneers of the comparative arts used this training to

evolve into an art which uses only what a man is born with — his arms and his legs — to manoeuvre even armed opponents. But no matter where it went the training showed the same marvellous result — their bodies were fine and slim, their complexions were healthy, their movements were faster than those of animals and they maintained a complete calm and sereve look on their faces.

CONCEPT

Then communications between countries improved. More education and freedom for the young started to revolutionise the world aiming at one philosophy and the concept of Universalism. With this concept the practice of keeping one's knowledge and wisdom to one's own self and passing only to the devoted ones started to fade out, and the philosophy of the Orient along with its mystical methods of training began to spread.

The minds were eager to learn the mysterious ways of the Orient and so they readily took to the concepts of the East. As the languages of the world internationalised and education in linguistics improved the world started to name phenomenas of each other's countries. And so popularised the training method of Zen, and so also did the martial arts which evolved from the physical and mental training of Zen. Then the world called the training of Zen-Yoga, and the world called these martial Arts by Judo, Ka-

rate, Ju-Jitso, Kempo ..... etc.

PHENOMENON

Once a phenomenon is labelled and the label is popularised, people have a tendency to follow that label. Where English Dictionaries started to carry the meanings of Judo and Karate, the readers of English started seeking places where these arts could be taught. Where they started learning and discovered its multifold advantages they spoke to their friends about it. And so these two arts popularised. So much that they have now become best spectator-sports of the USA and Northern European countries, and their inclusion into the Olympics is very likely. And because it so happens that today's women go along men in all walks of life, they readily adopted these sports also.

Then through its training they found that they become better beautiful and graceful women. Physical tharapists, psychologists and medical doctors had diagnosed over the exercises in Karate and found that they are the ideal exercises for the human body.

These exercises regulate the blood flow to each and every part of the body improving skin texture and complexion. They reduce fat and develop sound symmetrical bodies. The regular training of Karate regulates the functions of all organs in the body eliminating most of the minor ailments —

such as weakness — spells, digestion problems, blood clots along the flow system, spasticism, and in many cases has been the remedy for muscular ailments and epilepticism.

DOCTORS

All these the doctors have found to be true — in short they have described Karate training as the best form of development for the body and mind. Karate also teaches the art of meditation which has been described as the ideal method of relieving nervous tension which is a common result of today's hurried life.

In all cases, women have experienced the following advantages as a result of the training of Karate. 1. They learnt the ultimate in the arts of self defence. 2. They gained confidence poise. 3. They improved their figures and complexion. 4. It cured their problem of feeling weak and spastic too often. 5. It relieved all their nervous tensions. 6 Biologically, it has improved the chromozone content, making them more feminine then ever. 7. Institutionally, they have made list of friends and a lot more advantages and various cases only to be cited by the person experiencing.

And as more and more women join the institutions they themselves realise the benefits of the training. It is only those that experienced the philosophy and science of Karate that really felt its advantages.

Grand Master Hwa Chong

Master Saleem Jehangir with his teacher Grand Master Hwa Chong after winning the trophy in the 1974 US Tae Kwon Do Championships.

Master Chong, as we all called him, and now the Grand Master Hwa Chong as the world calls him, was my teacher, my coach, my mentor, my trainer, my philosopher. I have not seen him after 1981, but he has been in my thoughts, and his philosophy and sayings still echo in my mind as I confront obstacles in my life, and I use the defensive dodge and offensive techniques to tackle them. This is what Master Chong left behind for all of us, a way to approach life and handle its problems. I remember once I was very depressed, I was unemployed, had a wife and a child to support, and the US economy was in shambles. I had applied for hundreds of jobs to no avail. So I went to Master Chong and asked him what should I do. He said in his typical calm philosophical demeanor: learn from the animals, when the weather gets bad, they go in hibernation. That one simple advice brought my spirits up, and I looked in the World of Nature around me and started to observe and learn how the animals survive the ups and downs of their lives, and found my answers.

Master Chong would constantly give us these simple, small pieces of advices. And they would stay with us and guide us throughout our lives. His latest advice to me was to change with the times, or else I will end up as The Last Warrior. He was of course referring to the movie and the message there in.

Master Chong was a student of Master Park Chull Hee, who was a 7th Dan Black Belt in 1966 and one of the senior most masters of his time. We never met Master Park till 1974 when he came to attend the First All American Inter-Collegiate Tae Kwon Do Championships in Ann Arbor, Michigan. We knew him through Master Chong and through his book that he had written in Korea. Master Park was the senior student of the Great Grand Master Yoon Byung-in who was a very famous figure of his times and a pioneer of the art of Tae Kwon Do in history. They all belonged to the Kang Duk Won Association in Korea. Kang Duk Won was one of the original 9 Kwans (clubs or academies) that eventually merged to create the Kukkiwon system. This Kwan was founded in the late 1950s by former students of the YMCA Kwon Bop Bu (Chang Moo Kwan), Yoon Byung-In, Hong Jong-Pyo, and Park Chull Hee. Today, Kang Duk Won still exists in Korea and is officially known as the World Kang Duk Won Tae Kwon Do Federation with Grand Master Hwa Chong as its President.

Master Chong came to East Lansing in 1966, and joined the Michigan State University to complete his Master's Degree in Economics. He was requested by the University of Michigan to lead the Tae Kwon Do program at the UM Physical Education Department. He graciously accepted the assignment and began commuting two days a week from East Lansing to Ann Arbor to teach the classes. We were thrilled to see a Korean master of the art teaching us. It was The Real Thing. It is our fortune and good luck that he would later turn out to be the one and only, Grand Master Hwa Chong. But it is not his fame that benefitted his students as much as his training and philosophy. He would make the physical part of the training subservient to the philosophy of the art. His oriental accent made him even more mystical and attractive. His limited vocabulary actually helped him in teaching us the philosophy in a few words. He used to call me Saalem. I must have been one of his favorite students because he used me to demonstrate all the techniques by whipping me around. He paid special attention to my weaknesses and delayed my black belt a whole year till I harnessed my temper. In my first black belt exam when I completed four years of training, he made me fight a very skilled fighter of Italian descent who was a third degree black belt. That fighter literally floored me twice with his kicks to my head. He was limber, very athletic, very fast and focused. I was no match for him. When he floored me the third time, the Pakistani in me woke up and I lost my cool. I picked him up and threw him to the ground. Most of my colleagues were joyous at this, because he had whipped many of them before. But Master Chong became angry that I had lost my temper. He said: Saalem, you are not ready for Black Belt yet. I trained for one full additional year, after which he tested me again against a fighter who was one of the black belt champions in Michigan. I fought him with full composure and force, and showed full control of my temper. The fighter was very rough and agile. But I repeatedly scored with my reverse right punch. In the black belt exam you have to show one outstanding technique with which you can consistently overcome your opponent. In my case it was my reverse punch. At the end of the ceremony, Master Chong awarded me with a Black Belt, saying: now not only you are a black belt, you are a strong black belt. It took me five years to get my black belt, but that was Master Chong's philosophy and style.

We used to train in the old gym on the main campus. It was called the Waterman Gym. It is not there anymore. It had a large wooden floor that could accommodate 200 students. The Physical Education classes that we held there were very large. The UM TKD club classes were smaller and included mainly the senior students. Joe Lloyd and Terry Goebel were some of my colleagues who had the same amount of time in the club. We went through the belt progressions almost simultaneously till I was delayed for my black belt.

1969 All Michigan State Championships

Master Chong organized the first All Michigan State Championships in East Lansing in 1969. I travelled with the UM club to participate in it. I was a brown belt then and so completed in the same category. I reached the final round in the sparring competition but lost to a very speedy fighter. Later when Master Chong saw the bruises on my face, he said that the fighter who won should have been disqualified for making contact to the face. Back then, contact to the face was not allowed because we did not use guards. The championships were very successful and I achieved instant fame from my second place win in the Brown Belt category.

1974 Championships

We all helped in organizing the First TKD All American Inter-Collegiate Championships in Ann Arbor under Master Chong in 1974. He invited all the senior masters from all over US and Korea. Joe and I competed in it also. We both lost in the sparring competitions somewhere mid-way in the tournament, but reached the finals in the forms competition. This was expected, because Master Chong taught the old Traditional Tae Kwon Do style which was not conducive to winning in sport TKD sparring. But his forms were the best and that is what we ended up winning. Joe had performed his form in the best manner till the finals. All day was spent on eliminations. And then the finals took place in the evening. There were hundreds of spectators in the Yost Field House gymnasium on State Street. It was a huge gym. Having stayed out of touch with the new developments from 1971-73 (the time I was in Pakistan), I had not expected to reach the finals. I had gained 30 lbs in Pakistan and my movements had become slow. That is why despite winning some fights, I lost to the good fighters in the eliminations. They were fast and focused. But I managed to reach the finals in the form competition. I was nervous. The reason I reached the finals is because Master Chong had taught me a 5th Dan level form called Chang Kwan. It had fluid movements and was very graceful, something that fit my temperament and style. When I performed it, most of the Korean masters expressed their displeasure at Master Chong for teaching me that form. It was supposed to be taught only to high Dan masters. Anyway, when performing the form in the finals in front of a large crowd, I became a little nervous and rushed through the form. And Joe forgot the moves in the middle of his display. Consequently, Joe was placed third, I was placed second and the one who performed a lower level form but did it with full composure and stability, got the first position. Later as we celebrated our wins in a restaurant with the club members, we talked about how we never expected to do even this good. It was a very good experience. And a memorable one. And it was all due to Master Chong's efforts.

There was a picture taken of all the participants in the tournament, I am missing in the picture, and the reason is that I was up there taking this picture. But I still have my trophy, and the article in the 1976 Black Belt magazine, and the letter from Master Chong, all of which are testimony to my achievements.

Master Chong's achievements would become his launching pad into the national fame, he was then selected to lead the introduction of Tae Kwon Do in the American Athletic Union (the US government body, similar to Pakistan Sports Board, that governs all sports at the national level). He then became the Chairman of the AAU Tae Kwon Do Committee and introduced Tae Kwon Do in the 1988 Olympics. Tae Kwon Do was then included in the 1992 Olympics in Barcelona as an Olympic sport with Master Chong leading the US team as team manager. Some of his students won the gold medal in the 1992 Olympics. Later, Master Chong was appointed as the President of the United States Tae Kwon Do Union (USTU) from 1993 to 1996.

Today his name is in the Hall of Fame of Martial Arts. And I feel lucky and thankful for being one of his pupils.

A brief resume of Grand Master Hwa Chong

10th Degree Black Belt

President World Kang Duk Won Tae Kwon Do Federation

Member of the executive council of the World Taekwondo Federation

Member of the Kukkiwon Advisory Board

Chairman, Michigan AAU Tae Kwon Do Committee 1969

US Olympic Tae Kwon Do Team Manager, 1988 & 1992

President of AAU National Committee for Tae Kwon Do (USTU) 1993-96

Owner of Grand Master Master Hwa Chong Tae Kwon Do-Karate Institute, Detroit, Michigan

Professor of Physical Education, University of Michigan Tae Kwon Do Club 1966-2013

Director of the First All American Tae Kwon Do Inter-Collegiate Championships 1974

Director American Mid-West Tae Kwon Do-Karate Federation 1969

Director First Michigan Tae Kwon Do Championship 1969

Tae Kwon Do Instructor US 8th Army, South Korea 1964-67

Korean national sparring champion in Tae Kwon Do

National Referee Korea Tae Kwon Do Association, Seoul, Korea 1962-67

Tae Kwon Do Instructor, Presidential Police for the late Sigman Rhee, President of South Korea, 1958-59

M.A. Economics, Michigan State University, East Lansing, Michigan 1970

B.A. Korean University, 1966

For additional information on Grand Master Hwa Chong, look up into the following websites for more information on Master Chong:

Eastgatemartialartsclub.com

Studentorgs.umich.edu

Webservices.itcs.umich.edu

**Great Grandmaster
Chul Hee Park
1933 -**

MASTER PARK CHUL KARATE INSTITUTE
⮞ U. S. CENTER OF KANG DUK-WON TAE KWON KARATE ⮜

106 REISTERSTOWN ROAD ✖ BALTIMORE, MD. 21208

TELEPHONES: (301) 727-4484 727-4485

March 6, 1972

Dear Instructor:

First allow me to introduce myself at this time.
As a founder president of the Kang Duk Won Taekwondo-
karate Association in 1956, I was a former professor of
Physical Education of Korea Military Academy and an
instructor for the presidential police of the late Korean
president Syungman Rhee.

Through my Kang Duk Won Gymnagium, there are many
distinguished instructors who are active in the United States
now; Kang Rhee (Memphis, Tenn.), Hwa Chong (Ann Arbor, Michigan),
Young Ik Shu (Los Angeles, Calif.), Ik Jin Choi (San Francisco,
Calif.), Il Joo Kim (Akron, Ohio), Sang O Moon (Cleveland, Ohio),
Chul Soo Choi (Albuqueque, New Mexico), Joo Sub Chi (Oklahoma,
Oklahoma), Kyung Lee (Toronto, Canada), Young Il Park (Houston,
Texas), and Young Ho Jun and Myong Kim in Baltimore, Md.

This year our 1st U.S. TAEKWONDO-KARATE SILVER CUP
CHAMPIONSHIP TOURNAMENT will be held on April 8, 1972
at the New Gymnagium of University of Maryland Baltimore
County, Baltimore, Md., sponsored by the U.S. Kang Duk Won
Center.

We wish to invite as many different styles of Karate
as possible in this Tournament, spontaneously, to show
Korean style protection equipment fighting.

If you have any questions concerning this event,
please call or write to the above address.

I am cordially inviting you and expecting to see you
to make for the success of this Tournament.

Sincerely yours,

Chull Hee Park
President &
Tournament Director

CHP/is

1st AMERICAN INTERCOLLEGIATE AND OPEN TAEKWON DO - KARATE CHAMPIONSHIPS   March 30

Date Mar. 30, 1974   Location Intramural Sports Bldg., U. of Michigan

Sponsors U. of Michigan and U. of M. Taekwon Do Club, Ann Arbor, Mich.

Time Registration, 8:30-10:00 a.m.; Preliminaries, start 10:00 a.m.; Finals, start 7 p.m. Instructions for referees and umpires, 8:30 a.m.

Divisions Competition in forms and sparring will be held in five main divisions: (1) intercollegiate, (2) open, (3) high school, (4) women, and (5) junior, ages 12-15. Forms competition will also be available in a special division for students 11 years old and younger. Team competition will be held in the college division only. A team can be made up of five students of any rank and will spar with "blank" belts. A college or university can enter as many as five teams. Regular individual competition will be held in all five main divisions, in addition to the team competition in the college division only.
Rank partitioning will be: white, 7-8 kup; blue, 4-6 kup; brown, 1-3 kup; and black, 1st Dan and above. Black belts may participage in the open division only.

Fees Entrance fees are $5.00 for one event and $8.00 for both forms and sparring. Admission charge is $1.00 for adults and children.

Trophies Over 140 trophies will be awarded, including the Governor of Michigan trophy; President, U. of M trophy; Korea U. trophy.

Information Write championships director Hwa Chong, U. of M., Intramurals Sports Building, 606 E. Hoover, Ann Arbor, Mich. 48104

THE FIRST MICHIGAN REGIONAL
TAE KWON DO TOURNAMENT

Tournament Committee:

Jae Joon Kim *	Ho Yung Chung
Hwa Chong *	Chang Soo Lim
Tae Zee Park	Chang Hwang Park
Myung Nom Kim	Won Chik Park
Carl Stolberg	Frank Rogers
James Expose	BoBo Maurice
Eugene Humesky	Dayton Matlick
Joe Lloyd	Gregory Park
Saleem Jehangir	Byung Moon Park
Leonard Wilkenson	James Young

Master of Ceremony   Dayton Matlick

Guest of Honor
       Mr. Jack Garris   Dr. Dennis Sprandel

Tournament Doctor   Dr. Dennis Burke M.D.

Secretary/Treasurer   Mr. James Wigginton C.P.A.

Administration Officials:
       Patrick Harrigan   Frank Stasa
       Jackie Adler   Len Gil
       Don Peterson   Randy Hall
              University of Michigan Tae Kwon Do Club

Ring Officials:
Ring 1
Director: Ho Yung Chung
Co-ordinator: BoBo Maurice
Referees: James Judan Jr. (M)
               Ray Plunler (J)
               Brigid Archer (CD)
               Oatess Archey (CM)
               Len Gill (K)

Ring 2
Chang Soo Lim
James Expose
Alex Laquian (J)
Jackie Adler (K)
Timothy Williams (J)
Richard Weatherford (CD)
Bob Cockrill (CD)

Ring 3
Director: Won Chik Park
Co-ordinator: Joe Lloyd
Referees: Carlos Marin (K)
               Joe Sanna (J)
               Charlie Watkins (CD)
               Richard Himerson (M)
               Larry George (CM)

Ring 4
Tae Zee Park
Frank Rogers
David Novals (CD)
Douglas Larkins (CD)
Saleem Jehangir (K)
Thorton Kelly (JI)
James Cox (CM)

* Arbitration Panel

Some memorable pictures of Grand Master Chong coaching
Master Saleem Jehangir

Grand Master Hwa Chong demonstrating a high level form at his club

114

HWA CHONG

Head Instructor, University of Michigan Tae Kwon Do Club

Director, American Midwest Tae Kwon Do-Karate Federation

1969 Director, First Michigan Tae Kwon Do-Karate Championship in Lansing, Michigan

1964-67 Instructor, U.S. 8th Army in Korea

1962-67 National Referee, Korea Tae Kwon Do Association in Seoul, Korea

1958-59 Instructor, Presidential Police for the late Sigman Rhee, President of South Korea

Graduate, Korean University, B.A. (1966) and Michigan State University, M.A. (1970).

HWA CHONG - MASTER INSTRUCTOR
7th Degree Black Belt.

What will you learn from HWA CHONG KARATE INSTITUTE ?

Our industrial age has brought with it conflict and separation — between rich and poor, young and old, management and labor, radical and conservative, between races and between the sexes.

The Martial Arts (Tae Kwon Do-Karate) gives the individual an indomitable spirit and inexhaustible strength. Students are taught to develop their bodies, minds and spirits. Natural intelligence is developed. The difficult becomes easy. The dangerous path becomes smooth.

Master Hwa Chong welcomes students of all ages, colors and creeds — male and female.

ON THE MAT, ALL ARE EQUAL.

Master Hwa Chong believes that the Martial Arts (Tae Kwon Do) should offer society a spiritual force, a philosophy of life, a value system, and a communication between people.

MASTER HWA CHONG KARATE INSTITUTE

Date: **January 15, 1973**

This certificate entitles _____ to one FREE TRIAL LESSON at the Master Hwa Chong Tae Kwon Do Karate Institute within three months of the above date.

Approved by: *Hwa Chong*
Hwa Chong, Master Instr.

Call: 313/532-6660
18923 W. 7 Mile Road, Detroit
(between Southfield Freeway and Evergreen Road)

Call: 313/532-6660
Address: 18923 W. 7 Mile Road, Detroit (Between Southfield Freeway and Evergreen Road, 7 blocks west of Southfield Freeway)

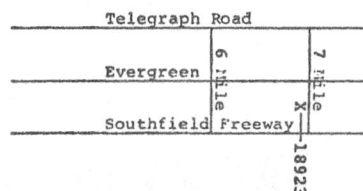

Telegraph Road

Evergreen

6 Mile

7 Mile

Southfield Freeway

18923

115

GRAND OPENING!

MASTER HWA CHONG

TAE KWON DO KARATE INSTITUTE

OPEN 7 DAYS-WEEK

SUPERIOR FEATURES OF MASTER CHONG'S TEACHING

- Efficient foot and hand techniques of Tae Kwon Do-Karate
- Dynamic soft and hard blow variations of Northern Chinese KUNG FU (Offensive-defensive forms)
- Dynamic throwing and self defense techniques
- Oriental philosophy for the cultivation of Chi (internal energy)

AMERICAN MIDWEST TAE KWON DO-KARATE FEDERATION

18923 w. 7mile, Detroit
tel. 313-532 6660   (Between Southfield & Telegraph)

A History of the University of Michigan Taekwondo Club

(Borrowed from the UM TKD Website)

The University of Michigan Taekwondo Club was founded by Master James G. Young in 1964. Master Young began training in 1959 in the Korean martial art style known as Tang Soo Do, under the instruction of Master Dale Droulliard. During his military service in Korea, Master Droulliard was the first American to be trained in this style and the first to open a club in the Detroit area. As a 2nd Dan, Master Young founded the UM club so he could continue training and to share this relatively new martial art. The club grew in membership and plans were made for continuation of the club after Master Young's graduation. In 1968, Professor Ergun Ar, who was not only a club member, but also the club's faculty advisor, located a number of instructors from various Korean styles. This was a time prior to the "unification" of various Korean styles into modern day Tae Kwon Do. Master Young, Dr. Ar and senior club members interviewed prospective instructors and also watched them train and compete. At this time, club members included Ed Bell, Terry Goebel, Jack Hoyt, Joe Lloyd, and Saleem Jehangir.

After considering skill level, technique and the intangible qualities of leadership and strength of character that martial arts training is supposed to foster, a unanimous decision was made to ask a young 5th Dan named Master Hwa Chong to be the primary instructor at the club. A student of Kang Duk Kwon founder, Master Park Chull Hee, and a former Korean sparring champion, Master Chong was in a master's degree program at Michigan State. After agreeing to teach at the club, Master Chong showed his dedication by driving from Lansing twice a week to teach at the University of Michigan.

By 1970, the club had almost 100 members and worked out in the Waterman Gym. During summers, club members would drive to Lansing to train with Master Chong (as he was completing his Masters Degree). The club actively participated in martial arts competitions throughout the Midwest.

Following his graduation from MSU, Master Chong took a job with General Motors and moved to the Detroit area, where he opened up a school. At this time, the UM club was struggling with workout space. There was an old bowling alley in the Women's Athletic Building. Jack Hoyt received permission to renovate this space for the club. Club members refinished the floor and installed mirrors. This became the club's workout room for several years. When the women's gym was scheduled for demolition to make way for the CCRB, University officials sought out the club for help with the design of a martial arts room.

Shortly after the opening of the CCRB in the mid-1970s, Dr. Rodney Grambeau asked Master Chong if he would teach a Phys Ed class. This eventually evolved into the Kinesiology/U-Move class. At that point, club reached the structure we see today, with Master Chong teaching the class, and his senior students leading club. Key Club members during these formative years included Masters Joe Lloyd, Jackie Adler, Dr. Dennis Burke, Greg Gorrin, Randy Hall, Don Peterson, Patrick Harrigan, Donna Valerie, Dr. Mahommed (Cubby) Khazaeli, Lonnie Odom, Dr. Harvey Slaughter, Cliff Price, and Jim Wigginton.

Club produces an Olympian

During the summer of 1976, club was working out in the track area behind the Intramural building. A 14 year old Korean boy named Han Won Lee would watch them from the side. His family had recently emigrated from Korea. Although he had never practiced Taekwondo in Korea, it was familiar to him. Han joined the club, worked his way through the ranks, and earned his black belt. He trained extensively with Joanne Hamilton and Eric Erickson. When he could, he also went to Detroit, where he would spar with Owen Pope, Lynette Love, and the other students there. Later sparring partners of Han included David Kim, John Vincent, and Master Chong's sons, Hoon and Sean.

In the early 1980s, Master Chong became involved in the founding of the United States Taekwondo Union (USTU). This group became the national governing body for the World Taekwondo Federation in the United States. Master Chong served as President of the Michigan State Association for a number of years. During this time, the club hosted the state championships each year.

In 1982, the University of Michigan Taekwondo Club hosted the national championships at Pioneer High School. Taking advantage of a home court, Han won the first of five national championships. In 1988, Han won the U.S. Team Trials and went to the Olympics in Seoul, Korea. Han won the Bronze medal, losing to the Gold medalist in the semi-finals. When he returned, Han took advantage of his publicity to open his own school.

In 1992, Han got the competition bug again and tried out for the U.S. team again. He won the team trials and went to Barcelona as the team captain. Unfortunately, Han injured his knee early in the competition and did not win any medal. A short while after the 1992 Olympics, Han was asked to come out to Colorado Springs to become the resident Head Coach at the Olympic Training Center.

At the same time, Master Chong was elected President of the USTU, a position he held from 1993 – 1996. During all of this, club continued on. Key members from the mid-1980s to the mid-1990s included Masters Tim Frye, Steve Busch, Sahba La'al, Garry Gross, James Marks, Susanne Kopecky, Jerilyn Bell, Matt Birchmeier, Terry Hull, Shana Milkie, Roland Spickerman, Laura Kistler, Tony Winkler, and Mike Spigarelli.

One of the constants of club from 1968 to 1999 was Master Joseph Lloyd. Master Lloyd served as Head Club Instructor for most of that time. Master Lloyd also supported Master Chong in the USTU, serving as Legal Counsel for a number of years.

In 2000, the first Big Ten Taekwondo Conference Championship was held at Michigan State University in East Lansing, Michigan. The club sent a team that took second place. President Josh Rosenblatt volunteered to host the 2001 championships. The tournament was a success. The University of Michigan took first place, narrowly defeating MSU. Ohio State University, Purdue University, and University of Indiana all sent teams.

Epilogue

The University of Michigan Taekwondo club is the oldest, and arguably most successful, martial arts club among the campuses in the USA. It can boast more alumni and Olympic medalists than most campuses. The source of this success has been its strong club members, alumni, combined with the constant support of its instructors, particularly Grand Master Chong, Master Lloyd, and Master Bissoon-Dath, who have formed a base that the current club members can build upon. Other clubs have lacked this, and many have either folded after the founder left or required regular support from an outside school. Many students have earned their black belts. Others have come as black belts and continued their training. Equally important are the contributions of the club alumni who are successful doctors, lawyers, scientists, engineers, and business leaders.

One of the great lessons that many club members have learned is the value of a true student-teacher relationship. Grand Master Chong has supported the club for many years and made many sacrifices. Grand Master Chong's peers stopped teaching classes many years ago, while he continues to teach on a regular basis. Recently awarded his Tenth Dan, Grand Master Chong is one of the top Tae Kwon Do masters in the world. He recently served on the executive council of the World Taekwondo Federation and is now on the Kukkiwon Advisory Board.

1988 The US Tae Kwon Do Olympic Team

- First Tae Kwon Do Team to compete in the Olympic Games

- Women's Team wins 3 Gold Medals, 1 Silver and 2 Bronze

Lynnette Love-Olympic Gold Medalist-Heavyweight Division 1988 Olympics

Testimony

My name is Lynnette Alicia Love. I have had a passion for Taekwondo for over 30 years. As a student and competitor I know the benefits of concentration, self respect and confidence that I have developed since walking into my first dojang with my instructor Master Hwa Chong and my development as a athlete with my Olympic coach Grand Master Sang Chul Lee.

I developed the ability to believe I can do anything I desire. Through this strength I realized many of my own dreams as a Gold and Bronze Medalist in the 1988 and 1992 Olympics. While these are a few victories, living a victorious life is a daily decision. At every match I knew "If I can make you believe I am "King Kong" then I have won the match". Knowing no battle is ever won on the mat but in the mental and physical preparation in the years, months and days proceeding it. Training with a champion isn't the key to being one, training like one is However, martial arts is so much more.

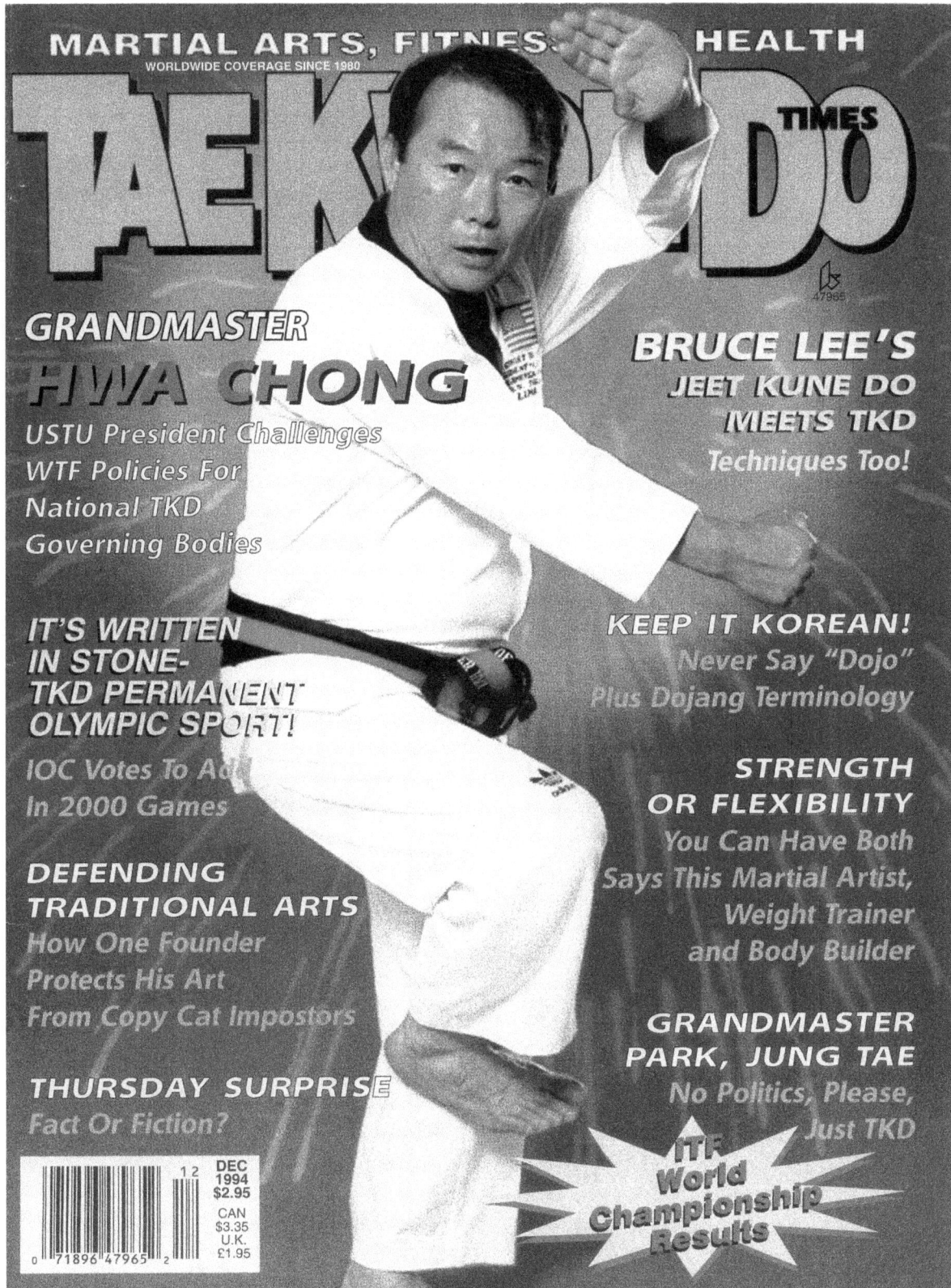

MARTIAL ARTS, FITNESS, HEALTH
WORLDWIDE COVERAGE SINCE 1980

TAEKWONDO TIMES

GRANDMASTER HWA CHONG
USTU President Challenges WTF Policies For National TKD Governing Bodies

IT'S WRITTEN IN STONE- TKD PERMANENT OLYMPIC SPORT!
IOC Votes To Add In 2000 Games

DEFENDING TRADITIONAL ARTS
How One Founder Protects His Art From Copy Cat Impostors

THURSDAY SURPRISE
Fact Or Fiction?

BRUCE LEE'S JEET KUNE DO MEETS TKD
Techniques Too!

KEEP IT KOREAN!
Never Say "Dojo" Plus Dojang Terminology

STRENGTH OR FLEXIBILITY
You Can Have Both Says This Martial Artist, Weight Trainer and Body Builder

GRANDMASTER PARK, JUNG TAE
No Politics, Please, Just TKD

ITF World Championship Results

DEC 1994 $2.95
CAN $3.35
U.K. £1.95
0 71896 47965 2

Article on Grand Master Hwa Chong in the Dec. 1994 Tae Kwon Do Times

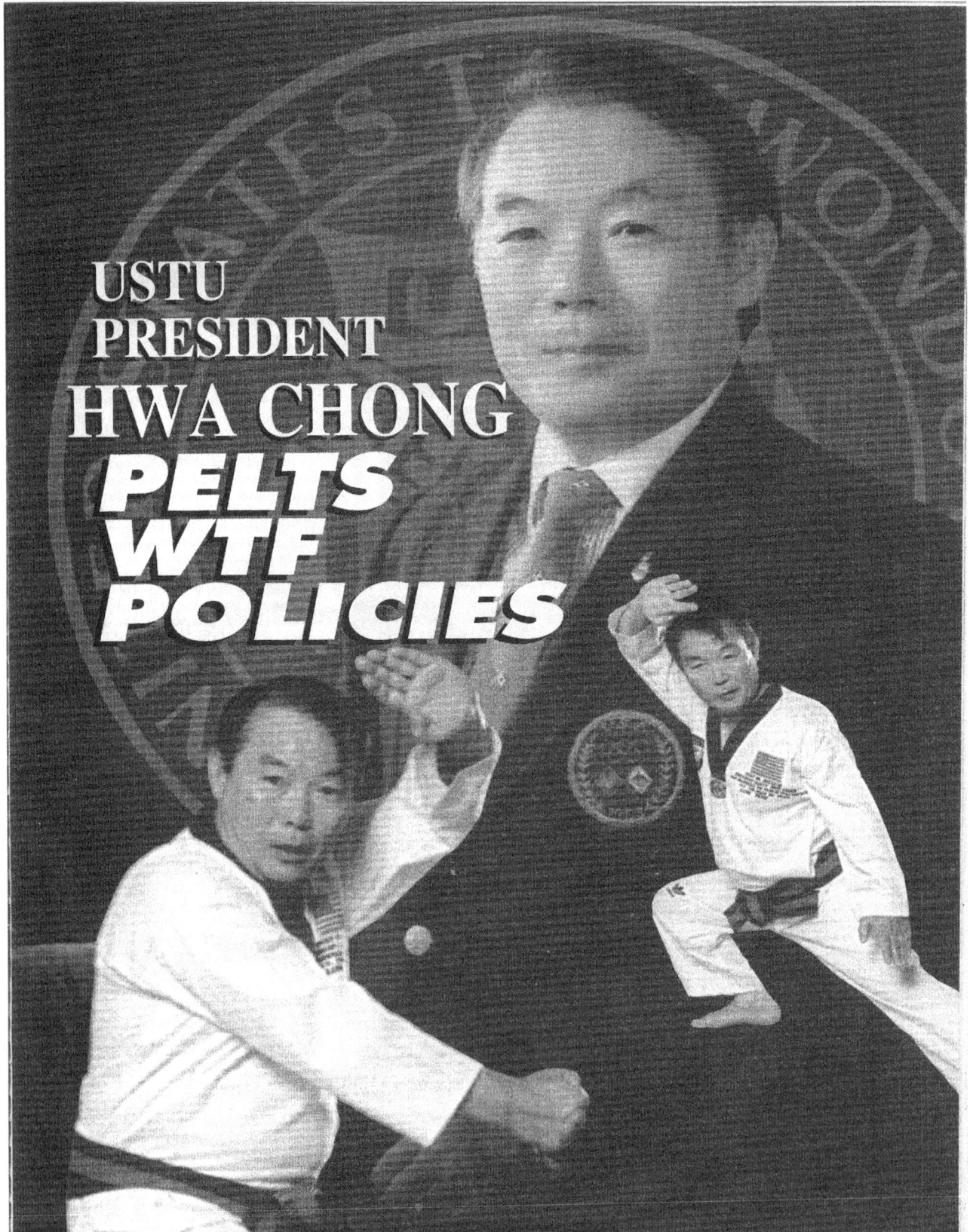

USTU
PRESIDENT
HWA CHONG
PELTS
WTF
POLICIES

MARTIAL ARTS, FITNESS AND HEALTH

TAE KWON DO
MAGAZINE
Established 1980

In an exclusive interview with Grandmaster Chong, TKDT Publisher, Grandmaster Chung Eun Kim delves into the sacred domain of the WTF with some startling answers from the head of the U.S. Tae Kwon Do governing body.

Grandmaster Kim

Grandmaster Chong

TKDT: *Welcome to "Tae Kwon Do Times." I have wanted to interview you for a long time but our schedules would not permit it. I'm so glad the timing is right now. I am so pleased that as martial artists we can sit together and talk about the future of Tae Kwon Do, not just the future of the USTU, which is the official governing body for Tae Kwon Do in this country. I hope that our publication and the USTU can help each other for the betterment of Tae Kwon Do.*

First, I would like to talk about the real possibility of Tae Kwon Do becoming an Olympic sport. (Editor's Note: This interview took place in August 1994, before the final vote in Paris. IOC members voted unanimously to include Tae Kwon Do as a permanent sport in the 2000 Games in Sydney, Australia.)

HWA CHONG: First of all, I want to thank "Tae Kwon Do Times" for helping us for the past ten years. For many years it was the only Tae Kwon Do martial art magazine.

To answer your question, the possibility of Tae Kwon Do becoming an Olympic sport is very close. Last June 15, the U.S. Olympic Committee had a meeting with the President of the IOC, Mr. Juan Samaranch in Colorado Springs. At that meeting Mr. Samaranch told us that Tae Kwon Do and Triathlon will be Olympic sports in the year 2000. The final decision will be made in September at a meeting in Paris. If it is voted in, Tae Kwon Do will be an exhibition in the 1996 Olympics in Atlanta, Georgia.

TKDT: *If Tae Kwon Do is in the Olympics, how can all styles compete? There are many different ways of competing.*

HC: This is a very difficult question. The United States is a country devoted to freedom where people follow their own beliefs, their own philosophy. This is not like Korea where the government says one thing and everyone follows it.

Hopefully, Tae Kwon Do will be taught in high schools and in colleges in the near future. If this is happens, maybe the rules will be more homogenous.

TKDT: *Who will be able to compete in Olympic Tae Kwon Do? Will it be only those who have a USTU certificate, a WTF certificate? In Judo, anyone can be in the Olympics, you don't have to be certified with the world body; any federation member can participate. They can be members of the Kodowan, which as you know is the Judo headquarters in Japan; The U.S. Judo Association; the U.S. Judo Federation; and the U.S. Judo Incorporation. Any of these organization members can be in the Olympics. At this time, Tae Kwon Do*

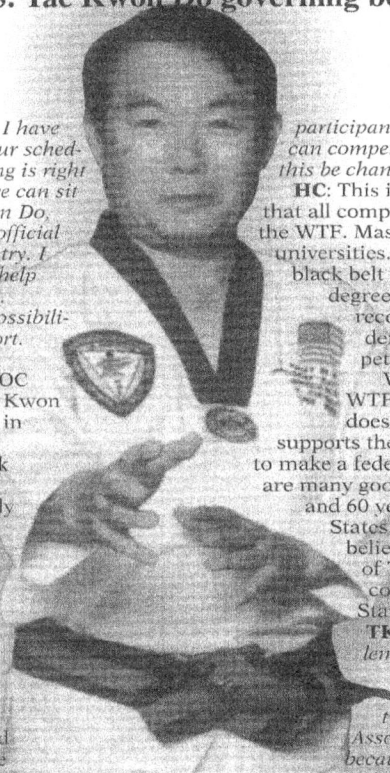

> **"...Tae Kwon Do will be an exhibition in the 1996 Olympics in Atlanta, Georgia."**

participants need WTF certification before they can compete in the Olympics. Is this fair? Can this be changed?

HC: This is an important point. I don't think that all competitors need to be certified through the WTF. Masters are like professors who teach at universities. Once students have reached the black belt level, it is like earning a college degree. The USTU and the WTF should recognize that level and give the students the credentials needed to compete in the Olympics.

We cannot force students to become WTF or Kukkiwon members. The WTF does support the USTU and the USTU supports the WTF. I don't think it is necessary to make a federation in the United States. There are many good masters between the ages of 50 and 60 years of age living in the United States. If these masters get together, I believe that the U.S. would be the leader of Tae Kwon Do in the world. Now, of course, it is Korea, with the United States in second place.

TKDT: *There seem to be many problems with issuing WTF certification. In fact, we received a letter concerning this issue. It stated that ten or twelve masters, Georgia State Association members, were incensed because the Kukkiwon gave certification to individuals not qualified for the higher rank. For example, first degrees were made third degrees, or a second degree was made a fifth degree. The letter also told of someone in New York that was made a ninth degree without any documentation.*

I know for a fact that Kukkiwon people have come to this country to give seminars or attend championships and sell WTF certification--eighth and ninth degrees-- to unqualified persons. Many people in this country think that you can get WTF certification by paying for it. How can this be? How can this problem be solved?

I know that the USTU has sent between $600,000 to one million dollars every year to the WTF for certificates. Instead of sending it to Korea, why couldn't the money be kept in the United States by starting a national federation?

HC: This is a good point. But, for the past several years my main goal and the goal of the USTU has been trying to help the WTF get into the Olympics. Currently we are doing fund raising to help build a Tae Kwon Do center in

Right: At the 1992 USTU Team Trials, from left: Hwa Chong, Lynette Love, Han Won Lee, Dong Keun Park and Y.H. Park.

Above from left: USTU President-Elect Sang Chul Lee, gold medalist Edwin Moses, Lynette Love and President Hwa Chong at the 1991 Olympic Festival in Minneapolis.

Above left: Keun Hong Lee, Jong Soo Hong, Vice-president of Korea, Un Kyu Um, WTF Vice-president, Dr. Jip Kim, Hwa Chong, Bong Sik Kim, James Wigginton at the 1994 Invitational Int'l TKD Championship in Seoul. Above Right: Family portrait, from left: Hoon, Sean and Jean who was graduating from high school, Mrs. Doja Chong and Grandmaster Chong.

Colorado Springs.

Between 1989 to 1991 WTF policy allowed each nation to issue its own certificate, but now it has changed. Kukkiwon issued a policy that each national governing body would need to have 80% of all Tae Kwon Do practitioners as members before they could issue promotion certificates. Now the USTU has only 20%. I don't think this is fair. For example, in the U.S. presidential election, only 52% of the population may vote, of that there may be only 27% of the total population that votes to elect the president. With the WTF policy, this is like saying that 80% of the adult population of the U.S. would have to vote before the president could be elected.

The USTU is open to everyone; it is not our fault if those practicing Tae Kwon Do do not join. I don't think the WTF should penalize us.

TKDT: *In a recent issue of "Tae Kwon Do Times," an article about consolidating the WTF and ITF was published. I understand the WTF is busy lobbying to get into the Olympics. I also know that the ITF wanted very much to work together to enter the Olympics. Do you know why the WTF did not respond? Does the WTF want all the attention, all the glory?*

HC: Karate has two organizations, that is why Karate cannot be recognized by the Olympics. This is not the same case as Tae Kwon Do. As you know, the IOC recognized the WTF first. Because of this, I think that all organizations can go to the Olympics through the WTF.

Concerning the consolidation of the two organizations, I frankly don't know the best way to do it. Before anything could happen, Dr. Kim and General Choi have to meet and talk. I know that many masters support this stand for unification. It seems that everyone, all the masters, want it. We should find the solution.

TKDT: *Not long ago about 60 masters living in the U.S. signed a petition to unite the ITF and WTF. It was a full page ad printed in "The Korea Times" newspaper. After this, the WTF treated them as communists. The WTF tried to find a connection with each name on the list to North Korea. This happened to "Tae Kwon Do Times" Vice-president Woo Jin Jung who traveled to North Korea as an invited guest of the ITF to view their World Championships. They tried to find a link between him and North Korea. Jimmy Carter went to North Korea, is he a communist now?*

I know that those who signed the petition are not involved in communist politics, they just want Tae Kwon Do to be better. Also, I have learned that the WTF has rejected any eighth and ninth dan promotions that these masters applied for through the federation. Is this right? It seems to me that WTF leaders just want to keep all the power and financial benefits for South Korea.

HC: Calling these people communists is not proper. There is no law that says you cannot go to North Korea. This happens because of political problems. I don't think the accusation from the WTF about these masters being communist is anything to worry about.

TKDT: *Grandmaster Chong, between us, we have over 80 years of martial art experience. With your 40 years of martial art knowledge, what problems, if any, have you identified with those of us on the master level?*

HC: There is one thing I would like to say to all the masters that I believe is very important. How can people who started training in the 1960's and 70's say they are eighth and ninth degrees? Only people who started training in the 1950's could have reached the level of eighth or ninth degree at this time. We should not be so concerned about a higher degree that we stoop to this level of dishonesty.

TKDT: *I understand the WTF is changing the regulations for becoming an eighth or ninth degree. I heard that those applying will have to go to Korea and physically test instead of just doing the paperwork and docu-*

At the Goodwill Games in St. Petersburg, Russia, American heavyweight Robin Umpry, third from left, won a bronze medal.

menting their Tae Kwon Do history. Now you have to travel to the Kukkiwon and do forms and sparring. Is that true? If you have heard about this, what is your opinion?

HC: I received a letter about it. I told the WTF my opinion: I don't agree with it. I teach three times a week, but my physical power is not that of a man of 20 or 30-years-old. The physical exam is not important. The mental portion, the maturity of the master is what is impor-

"I don't think the accusation from the WTF about these masters being communist is anything to worry about."

tant at eighth and ninth degree.

For example, a Ph.D. in physical education is not tested on his physical prowess. He has to write a thesis. If Kukkiwon begins this procedure, it goes against what I believe is important at this level of Tae Kwon Do education and development.

My opinion may not be right all the time, but neither are the policies of the Kukkiwon right all the time. Testing for eighth and ninth degree should be about organizational skills, teaching

skills, instead of actual physical prowess. This is why I do not agree with the changes.

TKDT: *Now in the U.S. there are many grandmasters and kwan jang nims. For example Won Gook Lee, Nam Suk Lee, Pyung Jik Noh, Duk Sung Song, Suh Jong Kang, Hwang Kee and Eugene Kim, etc. Has the USTU ever thought about a retirement plan for these men? If the USTU didn't send all the money to Kukkiwon—around one million per year—couldn't it be used as a retirement program for these men?*

HC: I've been thinking about this for a long time. Not only kwan jang nims, but masters too. About 70% of the masters do not have a retirement plan. I am thinking about launching an equipment company owned by the masters who own stock. They would buy their equipment through this company and earn stock by this. After they retire, they would earn dividends through the company. I am just thinking about this right now. Now there is no pension plan or anything.

TKDT: *I am invited to many tournaments and have attended the USTU tournament on several occasions. When I went to the WTF World Championships in New York City, I saw that the kwan jang nims were treated with disre-*

Top: Dr. Un Yong Kim, WTF President, with Hwa Chong at GAISF meeting in Monte Carlo. Left: Keum Hong Lee, USOC Exec. Director, Dr. Harvey Schiller and Pres. Chong at USOC Training Center. Right: Pres. Chong with IOC President Samaranch at PASO meeting in Acapulco, Mexico.

29

Right: At the 1994 Good Will Games. Front row, from left: Coach Jay Warwick, U.S. Team Head Soon Ho Kim, Head Coach Dong Keun Park, WTF VP Joe Hensen, President Chong and Robert Fugimura, USTU Executive Director. Below: Joe Hensen, M. Gunnar Ericsson and President Chong.

spect. Instead of being seated in the VIP seats, IOC members were seated there. I don't like to see this and many masters attending the event were appalled by it. Don't you think the USTU should be more respectful of the kwan jang nims?

(Editor's Note: Kwan jang nims are the heads of the kwans that formed Tae Kwon Do.)

HC: This is another good point. I agree with you. Because Tae Kwon Do is participating in the Olympic movement, both IOC members and the kwan jang nims should have been seated in the VIP section. In the future, I would like to see this corrected. I apologize in this matter.

UNITY THROUGH COMMUNITY: THE SPORT OF TAE KWON DO

While a warrior once used his martial art skills to defeat and often kills enemies, today's martial art warrior is typically not a soldier. He or she is a common worker seeking good health and values. These differences do not necessarily make one better than the other, only that the application is different.

Students trained solely for competition develop differently from those with well-rounded classes. This is somewhat akin to a doctor specializing in pediatric cardiology rather than general practice medicine. They may not develop all the skills within their potential or fully explore all that Tae Kwon Do has to offer, but they excel in the abilities they try to acquire. Tournament competitors who win repeatedly, however, are usually those wise enough to incorporate all aspects of Tae Kwon Do into their training: meditation, the execution of forms, the power of kicking, and the strategy afforded through philosophy. These students ride the emotional wave of winning and losing, practicing long hours, trying to remain motivated. This is the nature of the sport. And so is born the Tae Kwon Do athlete, the player of the game.

The techniques used in tournament sparring will vary depending on the rules. The quality of the tournament will vary depending on the referees and organization. Nevertheless, these competitions allow students to get together and practice their skills in the spirit of fair play without the risk of serious injury.

Tournaments are more than a showcase for skills. Participants develop mental strength and courage in preparation for the simple act of stepping onto the competition floor. Competitors must mature confidence and control fear to overcome stress and function under pressure. They learn about their strengths and weaknesses and to respect their opponents. The Tae Kwon Do athlete requires stamina, strength, and speed in sparring which demands proper diet and fitness. Training for competition can be more intense and purposeful when the motivation of achieving a specific goal, like qualifying for a national tournament, is present.

"It really does take a tremendous amount of courage to face an opponent, and it takes even more to test one's skills while risking the possibility of being scored upon, and perhaps receive the occasional bruise." From *TKDT*, September 1994

"Ideally, if an instructor is reasonably versed in philosophy, just the fact that the student is willing to face an opponent to test his skill shows courage. The student is a winner, outcome notwithstanding. Students of Tae Kwon Do also learn how difficult it

1988 USTU Olympic Mens Team with Head Coach Sang Chul Lee, second row, first on left, and President-elect Chong, first row on right.

Without a father there is no son. Without kwan jang nims there would be no masters.

In Korea, among the Judo people, two people are chosen to be Yusung, to be in the Korean Hall of Fame. I want to do the same thing for Tae Kwon Do only call it Taesung. I want to do this not only in the U.S., but on a world-wide level. This is one of my goals to accomplish before my term as USTU president is over. With this

Left: In St. Petersburg at the 1994 Goodwill Games. Mrs. Kim, Joe Hensen and Mr. Chong with two uni-dentifed sightseers. Below: Featherweight Kelly Thorte, center, wins gold at the Goodwill Games.

we can recognize and pay respect to the kwan jang nims.

TKDT: *Thank you for coming to "Tae Kwon Do Times." Good health and good luck to you!*

HC: Thank you for inviting me and good luck to your magazine.

Left, from left: Pyung D. Ko, Sang Lee, Y.C. Kim, Dong Keun Park, Hwa Chong, Yeon Hee Park, Sok Ho Kang, Koang Woang Kim and Yeon Hwan Park at the 1991 WTF Championships in Athens, Greece

is to land a kick or punch on another with similar training and effort, and perhaps most importantly, students learn respect for the power of Tae Kwon Do techniques." From *TKDT*, September 1994

"It is possible to rationalize competition in a number of ways. Some martial arts teachers hold tournaments to give their students a chance to observe their functioning under more stressful conditions. Also, if we must function in a competitive environment, we can learn to maintain our mental equilibrium by developing a large measure of detachment both from the actual competition and from its outcome." From *A Path To Liberation*

Besides personal growth, competitors share their experiences with fellow players and form the emotional bonds associated with all sports. Students who train together and enter competitions together may often also jog and eat together, forming deep friendships along the way. It is the sport of Tae Kwon Do that can unite the various styles and schools to find harmony and value in the sharing of individual accomplishments. This is accomplished through camaraderie and the spirit of competition.

"Through sport boys acquire virtues that no books can give them."

Charles Kingsley

The sport of Tae Kwon Do has evolved through these competitions. Tournaments have grown from local to regional and national events, all the way to the inclusion of Tae Kwon Do as an Olympic sport. Tae Kwon Do at this level takes on new meaning as it joins the sports community in uniting nations, shaping world politics, and becoming entertaining—for better or worse.

From nation to nation, school to school—even though the methods of instruction and modes of practice may differ—the sport of Tae Kwon Do ought to be the common thread that enables martial artists to interact while testing their skills. Sport Tae Kwon Do can and does provide a sense of fellowship in an art that otherwise

focuses on personal growth and inner discipline. Now these principles will be permanently tested on new ground, the Olympic Games.

According to the Fundamental Principles from the Olympic Charter of the International Olympic Committee, "Olympism is a philosophy of life, exalting and combining in a balanced whole the qualities of body, will and mind. Blending sport with culture and education, Olympism seeks to create a way of life based on the joy found in effort, the educational value of good example and respect for universal fundamental ethical principles.

"The goal of the Olympic Movement is to contribute to building a peaceful and better world by educating youth through sport practiced without discrimination of any kind and in the Olympic spirit, which requires mutual understanding with a spirit of friendship, solidarity and fair play."

The Olympic Games have become a business, with its television rights and endorsements, but any possible negative exposure gets easily buried under the Olympic ideals and traditions. The Games symbolize opportunity for both individuals and nations. The Olympics capture the drama of the human spirit and the dreams of young athletes. The admission of Tae Kwon Do into the Olympic Games will breathe new life into the ancient martial art.

1988 USTU Women's Olympic Team with coaches and then President-Elect Chong in Los Angeles before their departure to the Seoul Games.

Tae Kwon Do is a martial art, but it can be a sport too. Inclusion of Tae Kwon Do in the Olympic Games will provide exposure for the sport, heightening awareness, increasing participation in the study of the martial art, and not just the sport. As a spectator, the viewing public will see the explosive highlights of knockouts and quick snapshots of sparring matches along with background material on the history and practice of traditional Tae Kwon Do. With proper media coverage, people will realize that Tae Kwon Do is not a spectator sport, but a participatory activity for the whole family that instills discipline, confidence, and respect through basic skills and perceptive philosophy.

Just as Tae Kwon Do can help to unify the world through sport, the sport of Tae Kwon Do can surely help to unify the Tae Kwon Do community.

By Laura Kistler

Master Saleem Jehangir

- First Tae Kwon Do Black Belt from the sub-continent, 1970

- Pioneer of Tae Kwon Do (Korean Martial Art) in Pakistan

- Founder-President Tae Kwon Do-Karate Association of Pakistan, 1972

- Founder Tae Kwon Do Club at National Sports Training & Coaching Center, Karachi, 1971

- Founder of Rochester Institute of Technology Tae Kwon Do Club, Rochester, NY 1970

- Vice-President, World Kang Duk Won Tae Kwon Do Federation 2012

- President, Pakistan Kang Duk Won Tae Kwon Do Federation 2012

- http://www.saleemjehangir.info

Normally someone else should be writing this chapter, but since I am writing this book to tell the story in first person, I chose to write it myself. I have called myself Master Jehangir because, firstly, that is what Master Chong calls me, and secondly, this is the etiquette observed throughout this book. I have included more details about myself because this book is about Tae Kwon Do Pakistan.

Ancestral History On the Paternal Side
My grandfather from my father's side was Shahzada Mirza Mohammed Ashraf, who was from among the descendants of the Mughal king, Aurangzeb Alamgir. Mirza Mohammed Ashraf was from Delhi, and was appointed a professor of Mathematics at the Edjerton College in Bahawalpur during the British Rule. He was also the Ataleeq (personal teacher) of Nawab of Bahawalpur, Sadiq Mohammed, and was later appointed as the Revenue Minister of the State of Bahawalpur. He retired as the first Nazim (mayor) of District Rahimyarkhan. It is here that he purchased some 2500 acres of agriculture lands which were later inherited by his sons and now by my generation.

Mirza Mohammed Ashraf was ranked among the princes of Delhi. Even the tombstone on his grave in Jaipur is inscribed as "Marqade Shazada Mohammed Ashraf" and the whole family grave yard is maintained in mint condition by the Auqaf Department of the Government of India. He was also a very religious scholar and was well known among the literary circles of his time. He authored two books, Shyama Shami and Bin Baasi Rustom. An extract from the Bin Baasi Rustom is included in the school books in Pakistan today.

Ancestral History on the Maternal Side
My grandfather from my mother's side was Nawab Ahsan Ali Khan who was from among the descendants of Sultan Mahmud of Ghazni. He was the son of Nawab Haji Mohammed Ali Khan who retired as the member of the Supreme Council of Jaipur. Haji Mohammed Ali Khan also wrote the first compilation of Ayats and Hadith's by topic in Urdu, the published book was called Falah Din o Dunya.
Ahsan Ali Khan was the District Magistrate of Jaipur but was more known for his wealth and status, and for being the son of a member of the Supreme Council. He owned large orchards, lands and property in the form of Havelis, and commercial buildings on the main road of Jaipur, called Mirza Ismail Khan Road. Among his many passions was Pahelwani (wrestling), which he conducted at the Mardana Haveli he lived in. He was also the captain of the Jaipur cricket team in which the Maharaja played himself. There are still stories that people narrate on how he used to train local wrestlers who would end up

defeating national champions of their times. Among the notable wrestlers of those days who he trained were Amanullah Khan Shaikhu Wale, Majeed Pahelwan, and Husaini Dewee Lal Jee. His own Ustad was Juma Khan Nahar Wale from Delhi. During my visit to Jaipur in 2007, I was trying to find his grave in the graveyard that had become now very big, failing in my attempt I asked a man sitting idle if he knew where Ahsan Ali Khan was buried. The man replied by asking: that Ahsan Ali Khan who was the Ustaad of Pahelwani and had an Akhara (wrestling ring) at his Haveli? Being a student of martial art, I felt very proud of my grandfather's fame as a wrestling Ustaad.

The complex of Havelis was called Haji Bagh, and so was its address in Jaipur. The area occupied by these Havelis encompasses 3 blocks and has now been commercialized with hotels and shops.

Family History

My parents lived in Jaipur, and that is where I was born in 1945. The homes, located on Mirza Ismail Khan Road, were big. One belonged to my paternal grandfather, and two belonged to my maternal grandfather, the families with children lived in one and Nawab Ahsan Ali Khan lived in the other, alone by himself. They enjoyed a very privileged life style in Jaipur, only associating themselves with the elite and the Maharaja of Jaipur. But good times don't last long, to the misfortune of millions, the great Indian sub-continent was divided into three parts in 1947. My paternal grandfather, Shahzada Mohammed Ashraf, also owned lands in Rahimyarkhan, which fell in the newly formed Pakistan territory. Since he had been farming in that region already, my father loaded the family on a train and with good luck and God's help came through safely into Pakistan.

Early Schooling

I was born in Jaipur at Fajr time on Eid al Adha, November 16, 1945. I was hardly two years old when my father, Mirza Shamsul Huda Ashraf, brought the family to Rahimyarkhan. He was a graduate of Sadiq Edjerton College, Bahawalpur. After living a short period in Rahimyarkhan, he found a job with the Government of Pakistan and moved to the city of Multan, while his younger brother, Mirza Badr-ud-Duja Ashraf, managed the farming of the lands.

For a very short time I received my very early education in Rahimyarkhan, then at St. Mary's Convent School in Multan, then at the famous Sadiq Public School in Bahawalpur. In 1960, we moved to Karachi where I finished my Matric with distinction from Greenwood Secondary School in Karachi in 1962.

College

After finishing my Secondary School education, I joined DJ Science College and completed my Intermediate Science, also with distinction, in 1964. DJ was ranked among the best science colleges in the Indo-Pak sub-continent, and I am very proud that I attended it. Throughout my academic period in Pakistan I always topped in my class. From DJ, the normal progression was to go into NED Engineering College, which is now NED Engineering University. Conditions in Pakistan were getting from bad to worse, especially for students. Strikes, protest marches, class cancellations were becoming more and more frequent. I could foresee wastage of valuable years of my life, and decided to proceed to the USA for further studies.

(The University of Michigan (1965-1968

In 1965, I proceeded to the USA where I complete my Bachelor's Degree in Mechanical Engineering from the University of Michigan, Ann Arbor, Michigan, in 1968.

DAILY NEWS

Vol. 4, No. 171   Karachi, Tuesday

June 22, 1965 Safar 20, 1385

Mr. Walter P. McConaughy, U.S. Ambassador, welcomed 46 Pakistani Fulbright grantees and other scholars during an orientation programme held at the headquarters of the U.S. Education Foundation (Pakistan), Karachi on Monday prior to their departure to the United States where they will take advanced higher studies at major American universities.

Newspaper clipping showing the 1965 batch of students that proceed to the USA.

At the U of M, I completed a four year curriculum in 3 years and even appeared on the Dean's List for scholastic achievement for two semesters. It is here at the U of M that I also studied Tae Kwon Do from 1965 and received my Black Belt in 1970.

Saleem Jehangir at the University of Michigan 1965

Saleem Jehangir in 1967

Saleem Jehangir at College Graduation 1968

Eastern Michigan University (1975-77)

While working with Ford Motor Company, I joined EMU in the evening program for MBA, in 1975. I completed my MBA in 1977.

I secured my Professional Engineering License in Texas in 1982. In addition, I took numerous seminars and courses to enhance my knowledge in the profession as an engineer and a manager.

Professional Career

Immediately after graduation, in 1968, I started to work with the Ford Motor Company as an Advance Manufacturing Engineer. The job was eliminated after 2 years due to a downturn in the auto sales and consequent reduction in work force.

In 1970, I joined Xerox Corporation as Process Engineer. This job lasted only a year as economic conditions worsened in the USA and more and more companies resorted to work force reduction.

I then decided that it was time to go back and serve my country, Pakistan. I was hired immediately at Esso Eastern oil company in July 1971 as Terminal Engineer in charge of Bulk Operations. I worked with them till the end of 1973 before returning to the USA in January 1974 with my newly wedded wife.

I started back with Ford Motor Company in 1974 as Manufacturing Engineer and worked with them till July of 1981, at which point I was offered a job as Facilities Manager with Sii McEvoy in Houston, Texas. Seeing the auto industry going into another recession, I grabbed the opportunity. With McEvoy I led their expansion program and managed multiple projects for them in Texas and Louisiana. The oil prices sank in 1982-83, and many oil field drilling related companies folded in those years. McEvoy, too, went out of business.

In 1984, I joined Schlumberger in Austin, Texas, as Facilities Manager and managed their leased facilities, simultaneously building a new Research and Development complex for them. This job lasted 4 years when Schlumberger folded their business in Austin. Once again foreseeing an economic downturn in the USA, I decided to return to Pakistan with HinoPak Motor Company in Karachi as Director Production. I moved with the family to Karachi where my children joined the Karachi American School and my wife taught there as a librarian for the next four years. At HinoPak I introduced many new designs of buses and specialized vehicles, set up the engine and axle assembly plants, established their Quality Management

**Saleem Jehangir as Director Production,
HinoPak Motor Company, 1988**

System, and quadrupled their production of vehicles.

The law and order in Karachi gradually deteriorated to a point that it was no longer safe to live in Karachi as a family. So we decided to come back to the USA. I came back first in 1992 and started to work with Peterbilt Motor Company in Denton, Texas. This job was in the truck design department, which was not my forte. So I joined a Toyota owned company, Tokai Rika, in Battle Creek, Michigan. As head of Production I managed all its production operations for 2 ½ years before we decided to move back to Austin, a city that we liked most.

In 1996, I joined Applied Materials as head of their Lean Manufacturing Center and converted all their manufacturing operations to Lean Production System (aka The Toyota Production System).

**Saleem Jehangir with MIT professor Womack,
author of The Lean Machine**

In 1998, Applied Materials decided to outsource their manufacturing, and I ended up working with one of its suppliers, QuickTurn Precision Sheet Metal company, as head of Production. QuickTurn went out of business and I joined Horton Automatic Door company in 2001 as Project Manager, managing their automatic door systems installation at 14 monorail stations in Las Vegas, Nevada.

When this project finished in 2004, I came to Pakistan and joined Adam Motor Company in Karachi as Director Production and launched Pakistan's first designed car in production. It was destined to be a short tenure as the company went into financial difficulties and finally folded. I returned to the USA in late 2005.

In 2006, I joined Southwest Engineering Company as Project Manager in Malibu, California, and managed the construction of 18 water chlorination and disinfection stations for the Los Angeles County.

When the projects finished, I returned to Austin and joined St. Edward's University as Project Manager in 2008 managing a host of projects for them including design and construction of playfields, dormitories, class room and office buildings. I had a heart surgery (quadruple bypass) in 2009 and decided to retire in 2011 at the age of 66.

> At the end of my career in 2011, I had totaled 43 years of experience in management of manufacturing operations and projects. I won numerous rewards and recognitions during my professional life and also appeared on TV for a half hour presentation on the award winning project that I managed in Austin, Texas, for Schlumberger.

It is the year 2012 and I am writing this book.

Although this book is about Tae Kwon Do, but I have included my professional history for a reason. I lead a very hard life in my profession, changing jobs frequently due to economic conditions that befell the companies that I worked with. But martial arts taught me to weather the storms and come out struggling from life's calamities. My wife and children also supported me in this struggle in which we led a transient, but successful life. Alhamdolillah.

Family Status

I was married in the January of 1973 to a girl from Lahore. I have two daughters and one son. My eldest daughter is a Gynecologist, my second daughter is a legal assistant to the Attorney General of Texas, and my son is an Events Planning Manager at a well-known hotel in Las Vegas, Nevada. My son, Noor has also appeared on Television shows in the USA and plays in the US Rugby team. I have three grandchildren from my daughters, two girls and a boy, who are my Qurratil Aayunin.

Extra Curricular

I was extra ordinarily active in my extracurricular activities which covered a wide spectrum.

Tae Kwon Do

I will best be remembered for my contributions in Martial Arts where I gained fame and acclaim. Although most of the details are written in the chapter on The History of Tae Kwon Do in Pakistan, I have also summarized them here. I studied Tae Kwon Do under Grand Master Hwa Chong at the University of Michigan from 1965 thru 1981, and taught the same at the University of Michigan and at Master Chong's Tae Kwon Do Institute. Master Hwa Chong was the pupil of Master Park Chull Hee in Korea, one of the senior most pioneers of modern day Tae Kwon Do.

In the history of Martial Arts, I was the first black belt from the Indo-Pak sub-continent. I took part in numerous tournaments, and in organizing many championships. In 1970 I established the first school of Tae Kwon Do at the Rochester Institute of Technology in Rochester, New York. In 1971, I came to Pakistan and established the first school of martial arts in Karachi, promoting specifically Tae Kwon Do. I was featured in many newspapers magazines, and television shows in Pakistan. My name is now included as one of the Pioneers in History of Martial Arts, and appears in the Encyclopedia of Martial Arts and many other books written on the subject. Pakistan can boast of being one of the first few countries in history to nurture modern day Tae Kwon Do, and having thousands of followers today.

I competed in numerous tournaments across USA. I was placed second in sparring in the First All Michigan Tae Kwon Do Championships in 1969. I took part in the organization of the first All American Inter-Collegiate Tae Kwon Do Championships held in Ann Arbor, Michigan, in 1974, and competed in the same, winning 2nd place in Forms (Kata). I was featured in the December 1975 issue of the Black Belt magazine, and was included in the Martial Arts Traditions, History, and People, and the Original Martial Arts Encyclopedia among the Pioneers in History of Martial Arts, and in other books written on Martial Arts.

I moved to Pakistan in 1971, started the training of Martial Arts at the National Sports Training and Coaching Center in Karachi in late 1971. Formed the first martial arts association in Pakistan under the name of Tae Kwon Do-Karate Association of Pakistan in 1972. This is the first time in the history of the Indo-Pak sub-continent that formal training of the martial arts was established.

I organized Pakistan's first Tae Kwon Do tournament in Karachi which was held in 1973. Also organized coaching camps in various cities of Pakistan including Lahore, Quetta, and for the Pakistan armed forces and selected police departments.

I Organized Judo & Karate demonstrations country wide. I invited Judo Masters from Japan and held the first demonstration of the art at the NSTCC in Karachi. I was featured in practically every magazine and newspaper of that time and also appeared on Pakistan Television in 1972 on the Zia Mohiuddin Show. I went back to the USA in 1974 but continued to conduct training sessions in Pakistan once every year till 1981. After 1981, I left the Tae Kwon Do Association matters with the senior students in Pakistan.

Master Saleem Jehangir (5th from right) at the UM TKD Club

Master Saleem Jehangir (right) in sparring competition in 1969 All Michigan State Championship

**Master Saleem Jehangir with 1974 All American
Championship trophy**

Sports

I captained the Greenwood School cricket team in 1961-62, played badminton and table tennis for DJ Science College in 1962-64, played soccer for the University of Michigan and Eastern Michigan University in 1965-77. Also played golf, and swam often. I was the Carom Board champion at Esso Eastern in Karachi. And at the age of 67 won the Table Tennis championship at the North Austin Muslim Community Center in 2012.

Community Organizations

I held the position of President of the Pakistan Student Association of the University of Michigan, the Pakistani Association of Detroit, Michigan, and was the founder-president of the Pakistan Association of Austin, Texas.

Religious Organizations

I was very active in the Islamic activities since 1981, serving the Muslim community as an Executive Committee member with Mosque organizations in Texas and Michigan, including four years as President of the North Austin Muslim Community Center in Austin, Texas. In 1994, I established the first mosque at Battle Creek, Michigan, and assisted in the construction of mosques in Houston and Austin. I am grateful to Allah Almighty for giving me the opportunity to serve the Muslim community wherever I lived in the USA.

Professional Organizations

I was always a member of professional organizations and held office in the Society of Manufacturing Engineers in Michigan, and the Internal Facility Managers Association in Texas.

Outdoors

I loved the outdoors, and frequently camped on lakes, rivers, and in state parks. I started with a tent, then bought a tent trailer, and finally a motor home.

I also loved hunting and fishing, and frequently embarked on these trips.

If I was not doing any of the above, I was found enjoying picnics on weekends.

Stage

I frequently organized and participated in stage activities throughout my life as a student. I played the guitar and sang in gatherings and stage shows, including the Zia Moheyuddin show in Karachi. Organized the All American Pakistan Students Association annual variety program held in Ann Arbor, Michigan in 1968. Organized the cultural variety program for the Pakistan Night at the United Nations, 1968. Appeared on the Zia Moheyuddin Show in 1972

Books, Magazines, and websites to read about Master Saleem Jehangir:

Martial Arts Traditions, History, People by John Concoron& Emil Farkas

The Original Martial Arts Encyclopedia by John Concoron& Emil Farkas

Black Belt Magazine December 1975 issue

Saleemjehangir.info

Photos

Master Saleem Jehangir's Flying Side Kick was included in Best Sports Photographs of 1972 by Sports Time Magazine

The Original Martial Arts
Encyclopedia
Tradition-History-Pioneers

John Corcoran and Emil Farkas
with Stuart Sobel

The book that included Master Saleem Jehangir among the Pioneers in History of Martial Arts (see following page)

JACKSON, HOWARD (1951-) American karate champion. Jackson began martial arts in 1968 under Harold Williams of Detroit, Mich. In 1970 he received a black belt from Hwang Kee in the Korean style of tang soo do.

After moving to southern California and gaining some notoriety as a fast-rising regional point fighter, Jackson trained with senior members of the Chuck Norris Studios and also with world heavyweight champion **Joe Lewis,** who had a profound influence on Jackson.

In 1973, when **Mike Anderson** introduced **semicontact** fighting at his **Top 10 Nationals** in St. Louis, Jackson won the grand championship and the first $1,000 purse in semicontact competition. *Black Belt* and *Professional Karate* magazines rated him the number-1 U.S. karate fighter of 1973; he was inducted into the **Black Belt Hall of Fame** as "Fighter of the Year," the first black fighter to be ranked number-one in the history of the sport. He is also the only two-time grand champion of the prestigious **Battle of Atlanta** (1973 and 1974).

Howard Jackson

A severe knee injury destroyed Jackson's chances of winning an inaugural world championship title at the World Professional Karate Championships of 1974, the event at which **full-contact** karate was spawned. He limped through a one-legged performance and retired bitter and frustrated shortly afterward. After two years of surgery and therapy, Jackson launched a comeback in 1976, competing in professional boxing, karate, and kick-boxing.

On January 26, 1980, Jackson, now with a record of 15-1 in full-contact karate and 21 wins in pro boxing, won a sanctioned

JAY, WALLY (1917-) American judo and jujutsu instructor and administrator. Jay began training in 1935 with Paul Kaelemakule in Honolulu and received his black belt in 1944. He is a past president of Jujitsu America and technical director and international head of jujutsu for the **Butokukai,** Kyoto, Japan. He is also technical advisor and black belt grading consultant of the Norwegian Jiu Jitsu Federation, technical advisor of jujutsu for the Independent Karate Association of London, and technical director of the Canadian Jiu Jitsu Association. An exponent of a "small circle theory," he was inducted into the **Black Belt Hall of Fame** in 1969 and entered *Who's Who in the Martial Arts* in 1975.

JEHANGIR, SALEEM Pakistani karate pioneer and instructor; founder and president of the Tae Kwon Do Karate Association of Pakistan. While studying in the U.S. he began tae kwon do with Hwa Chong in Ann Arbor. He received his black belt in 1970, and in 1971 he returned to Karachi, Pakistan, to work for an American oil company. Jehangir overcame Pakistani government objections to establish martial arts in his homeland. In 1971 he taught the first karate class held in Pakistan. Although he now lives in the U.S., he still returns to Pakistan to help promote the martial arts.

JINSUKE, HOJO Father of modern **iaijutsu.** Jinsuke founded the shin muso hayashizake ryu (also known as muso ryu), where he taught defensive swordsmanship. Some historians dispute that Jinsuke founded iaijutsu, but clear evidence has not come to light.

JIROKICHI, YAMADA (1863-1931) Japanese kendo master, 18th headmaster of the jikishin-kage ryu. All of his efforts in teaching went toward maintaining kendo's intrinsic spiritual essence. He devoted his life to kendo and influenced many people who were instrumental in the art's later development.

JIRO, NANGO (-1951) Japanese judo administrator, past president of the **Kodokan.** He began studying judo with founder **Jigoro Kano** in judo's embryonic era and received his black belt in 1884 while continuing a career in the navy, from which he retired as a rear admiral.

In 1938, when Prof. Kano died, the Kodokan board of trustees unanimously chose Jiro his successor, a post he held until September 1946, when he retired due to bad health. While president he established a system of judo for juveniles, fixed the kata of self-defense for women, and founded the institute for the training of teachers of judo. He was one of the few judans, 10th-degree black belts.

JOHNSON, PAT (1939-) American karate instructor, competitor, and referee; originator of the Johnson Rule, a penalty-point system

Pat Johnson, front row mustached. Also pictured, left of Johnson is Ron Marchini and the right of Johnson is Louis Delgado. Top row left is Bob Wall, next to him is Chuck Norris with black lapels.

Master Saleem Jehangir's name shown included among the Pioneers in History of Martial Arts

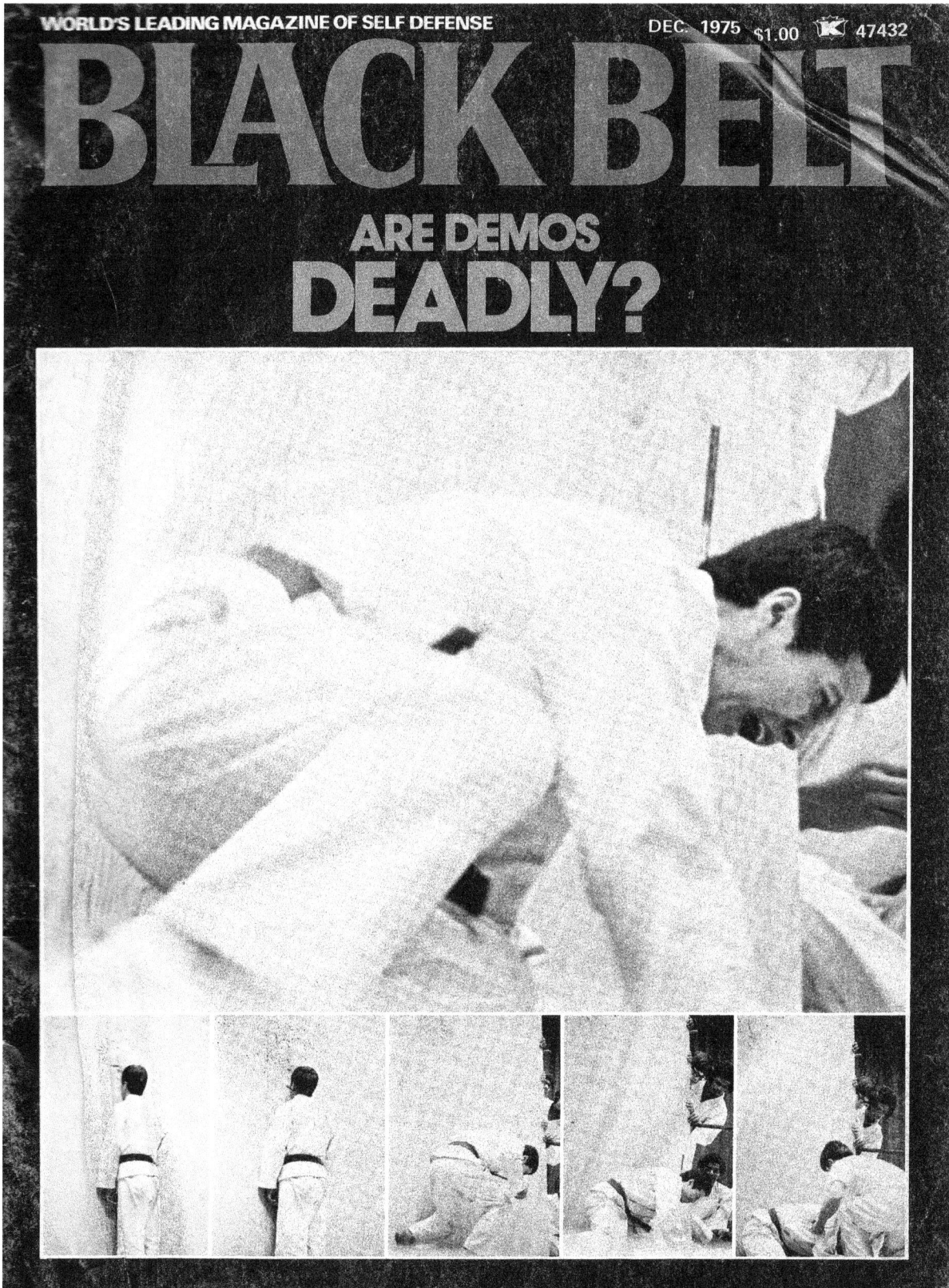

Black Belt Dec 1975 Issue featuring Master Saleem Jehangir
(following page)

BY RICHARD HIRNEISEN

Four years ago, the martial arts in Pakistan were dying. Considered by scholars to be the ancient birthplace of the martial arts, the India-Pakistan subcontinent had been subject to British colonial rule since 1707.

During that period all fighting arts were severely curtailed and by the time of India-Pakistani independence in 1947, there were no formal martial arts schools. Only a few masters, usually hidden in remote villages, hung on to the old

PAKISTAN: MAGIC CARPETS AND MARTIAL ARTS

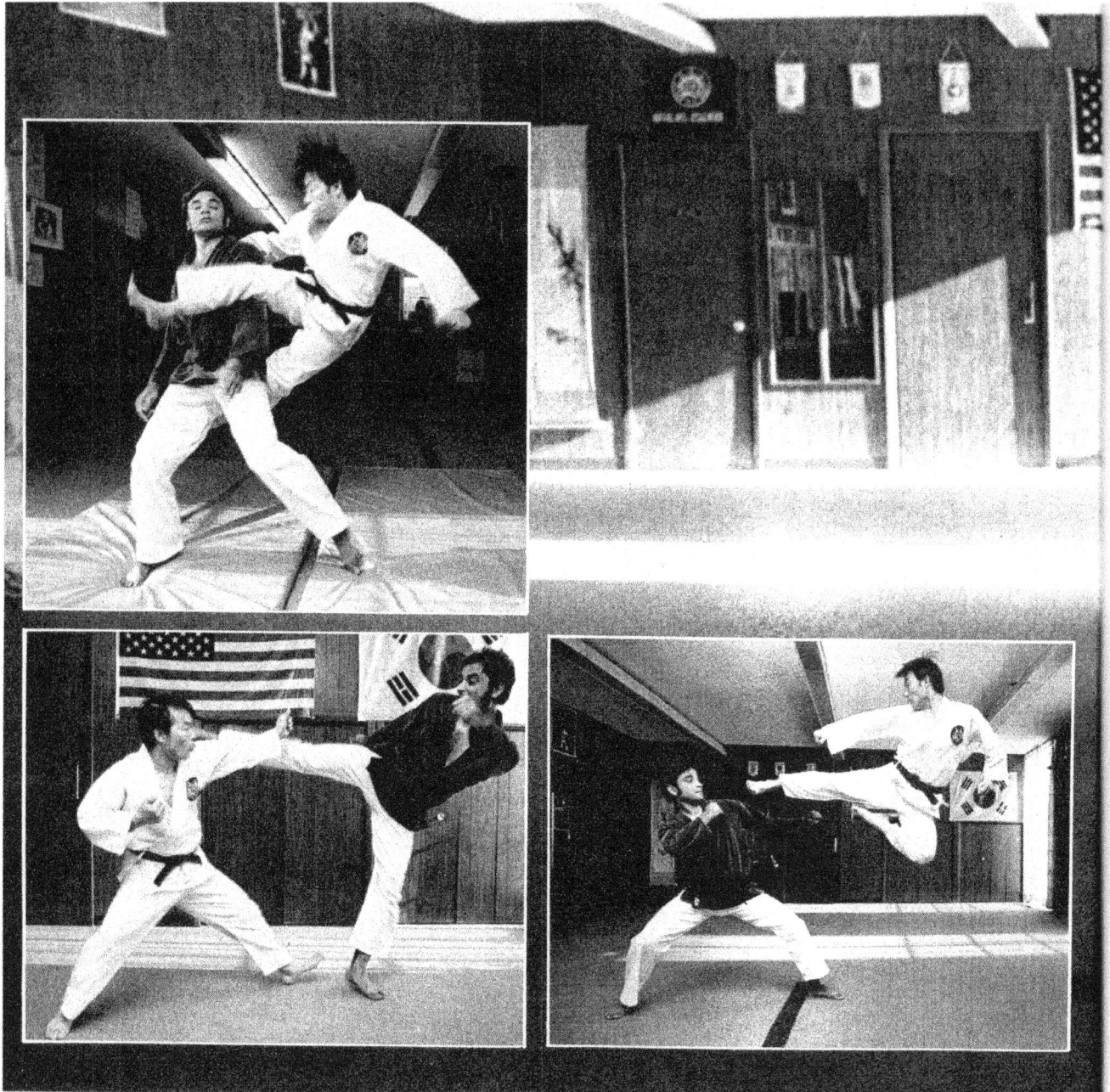

traditions, teaching a handful of students the intricacies of such martial esoterica as axe and stick-fighting and a form of wrestling similar to sumo. The empty-handed forms of combat had completely vanished.

But recently a remarkable renaissance began in Pakistan. The Pakistani government, which formerly prohibited all martial arts, now promotes and may soon help finance them as an asset to the country.

Saleem Jehangir, a 30-year-old Pakistani who received both his degree in engineering and his black belt in tae kwon do at the University of Michigan, is primarily responsible for this sudden turnabout.

As founder and president of the Tae Kwon Do-Karate Association of Pakistan, Jehangir has shown ingenuity and tenacity in a battle to overcome government hostility to the martial arts in his native land. Through the efforts of his organization, tae kwon do is becoming a household word in Karachi, the bustling capital of Moslem Pakistan. Masters of local arts are migrating from the villages to the cities, encouraged by public and civic support, and teachers from the Orient have established karate and kung-fu schools in major cities.

Jehangir's career in the martial arts began in Karachi in 1965, when he read an article in *Life* magazine that praised the academic virtues of the University of Michigan. Seeking a

SCISSORS TAKE-DOWN whips Jehangir to mat (above left). Student and master (above) perform double kata. Lured to the States by the U of M's worthy reputation, the Pakistani earned his black belt from Chong within five years and then returned to his native country to instruct.

Photos by Richard A. Hirneisen

degree in engineering, he decided to enroll.

Hwa Chong, a Korean pursuing a master's degree in economics at the U of M, had just begun teaching tae kwon do in Ann Arbor. Jehangir enrolled in Chong's tiny class and was soon a star pupil. "It is ironical," the soft-spoken Jehangir reflects, "that to learn an Eastern art I have come to the West. But such is the way of life. Western affluence has brought many masters to the United States."

Chong promoted Jehangir to black belt in 1970. In 1971 the new graduate returned to Karachi as an engineer for a US oil corporation with extensive facilities in Karachi. Jehangir found his homeland in turmoil, on the brink of war with its Hindu neighbors India and East Pakistan (now Bangladesh). Youths were rebellious, persistently confronting authorities with civil disobedience. In this tense, distrustful climate, civil authorities suppressed the teaching of the martial arts, afraid they might be used against them. The year Jehangir returned, a

Korean opened a karate school in Karachi but was promptly closed down by the police.

Undeterred by incidents like this, Jehangir tried to open a tae kwon do school but his employers tried to discourage his attempts and building owners refused to rent space. Through his father's influence in government, Jehangir was able to meet with Khwaja Saleem Ahmed, the director of the National Sports Training and Coaching Center. As director of the NSTCC, Ahmed held tremendous power over the direction sports would take in Pakistan. Unlike the US, where government is only minimally involved in sports programs, the Pakistani government actively directs and funds a national sports program. After discussion, Ahmed finally agreed to support the martial arts.

In October, 1971, the young engineer — his country's first black belt — taught the first karate class held in Pakistan. Twenty students met at the extensive NSTCC facilities in Karachi. Government approval had finally bestowed legitimacy upon the martial arts and police harrassment ceased. Tae kwon do took off. Jehangir was soon featured on television shows, sports and news magazines and became something of a celebrity. "Through this publicity," he recalls, "I was able to bring our philosophy of non-violence, peace and discipline to the people. This changed their view about karate, so that parents began bringing their kids into the institution with the idea of getting them disciplined. I soon got the impression," he continues, "that high government officials were in favor of tae kwon do as a method of disciplining the youth, channeling their energies."

Photos courtesy of Saleem Jehangir

PAKISTANI STUDENT takes part in promotional testing in Karachi (above). Jehangir (standing alone in center of photo below) and class pose on steps in front of NSTCC facilities. Currently studying with Chong in Michigan, Jehangir's major goal is to aid youths in becoming "an asset for the future" of Pakistan.

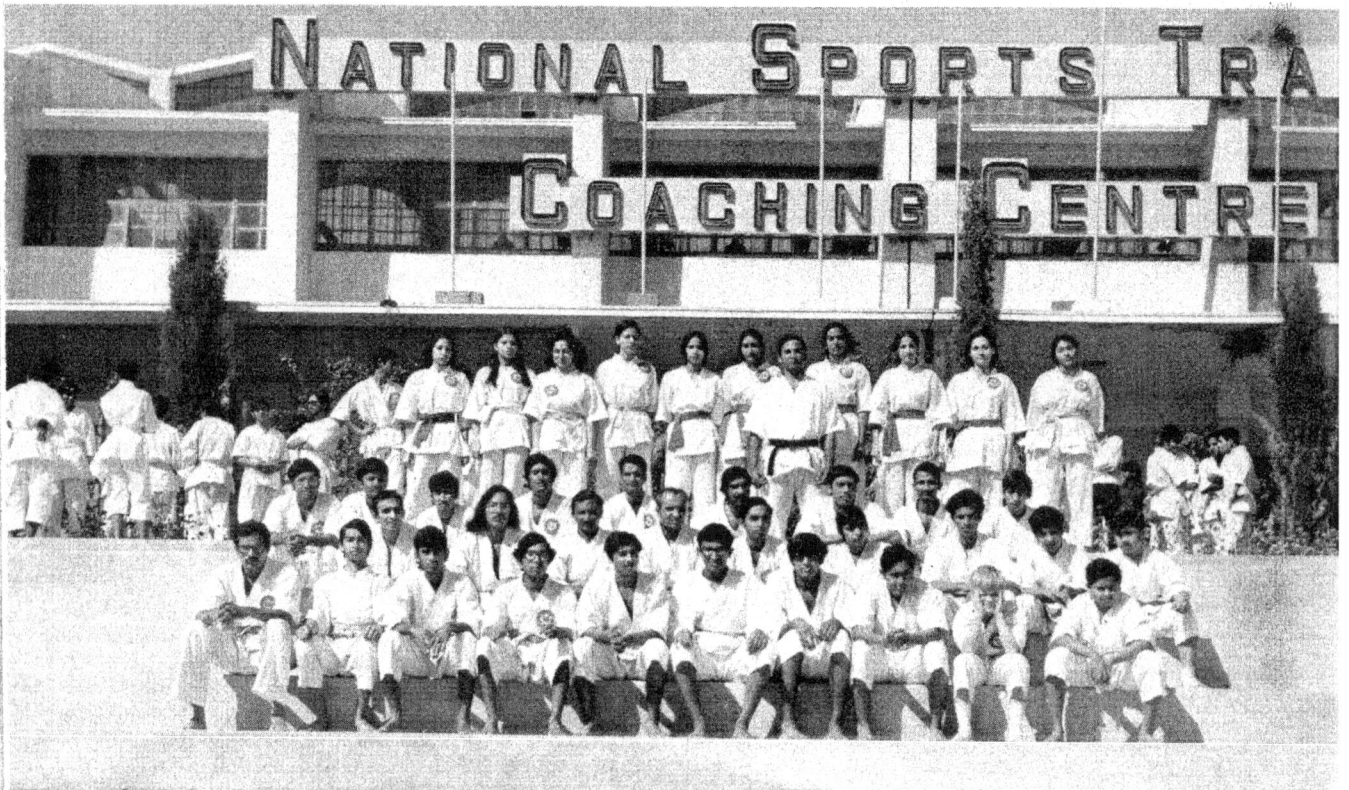

In two months the class had doubled to 40 students. When war erupted in December with India and Bangladesh, all classes at the NSTCC were suspended. After 14 days a cease-fire agreement ended the fighting, but a curfew that remained in effect for 45 days continued the blackout on karate.

With two months of momentum lost, Jehangir started his martial arts crusade once more. Featured for a 25-minute segment of a nationally popular television show, his fledgling class demonstrated tae kwon do and explained its philosophy. Within two months, Jehangir had 200 students, 40 of them women. "It was a very good trend," he comments. "In Pakistan, women don't get out of the house much and rarely participate in sports. We have a fixed-marriage system — pre-arranged marriages — and women rarely are allowed out in the evening or at night without parental escort. It is a major problem to get them to contribute to anything. But their parents actually began escorting them at night to study tae kwon do, an activity they had only months before thought unacceptable for their sons."

Jehangir scored a major success in 1972 when the police, whose role in the past had been to suppress the martial arts, came to him for instruction. "The inspector general of police," Jehangir recounts, "ordered one of the superintendents of police to have all the prime minister's bodyguards trained in tae kwon do. I heard that Prime Minister Zulfiquar Ali Bhuto himself gave the order to the inspector general."

In 1973 the Pakistan Sports Board (similar to the American Athletic Union) formed the Judo-Karate Federation of Paki-

stan, to promote the martial arts and to prepare teams for international competition. Jehangir's pioneering had paved the way for the introduction of other martial arts, Instructors from Burma and Taiwan opened schools in Karachi. Local indigenous martial arts that were very popular until the advent of British rule were revived by the few remaining masters.

In December of 1973 Jehangir returned to Michigan. "I came back," he explains, "to learn from Master Chong. My philosophy is to teach *all* of the art of tae kwon do. Master

Chong believes this also — that if he dies tomorrow, he will have taught as much as possible today. To bring the art to my people, I must know much more about it."

While Jehangir resides in Plymouth with his wife and daughter, the Tae Kwon-Karate Association of Pakistan keeps growing. The association now claims 3,000 active members, who each pay dues of 30 rupees (three dollars) a month.

In his absence, Jehangir's brown belts have published their own magazine and continue to ride the tidal wave of publicity established by Jehangir's earlier work. In February national TV covered the First All-Pakistan Karate Championships held in Karachi and Jehangir returned to host the event. "We decided only a week before to do it," he explains. "But we drew over one hundred competitors from all over Pakistan — a very encouraging number because no one even knew what a championship was and people are afraid to compete like that.

"For the four-hour duration, not one of the 2,000 spectators left the gymnasium, even though most of them knew nothing about karate," he continues. "They were so excited, so enthusiastic. The applause, the spirit was very encouraging. Sections cheered for their favorites so loudly that often I could not hear the point called or the bell that ended the round."

The Association is now trying to interest public school authorities in substituting karate exercises for the calisthenics the children now perform each morning. Jehangir thus claims that they will learn an art, as well as keep their bodies fit.

With money from dues and contributions, the Association recently purchased one acre of land in Karachi to serve as the site for the future headquarters of tae kwon do in Pakistan. Conceived by Jehangir to be an institution similar in function to the Kodokan in Japan, the interior is being designed by volunteer architects in the Association. To keep costs down, the exterior design will be kept simple and functional with 1977 as the target date to begin construction.

Fund-raising to support the growing non-profit Association goes on unabated in Jehangir's absence. Industrialists are being solicited for contributions and attempts are being made to enlist government assistance.

The Pakistani government has allocated several million dollars for the development of a national sports program. As the keeper of those purse strings, Ahmed, Jehangir's ally in the past, is now in a key position to help again.

Jehangir has not set a date for return to his homeland and continues to study diligently with Chong in Michigan. "Before I return to Pakistan," he explains, "I must learn as much as I possibly can from Master Chong. I am not like many people who will train two or three years and claim to be masters. I have much mental and spiritual development to accomplish," he continues. "When this goal is achieved, when I feel sufficiently confident that I can teach, I'll go back.

"I believe in this. I plan to have the youth follow me in a fight to construct the nation, rather than destroy it. I believe I have the access to them because they respect me. When I say something, they listen. All my thoughts are directed to one thing," he concludes, "to really promote the art, to bring it to the youth, so I can help the youth of Pakistan become an asset for the future."

His progress toward this goal has so far been remarkable — through his efforts and the devotion of his students, the healthy future of the martial arts in Pakistan has been assured.

Certificate of Honor

Awarded this day, Saturday, March 30, 1974, in recognition and in honor to

Saleem Jehangir

for outstanding contributions to the success of the 1st American Intercollegiate and Open Taekwon Do-Karate Championships, held at the University of Michigan, Ann Arbor, Michigan. Be it known that his efforts have forwarded the cause of intercollegiate Taekwon Do-Karate and of all martial arts.

Dr. Rodney Grambeau
Tournament President
Director of Intramural and
Recreational Sports Programs,
University of Michigan

Hwa Chong
Tournament Director
Instructor, University of Michigan
Taekwon Do Club

Certified Referee

SALEEM JEHANGIR

Be it known that the above named person has received information and training as to the laws and regulations governing Michigan AAU Tae Kwon Do competition.

Be it further known that said individual has further proven knowledge of these rules and regulations and is hereby classified as a Certified Referee.

Having completed the prerequisites, said individual is eligible to referee Michigan AAU Tae Kwon Do competition for the period 1975-1976.

A.A.U.

TAE KWON DO

Hwa Chong, chairman
Michigan AAU
Tae Kwan Do Committee

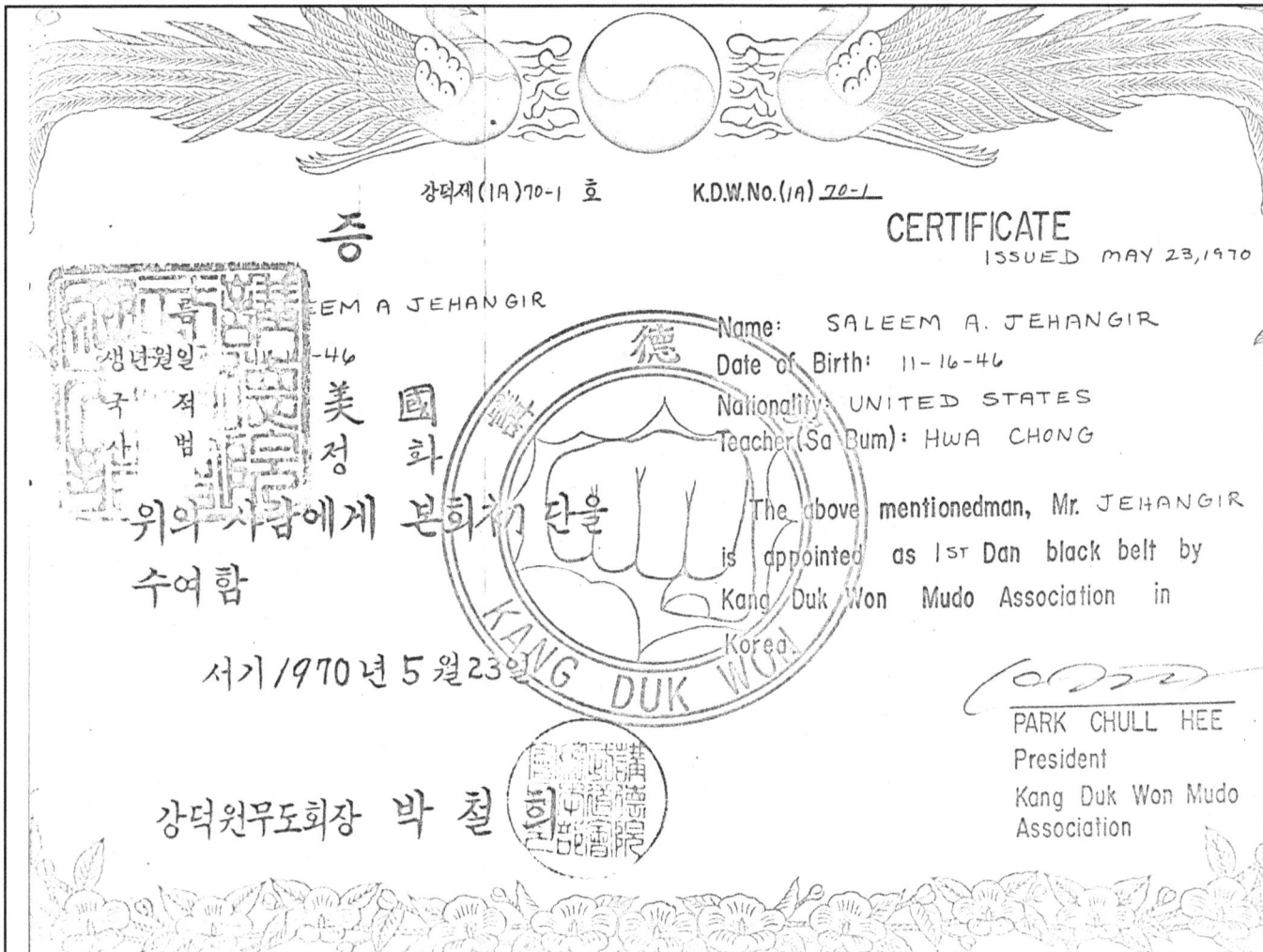

강덕제(IA)70-1 호   K.D.W.No.(IA) 70-1

CERTIFICATE
ISSUED MAY 23, 1970

증

Name: SALEEM A. JEHANGIR
Date of Birth: 11-16-46
Nationality: UNITED STATES
Teacher (Sa Bum): HWA CHONG

The above mentioned man, Mr. JEHANGIR is appointed as 1st Dan black belt by Kang Duk Won Mudo Association in Korea.

위의 사람에게 분하기 단을 수여함

서기 1970년 5월 23일

PARK CHULL HEE
President
Kang Duk Won Mudo
Association

강덕원무도회장 박 철 희

**Black Belt certificate of Master Saleem Jehangir
from Grand Master Park Chull Hee, 1970**

KNOW KARATE

By S. A. JEHANGIR

IN my previous articles I had talked about defensive moves, commonly called Blocks—Upper Blocks, Lower Blocks and Middle Blocks. Blocks are used to divert an oncoming strike. I had also discussed about offensive moves such as the lunge punch, a punch executed to the solar plexus in the front-stance. Let us go further into some more offensive moves.

Sudo is an open hand strike commonly executed to the neck. Notice in Picture 'A' how the strike begins and in picture 'B' how it ends in a front stance. The hand is held tight and the contact is made with the edge of the palm which is hardened through continuous conditioning. Sudo can be applied to the side or back of the neck. The effect is the same as if hit by a stick. Considerable force is concentrated in this type of strike. Sudo is a major part of Japanese Karate — the same signifies its importance, 'Karay' meaning 'empty' 'te' meaning hand —. The whole name of the art being Karate — 'Do' meaning 'the way with the empty hand' Korean Karate stresses more on kicks and punches. Hence the name TAE KWONDO — meaning 'the way with the kicks and punches'.

We have covered the empty hand and the KWON — meaning fist, now let us go into the 'TAE' meaning kicks. Among kicks we have already covered our preliminary kick, the front kick. Now let us go into the most strong kick of TAE KWONDO — the side kick.

Side kick

Look into Picture C: the leg is pulled up and then suddenly shot in a straight line to land in the posture shown in the picture. The contact is made with the edge of the foot. In Karate most strikes are made with the edges or tips — the science behind being that if you reduce the area of contact the force per unit area is increased. The side kick could be aimed to the head, mid section or the lower section — in each case resulting in serious damage to the opponent.

Combat

In combat the side kick can be executed from almost any stance. Look at Picture 'D'. To visualise the lifting effect of the kick when applied to the mid section. The side kick is the most powerful weapon in Korean Karate (TAE KWON DO) with multiple advantage to it such as the reach, the power

and the defensive posture of the body in which the side kick is completed.

Stance

Before we go any further let us understand the importance of 'STANCE'. Stance is the posture of the body that should be maintained during combat at all cost. We have covered the front stance in which all our defensive and offensive strikes were executed. Front stance is the preliminary stance in which all basic movements are taught. However during combat the defensive stance that is maintained is the 'CAT STANCE'. Look into picture 'E' to visualise this stance. Notice how the legs are maintained in a low bent posture. The feet are at right angle to each other for balance and stability. The hands in

THEORY OF POWER IN KARATE

By S. A. JAHANGIR

OFTEN we talk about Karate and the power and the mystical techniques lying behind it. It is not so much of the techniques as it is of the power, that impresses people. Where does this power come from and why is it non-e—istent in other combative arts? Let us see. This secret to this power is "continuous training", of course, but there is a whole scientific theory lying behind this tremendous moment of impact. Hence, assuming that the reader has had upto high school physics, I will go ahead to use the laws of physics to explain the theory of power.

MOMENTUM

Assume a mass travelling in a straight line at a certain velocity. If this mass collides with a stationary mass it results in an impact, and if the constituents of both the masses are the same, the mass that was in motion will shatter itself more than the stationary mass. Similarly asume a man running in a straight line at a certain velocity. If you just hold a stick in his way, be collides with the stick and his own momentum hurts him. Now assume the same man running towards you and you hold your fist in his direction of motion. He collides with your fist and hurts himself. Your fist you can aim at any of his pressure points and his own momentum will be used against him.

CASE II

Now assume two masses tra-velling against each other in a straight line at a certain va-locity. They will collide with each other resulting in a greater force of impact than in case I. Now assume the same man run-ning to you to beat you up. This time you put velocity in your fist to hit him, and you will find that your fist now does more damage to him than if you held it stationary because now it becomes the case of uti-lising the opponent's momen-tum and adding your own mo-mentum to use both against him. Thus we come to a scien-tific conclusion that you will hurt your opponent more when he cashes towards you, than if he were stationary. I used the fist as an example—the kick, the SUDO and other strikes can be used in the same man-ner.

CONSTRUCTION

What is power? Power is the stored energy in your body. If you lose this energy, you lose power. Hence you should learn to conserve your energy. How can you conserve energy? By not wasting it. How can you not waste energy? By keeping your muscles relaxed during physical combat and tensing them only at the time and point of strike. In simple, in Karate, you do not waste energy by keeping your muscles tense all through-out combat, instead, you con-centrate all energy at one point and that is the point that you are striking at. Using an analogy, just like the light rays from all directions, when passed through a lens converge, to a point; the energy in your body also collects to travel through the striking member and CON-VERGES at the point of strike. This way you have increased you energy per square inch to a much greater extent.

FORCE

If a man strikes your body, what is it that hurts you? In physics, it is described as the impact of the mass. This impact is due to the force existent in that mass. We know from physics that FORCE =MASS × Acceleration and acceleration = Rate of change of velocity.

Thus to increase force you increase either the mass or/ and the velocity. In your body, since the mass can not be changed the only way left to increase force is increase the velocity. Hence the speedier is your strike the more the force in it

Any mass travelling in a cer-tain direction is supposed to possess kinetic energy. If this mass collides with another, it is this kinetic energy that pro-duces the impact. From physics.

KINETIC ENERGY $= \frac{1}{2} \times$ mass $\times$ (velocity)^2.

Thus if you increase the ve-locity of your striking mem-ber you increase its kinetic ener-gy by multiple proportions. Similarly by increasing the ve-locity you increase the mo-mentum of your striking mem-ber because momentum=Mass× velocity.

Thus, we have seen how by increasing the speed alone we increase the force, kinetic ener-gy and momentum of your striking member. Hence all Karate motions involve high speeds resulting in tremendous impact at the point of strike.

All these major factors con-tribute to result in a concen-trated power that can be ascer-tained through pictures (1) and (2).

fession. He studied both engineering and Karate at Michigan University—"And it sure wasn't easy!!" says Saleem. For he had to walk to and from the Karate class—which was over four miles and he had to pay the equivalent of Rs. 300 a month for these clases which he attended for six years.

Why did he learn Karate?

Two things motivated him. The first was his violent temper which he desperately wanted to control and second an incident at Clifton where ten people without justification beat him tell he was a mass of bruises. Now Saleem is confident that he could fight singlehanded four healthy, strong, well built men and emerge as the victor. And surprising as it may sound Karate has had such a disciplining effect upon him that he feels he has his temper completely in check!

HOW DOES ONE BEGIN TO LEARN KARATE?

Simply by going over to the national coaching Centre and

enrolling as a Karate student. Classes for boys are held regularly every day in the evenings after 6 P.M., whereas Classes for girls are held only three times a week, also in the evenings.

The fees are rather nominal Rs. 15/- a month for girls and Rs. 25/- for boys.

advanced group of students, green belts showed the audience some of their daily exercises, which consist of attack and defence techniques, these are again divided into arm tricks and leg tricks. But, whilst learning how to defend oneself against all types of attacks, the student of Karate normally specializes in a few trick in which he becomes an expert.

The total strength of the students learning Karate was 125 but after the Karate demonstration on 14th June 1972; many more people have joined the classes.

The passing our examination cum demonstration was staged especially for those people who don't know what Karate is. At first the most

Demonstrated also at this function were techniques of breaking blocks of wood. The most famous is the breaking of wood with the side of the hand. However that is not the only way. We saw boys shattering these blocks of wood with the front kick and side kick, and a very impressive flying kick, where the student jumped over three boys and struck three blocks of wood with his foot and broke them. The last way to break the blocks is with the head . . . . a little dangerous but very unusual and impressive.

Girl students also demonstrated that day. One of the students, Pearly demonstrated Judo tricks whilst in combat with a boy. If she ever wants to join the film Industry to play the part of a spy or detective, she ought to have no trouble at all!

If you wish to learn you can start anytime. It's never too late to begin. There are men over 50 years old in the class! And its never too early either. The youngest student at the classes is a five year old boy.

Whereas many boys are seriously learning Karate as an art, I think most girls attend Karate classes mostly to keep trim and physically fit. If you happen to be one of those who can never find time to exercise at home, or find it boring to exercise, I think Karate Classes are the answer for you!

By Gul Hameed Bhatti

The Clean Art of 'Dirty Fighting'

Saleem Jehangir: Flying kick

Performing a difficult kata

I shall observe the principles of **Tae Kwon Do**. I shall respect the instructor and all senior ranks. I shall never misuse **Tae Kwon Do**. I shall be a champion of freedom. I shall build a more peaceful world."

That (though it's hard to believe) is the oath at one entrance to the world of "Dirty Fighting." The world of chop. kick, punch, blow; of **Emma** Peel and **Bruce Lee** — the world of **karate**.

It's enemies call it "dirty fighting." That's how the movies have popularised it, and the holy scriptures projected it.

Yet, behind it's mauled, bloodied face. lie the purifying qualities of the great eastern religions: self_control, respect for others, love of freedom. For every Tae Kwon Do (Korean for karate) student, or for that matter anyone learning any form of karate, his instructor or superiors are persons to be highly revered.

Yet the general concept about karate remains that of "Dirty Fighting." For Kung Fu movie addicts, karate is a "rear thunderbolt kick to the temples of your opponent, a back_hand slash to the jaws, the eye gouge, the groin kick and what have you." An unfair definition of the Martial Arts, perfected in the East centuries ago and now highly respected throughout the globe, for their power to achieve unification of the soul and the body through dexterity, speed, strength and above all, to the emphasis on respect for other human beings.

The art of karate (literally meaning 'empty-handed' in Japanese) is the most devastating and lethal method of unarmed combat yet devised. But there is a vast difference between karate for self-defence and karate as a sport. The

Hup... one, two

first permits the use of every tactic taught in a moment of need, as sport karate has its own rules and regulations, a system to recognise the fouls, and of course judges to watch and assess. In the 20th century, karate, has flourished throughout the world, both as a combat art and a very popular spectator sport. But it still suffers from a lack of organisation, while the contests, though excit_

ing, are somewhat unsatisfactory, because real blows cannot be landed.

Inevitably, for those in the movie business karate has become a great money-spinner, a purely commercial proposition. True, their characters depict the highest qualities of friendship, comradeship, perfect execution of the artistry of the fighting arts and great love for humanity, but the real attraction for the thousands of fans queuing up at the box office is the amount of blood spilled, jaws broken, temples smashed, bellies split open, eyes gouged out and groins kicked in.

In Pakistan, karate has achieved tremendous popularity over the last six years or so. Scores of enthusiastic young people including girls and children, have taken it up either as a pastime, or as a serious method of self-defence. But apart from those going about learning this martial art form with religious devotion in the various clubs dotted around the country, Pakistanis generally view the sport like other movie enthusiasts the world over. They are thrilled by the same blood-splashing orgies, which have enthralled European and Far Eastern countries. The number of **Bruce Lee** posters sold at bookshops in all the big cities of Pakistan is one indication of how popular the movie version of karate is; a life size pin-up comes for as little as twenty rupees.

But karate is not just Bruce Lee. Although it was developed in the Orient, particularly in **Japan**, it probably originated in ancient Greece where the Olympic Games included an event called the **Pankration**. This 'sport' was a combination of wrestling and fist fighting in which the participants were allowed to

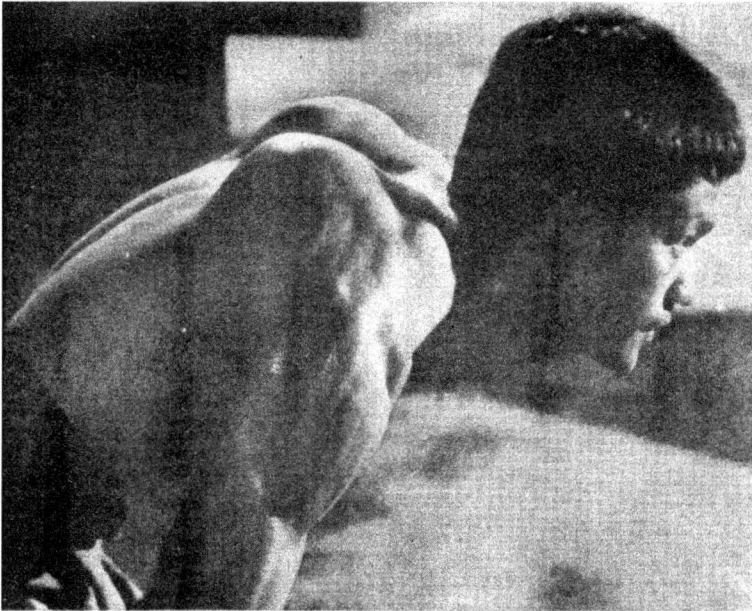

The "real" thing: **Bruce Lee**

use punches, kicks, throws and holds. It was so keenly contested that the loser invariably ended maimed or dead. But gradually it lost popularity and died its own death, giving way to boxing and wrestling in Europe. The martial arts then found their way into Asia, probably with the invasion of India by Alexander the Great in the fourth century B.C.

South Indian legend has it that in 525 A.D., an obscure Indian Buddhist monk, **Daruma Taishi** (more commonly known as **Tamo** or **Buddhadhrama**), made a sojourn from India to China to teach the people of that great nation the secrets of **Zen**. There, says the legend, the monk secluded himself in the Saloin Temple at Chung Shen in the Hunan Province. For nine years, it is said, the monk sat facing a wall listening to "the ants screaming." He later came to be represented in Chinese Art as a man of almost demonic spiritual powers. His secrets of Zen were very difficult to learn. The essence of his teachings was austerity and strict discipline, no matter what the odds. The intense austerity practised during the training periods weakened many a disciple both mentally and physically. To overcome this difficulty and to equip his disciples for the learning of Zen, the monk taught them a form of 'exercise which would help them control their actions. This was the doctrine of the inseparability of spirit and body. It was called **Ekikinkyo**. And that's how the present day sport of Chinese **Kempo** began.

Actually, the sub-continent has been considered by scholars as the birthplace of these arts. The British did not encourage these fighting arts during their rule and they seemed to be dying. There were no formal martial art schools in this area, but then, there were few organised set-ups to promote other forms of sporting activity either.

India. Many others taught various forms of martial esoterics to their students in obscure environment. These included axe and stick-fighting. The latter had a number of exponents in the Punjab, where it was known as **Gatka**, and in other areas where it was referred to as **Binot**, or literally "striking from a hiding place. But then those who excelled in these arts seldom passed on the intricacies of their techniques to their students, and the secrets either remained within the family or died with the masters. However, after the British left, traditional sports began to come into their own.

Perhaps the form closest to **Gatka** in the eastern martial arts accepted by worldwide organisations and developed as a spectator sport is **Kendo**, in which contestants wear padded armour and masks like fencers, and fight with bamboo or metal swords. Even traditional Indian wrestling was able

tests — **Kumite** (free sparring) and **Kata** (forms). In Kumite, a contestant attempts to pierce an opponent's guard with a blow, but withdraws it before striking him. In Kata, the performance of a series of set movements of attack and defence mark the contest, and competitors are marked on their precision and correct posture. Because, competitors are not allowed to inflict real blows on their opponents, sport karate's usefulness in moments of crisis is a little doubtful. Despite this, sport karate has more followers all over than practical karate which teaches defence against gang attacks and experienced street fighters.

Tae Kwon Do came to Pakistan in 1971 through a Karachi youngster named **Saleem Jehangir**, who received both his degree in engineering and his black belt in Tae Kown Do at the University of Michigan. His career in martial arts began purely by chance. **Hwa Chong**, a

Two bricks shattered in one action

Korean studying for a master's degree in economics at the same university, had just begun teaching Tae Kwon Do. Saleem joined Master Chong's small class and was soon his eager student, wanting to learn all the intricacies of the art. "It is ironical," Saleem reflects, "that to learn an Eastern art I had to go West. But that is the way of life. Western affluence has brought many masters to the United States." In 1970, Saleem became the first Pakistani to receive a black belt. The next year, he returned to Pakistan as an engineer with a Karachi-based US oil corporation and in October that year, he held the first karate class in Pakistan.

Saleem had to face hostility from official sports quarters who felt that the martial arts were some sort of unholy warfare technique. He showed remarkable calm and ingenuity in the face of sustained police harassment, and finally over-

All grace and poise

The Herald, December 1977

Miss Durdana Mirza
Pakistan's First Female Black Belt

Cover page article in Jang's Akhbar e Jahan, on DurdanaMirza, first Woman Black Belt of the Indo-Pak Sub-continent

بلیک بیلٹ دُردانہ مرزا سے نہایت دلچسپ انٹرویو

عکاسی: مرزا انتخاب رشید مسعود

سیکھنے کے ذمہ دار ہیں۔ ایسے لوگ کی بعض وقت منفی تبلیغ — اُن کی مشرقی اور اِن کی غربی ہے ۔۔۔ ہمارے ملک میں ہمیں یہ دُنیا بھر میں پائی جاتی ہے۔ اس لحاظ سے جو ذخیرہ کرنے کا فن مسلسل اختیار کر رکھا ہے اور اُن کی کون ذی کو اہمیت دی جا رہی ہے۔

دُردانہ آنسہ نے تقریباً پیچھے سال پکنگ نیشنل ایسوسی ایشن ٹریننگ کے چینگ سینڈرڈ نائی کون ڈو کی تربیت حاصل کی۔ مسٹر کون ڈو کی مہارت حاصل دیہان اُن کی سربراہی میں پاکستان نائی کون ڈو فیڈریشن سیکرٹری طالب العلم کو اس فن کے رشتہ سے کام لے رہا ہے۔

اس آنسہ سے متعلق دُردانہ سے ہماری تفصیلی بات چیت ہوئی اور ہم نے اُن سے پوچھا "آخر کب سے اس فن کو ہمارے ملک میں مقبولیت حاصل ہوئی؟ اور لوگوں نے اسے کس حد تک سیکھنا شروع کیا۔"

"پاکستان میں ۱۹۶۰ء میں اس فن کی ابتداء ہوئی اور ماسٹر سلیم جہانگیر نے اسے بہتر طور پر اس فن کو راستہ دیہان اُن کی سربراہی میں روشناس کرایا۔ اس سے قبل لوگ کہیں کہیں اسے بہت معمولی سا جانتے تھے۔ اب پہلے کی نسبت لوگ اس فن میں کہیں زیادہ دلچسپی لینے لگے ہیں۔ شرع میں تو مشرق ممالک کے علاوہ لوگوں کو اتنا بھی معلوم نہیں تھا کہ یہ کیا چیز ہے اور اس کی افادیت کتنی ہے۔ لیکن گزشتہ چند سات سال کے عرصے دوران عزیز کی نہیں ہمارے یہاں اپنی جوں اس فن کے حسن تھیں تو لوگوں کو سامنے لائے جانے اور دکھے کا مہ حلا اس لیے یہ مقبول عام ہو گیا۔"

"اس فن کو سیکھنے والوں میں مخواتین کو لڑکیوں کی تعداد زیادہ ہوتی ہے یا لڑکوں کی۔" یہ سوال خاصا دلچسپ ہے اور لوگ جاننا چاہتے بھی ہیں۔ مجھے آخر یہی بات پوچھی جاتی ہے۔ لیکن ہم تو سب ہی جانتے ہیں کہ جس معاشرے میں رہتے ہوئے ہم اپنی تمام روایتیں کو بار بار نکلنے کی مختی نہیں شائع جب اور ہر کی تعداد اور کردار کے مقابلے میں یہ یقینی بات ہے لیکن ہو لڑکیاں باہر نکلتی ہیں اور رہ سکتے ہیں۔ اس لحاظ سے اُن کی تعداد کا فی حوصلہ افزا اضافہ ہو رہا ہے۔"

"کیا لڑکیاں اسے سیکھنے میں خاصا وقت لیتی ہیں؟"

لڑکے اور لڑکیوں کے درمیان سیکھنے کا تناسب یا اسٹینڈرڈ ایک سا ہے — دونوں میں سے کوئی بھی جلدی سی سیکھ لیتا ہے اور دیر سے ۔۔۔۔۔ جتنا مختلف مدارج میں سیکھنے لگتا ہے وہ دونوں کے لیے برابر ہے۔ اس میں یہ نہیں کہہ سکتا کہ لڑکیاں چونکہ نازک ہوتی ہیں اس لیے اتنی مشکل فن کو سیکھنے کے لیے رشتہ آسان ہے۔"

"اسی ٹریننگ کے لیے عرصہ پیدا ہوتا ہے؟" یوں تو ٹریننگ ساری زندگی جاری رہتی ہے اگر تکبریہ تو ایک طرح ہم عملی زندگی ہے جس پر ہمارا تمام زندگی کا انحصار رہتا ہے ۔ ویسے مختلف احتمالات کے گزرنے یا پیشش حاصل کرنے میں ڈھائی سے تین سال لگتے ہیں۔ ہر دو ماہ بعد طالب علم کا ٹیسٹ لیا جاتا ہے اور جو کچھ وہ سیکھ چکے اس کے بارے میں آیا جو بہتر پرفارمنس کا مظاہرہ کرے تو پھر اسے بیلٹ دی جاتی ہے۔ سفید رنگ کی بیلٹ سے طالب علم کی تربیت کا آغاز ملتی۔ یہ دس بیلٹس ہوتی ہیں اور اس کی آخری بیلٹ بلیک ہوتی ہے۔"

"نئے طالب علموں کو سب سے پہلے کیا بتایا جاتا ہے۔"

ذہنی تربیت سب سے پہلے دی جاتی ہے اس میں طور طریقوں کی بات بتایا جاتا کسی نہیں یہاں کس طرح آنا اور جانا بات کسی طرح اتنا جھکنا۔ پھر اسے بچھانا یا بچھایا کہ وہ اس فن کو کیوں سیکھنا چاہتے ہیں اگر وہ صرف اسی فن کو سیکھ کر یہ فن سے باہر کسی کے لیے جھگڑنے یا کسی اپنی دشمنی

(باقی صفحہ ۳۵ پر)

ذاتی تحفظ اور دفاع کے حیثیت انگیز فن اِتائی کون ڈوکی

اخبارِ جہاں

اِزروِ حمیدہ نازش

"تائی کون ڈو" جو کراٹے کی طرح ایک حیرت انگیز فن ہے جو کہ آج سے پانچ ہزار سال پہلے قدیم ہندوستان کے شہر "کپل وستو" میں دریافت ہوا تھا۔ اس زمانے میں انسان کا مسئلہ کل نہیں بلکہ آن پر محیط تھا۔ اول کھانے پینے کا اور آخرمیں اپنی حفاظت کا۔ ذاتی دفاع اور حفاظت خود داختیاری اگر چہ ایک فطرت ہے تو۔ اس زمانے کا انسان طاقت کے بل پر کمزور کو زیر کرنے کی فکر میں رہتا تھا۔ اسی لئے انسان نے اپنے دفاع کے لئے سب سے پہلے پتھروں کے ہتھیارہ کا استعمال شروع کیا۔ پھر پتھرو کے دور کے گزرتے ہی لوہے کے بنانے اور اوزاروں سے کام لیا جانے لگا تو یہ تیر بنانے ہے۔ بعد ازاں فولاد کا دور شروع ہوا پھر بارود کا استعمال بھی عام ہو کیا۔ سب طاقت کو مضبوط اور بالادستی قائم رکھنے کے ذرائع بن گئے۔

قدیم دور میں کچھ مذاہب ایسے تھے جن میں خون بہانے کو بہت بڑا گناہ سمجھا جاتا تھا اور ایسے پسندیدگی کی نگاہ سے نہیں دیکھا جاتا تھا۔ وہ مذہب سے بیرو کا راستہ انسان کو تکلیف پہنچانے کو قطعی گوارا نہیں کرتے تھے یہاں کہ وہ جانور کو بھی ذبح نہ کرتے اور نباتات کھاکر انہیں کھاتے تھے۔ ان کے مذہب پیشوا..... ایک جگہ سے دوسری جگہ جب اپنے مذہب کا پرچار کرتے تو انہیں خطرناک راستوں سے ہوکر دوردراز علاقوں کا سفر کرنا پڑتا تھا۔ اس سفر میں ان کا گلہ لٹیرو اور ڈاکوؤں سے بھی ہوتا تھا۔ ایسے وقت پر مذہب کے مبلغوں پیشوا اور کرمی کے ذاتوں کا مسئلہ بڑا نازک تھا۔ وہ خون بہانے سے لے کر کسی کے قتل سے بچنے کی کوشش کرتے تھے۔ اسی وجہ سے انہوں نے اپنی حفاظت کے لئے ایک طریقہ یا انداز ایجاد کیا جس میں مدمقابل یا حریف کو جان کے ہاتھ بھی نہ دینے پڑیں اور اس طرح اپنا دفاع بھی ہو جاتے۔ دلچسپ بات یہ کہ یہ طریقہ انہوں نے جانوروں کی لڑائی کے انداز سے وضع کیا تھا جس میں جبوں اور پیروں کا استعمال کیا جاتا تھا۔ اسے آہستہ آہستہ انہوں نے اس آرٹ کے طور پر مزید دلکش منظر اور پر ووقا کرنا شروع کیا اور یوں یہ فن بہت زیادہ وسعت جانا چلا گیا۔ پہلے تو صرف ایک خاص عقیدے کے لوگوں میں ہی یہ پھیلا۔ لیکن آگے چل کر دنیا بھر میں متعارف ہو گیا۔ جولوگ اس فن کو استعمال کرتے اچھی پانے سیکھتے ہیں۔ وہ یہ جانتے ہیں کہ اسی فن کے ذریعے کوئی بھی انسان اپنا دفاع کتنی طرح اچھا کرسکتا ہے یا یہ کہ اس فن میں جوسب سے بڑی خوبی موجود ہے۔ وہ یہ ہے کہ بغیر خون خرابے کے خلاف کو زیر کر لینے کے لئے اس فن سے بہتر کوئی فن نہیں۔ اس فن کی شہرت اس وقت اور بڑھے گی جب پردہ دارخواتین اگر یہ فن سیکھنے لیں تو نوردوں کی مدد کے بغیر کسی بھی نازک مرحلے میں اپنی عزت، ناموس اور نسوانی وقار کی حفاظت خود ہی کر سکتی ہیں۔

درد انہ مرزا نے ایک لڑکی ہونے کے باوجود کی تائی کون ڈو میں کمال پیدا کیا ہے اور اس کی آخری ڈگری بھی "بلیک بیلٹ" حاصل کر لی ہے۔ اب تائی اور انگیز میں جو ڈو اور کراٹے کا فن اب اتنا پھیل گیا ہے کہ عام طور پر ہر شخص بھی اپنا بنتا ہے دنیا کی ہر دوسرے کرلے کہ سیکھنے کا خواہشمند ہے یا سکھدرورسا کہ کو اس فن کی جانب بہ اتنی زیادہ دلچسپی اسی سبب سے سیکھنے سیکھتے ہیں کہ اس کا پورا جذبہ جاتی رکھی موجود ہو جاتے ہیں۔ اس میں فکری، چالبازی اور اسی کسلی پیدا ہو جاتی ہے حوزم ملکا بھلا لکتے کہ اس کا بہادراسی سیکھ ہوجاتے ہے۔ لڑکیاں اسے سیکھ کر اپنی حفاظت خود کرنے کی اہل بن کتی ہیں اور بری اعتماد کا حوصلہ سیکھ کی نظر سے دیکھیے یہ آرٹ اب عینی شہرت کی حد کا اندازہ آن امارو میں لگایا جا سکتا ہے جہاں اس فن کو

لڑکیاں یہ فن سیکھنے میں لڑکوں سے پیچھے نہیں ہیں

Cover page article in the SundayMashriq Magazine April 1975

Cover page article in the April 1972 AkhbareKhwateen

Miss Jacqueline Adler

Jackie, as we called her, is mentioned here because she made her contribution, directly and indirectly, in the promotion of Tae Kwon Do in Pakistan. When I returned to the USA in 1974, I met her at Master Chong's club in Ann Arbor and requested her to take a visit to Pakistan and train my students, specially girls. She agreed. Jackie graduated in Architecture from the University of Michigan. While she was there she was Vice President of the U of M TKD Club for 1.5 years and President for 2 years. She also served as the Secretary of the American Midwest TKD Federation for 2 years, and Treasurer for the First Inter-collegiate TKD Championships in 1974. She also taught at the UM TKD Club as instructor for many years. Jackie was a Black Belt under Master Chong and a very good performer, both in forms and sparring. She competed in many tournaments and was placed in all of them, winning at least twenty trophies in sparring and forms by 1974.

The Pakistan Tae Kwon Do Association paid for her flight and her stay in Pakistan. She arrived in Karachi on the 29th of September, 1974, and coached at the NSTCC for many weeks before returning to the USA. Her efforts in Pakistan were rewarded with an article in the Black Belt magazine of December 1975, besides being featured in many magazines and newspapers in Pakistan.

She was loved by all the students, and at the end of her stay they treated her with a vacation trip to the northern areas of Pakistan.

Another student of Master Chong, Patrick Harrigan, also visited Pakistan in 1977, but he spent most of his time in India learning Yoga. I wish I had more details on his visit. But I did meet him in Karachi and introduced him to the students at the NSTCC where he trained them for sometime.

More about Jackie can be read in the articles from newspapers and magazines that I have included here, and on the U of M Tae Kwon Do Club website.

Miss Jackie Adler in 1974 with her trophies

**Miss Jackie Adler with Master Saleem Jehangir at Master
Chong's club in 1974**

BE IT EVER SO HUMBLE, SOME PLACES ARE BETTER THAN HOME

BY RICHARD HIRNEISEN

Female karateka finds recognition in Pakistan

Photos by Richard Hirneisen

Miss Jackie Adler in the Dec 1975 issue of the Black Belt Magazine

Karate is a man's world. Few women venture into it and only a very few stay long enough to get their black belts. Those who do face problems most men do not understand or choose to ignore.

A woman in karate — as in most sports and many professions — is caught in a demoralizing double bind. She must prove herself to be as competent as her male peers to earn their respect, but if she displays the aggressive toughness they prize, she is labeled pushy, unfeminine — or worse.

Jacqueline Adler, the first woman to wear a black belt in her instructor's Kang Duk Won organization, confronted this dilemma when she joined the University of Michigan Tae Kwon Do Club in 1970. For five years she has fought to stay on top in a man's world, where her actions have often been misunderstood, her anger ignored. Perhaps because of this conflict, because she is a woman — not despite it — she has been forced to excel to prove herself. She has won more trophies for both forms and fighting than any other student in the predominately male U of M club.

She was elected vice-president of the club in 1971 and president from 1972 to 1974, the first female officer of a traditionally male sports club in U of M history. In 1974 she was elected secretary of the Midwest Tae Kwon Do-Karate Federation, her club's parent organization.

She has assisted in teaching large classes, with as many as 100 white belts on the floor at once. In January, 1975, she took a class of 50 beginners — both men and women — and led 25 of them through to yellow belt promotions in April.

In 1974, shortly after her promotion to black belt, Adler spent four months in Pakistan as head instructor of the Pakistan Tae Kwon Do-Karate Association. She taught hundreds of men and women at the government-administered National Sports Training and Coaching Center (NSTCC) in Karachi and helped establish a women's karate organization that continues to flourish in her absence.

But despite such accomplishments that anyone — male or female — should respect, she is still fighting a battle to be recognized in her own club as a competent karateka. As a beginner she angrily confronted what she calls "sexual politics," challenging her instructors by refusing to obey them when they ordered men into one line, women into another. When Adler refused to obey such commands, she found some support and encouragement among the ranks and tolerance from her instructors. But the tolerance and support often proved more lip service than reality.

When she was promoted to brown belt in December of 1971, her frustrations began to surface. "I felt anger and hostility building up towards some of the men," she recalls. "It's a common thing with women. Every time I had a chance to teach in my own club I was constantly being overruled by men of either comparable rank and less experience or with less experience and less rank altogether. I felt that nobody really respected me for the abilities I had."

Hwa Chong, the head instructor of the Detroit-based Kang Duk Won organization, recognized her abilities and made her assistant instructor of the U of M club. But when organizational paperwork increased with the club's growth, she claims she was shuffled off to the typewriter and off the gym floor. "It was just wearing me down," she recalls. "It was like somebody taking a hammer and continually breaking down the mortar of something I spent four years to build. I just couldn't take that any longer. And if I believed at all in myself, something was going to have to change, if I really believed that anything I did in karate had any value."

A turning point came in March of 1974, after her club hosted a large tournament that drew competitors from all over the Midwest. Although she took the grand championship for forms, she was discouraged with her own and her club's performance. "That tournament made me stop and think that my beliefs and ideas about karate were going to need a lot of work," she explains. "I didn't know how I was going to do it, but I knew that if I wanted my black belt I was going to have to work really hard and consolidate everything I was in karate.

"I was getting really pissed that it would only take men in our club three to four years to get a black belt," she continues, "and here I was over the four-year mark. And dammit, I wanted to do it."

At this time Adler was working 60 hours a week as a draftsman and in her third year in architectural studies at the university. With little time to train, she was getting out of shape and out of favor in her club.

Adler's close friend at this time was Saleem Jehangir, a

JACQUELINE ADLER's long uphill effort to gain recognition for karate abilities was not easy. Even after becoming assistant instructor, sexual politics prevailed and Adler ended up with club's clerical duties rather than a teaching position.

lower abdominal muscles. On inhalation, if the exercise was done correctly, the abdomen could take a powerful blow or support great weight. The 120-pound woman lay down on the floor and asked Doc to step with all his weight onto her midsection. The audience gasped in amazement and Doc refused, but with Adler's insistence, lifted first one foot, then another, placing all his weight upon her body. Doc stepped off and the crowd roared its approval. Adler had scored a success.

The Pakistanis were anxious for her instruction and she immediately began a hectic teaching schedule. Six evenings a week she taught men and women at the NSTCC. In the afternoon she taught 90 young women at three girls' schools. At first few of the women could do little more than a single push-up, but by the time Adler left four months later, most could do ten. "I was overwhelmed by the women's enthusiasm," she smiles warmly. "The stronger they got, the happier they were."

Things didn't go as well with the men. Although they seemed to respect her teaching abilities and politely called her "sensei" in the gym, she guessed they had reservations about her fighting abilities. Asif Hussain, the highest ranking man in the club, had consistently refused to spar with her, making excuses she found difficult to accept. Hussain also had become one of Adler's closest friends in Pakistan. One day she forced the issue and demanded to spar with Hussain. "We squa[r] off," she recounts, "and we started fighting." Hussain [was] impressed with Adler's fighting techniques and did not han[dle] her as easily as he first thought. "And at that point," Ad[ler] continues, "Asif stood there and he said, 'Wow, you can figh[t.]' Those were his exact words. 'I didn't know a woman co[uld]

(Continued on page [ ]

166

Remember, 100 percent protein is out. Protein needs carbohydrate for protection, otherwise the protein goes for energy and is excreted. The kidneys will be strained, fats and waste will accumulate in your body and you'll go into an undesirable state called "ketosis." You'll also miss other nutrients.

Life begins with amino acids and protein. It is a good idea for athletes such as martial artists to get protein three times a day without depending on beef and pork too much. Individual protein needs vary, but if you feel "shaky," maybe you don't get enough. If you have doubts about your health in this respect, see a doctor as serious aspects may be involved here which can't be corrected by diet alone. Diabetes and hypoglycemia (low blood sugar) are a few problems a doctor can diagnose.

BETTER THAN HOME
(Continued from page 31)

fight.' And I just kind of threw my hands up in the air and turned around and laughed because I guess a woman is always going to have to prove herself.

"That was a realization for me too," she concludes, "and at that time even more honesty came out between us and more respect. They saw I could fight and this is the biggest thing these Pakistani people wanted to see."

But soon the meatless spicy Pakistani cuisine, blistering hot climate and grueling schedule exacted a heavy toll on Adler. She was fighting recurring bouts with dysentery, lost 15 pounds and was forced to cut down on her workouts.

The time was nearing for her return to the U.S. and just before Christmas Jehangir went to Pakistan to preside over a promotional test for the Association covered by national TV and press. "That was the high point and the culmination of the whole journey," Adler recalls. "The realization that I was there with Saleem and I had worked with his people and that I really did stand on foreign soil."

Finally, it was time for Adler's return — and all too soon. "I couldn't stay any longer. All of a sudden the next morning I was supposed to be on my plane and away. Maybe I'd come back and maybe I wouldn't. I cried and all those people were coming by to shake my hands and people wanted autographs. They were saying goodbye and I was just dying . . . because the realization was there that it was all over. I was very, very sad to leave because I had become immensely close to these people."

Back in Ann Arbor by Christmas, Adler was preparing for final exams, eating meat and gaining weight. "Somehow," she says, "I expected my trip to Pakistan to be a cure-all, but it wasn't. Because of my new self-confidence I became a threat to those close in rank to me. And because of my experience, I have become hard-core and radical in my beliefs, my desire to change things.

"I've now been forced," she continues, "to accept that my ideas and beliefs and the way I want to do karate might alienate me from those people I trained with for all these years. I may have to go somewhere else but I will always maintain my allegiance to Mr. Chong and kang duk won."

Adler's complaints and frustrations, victories and defeats are not unique. Most women, in many areas of our society, share them. Her conviction that things can be changed, that women should and will someday be respected for their abilities — which she is helping to define — is remarkable. Her contribution to the martial arts, her devotion to her art and her ideals, are fine examples for anyone, regardless of sex. ✄

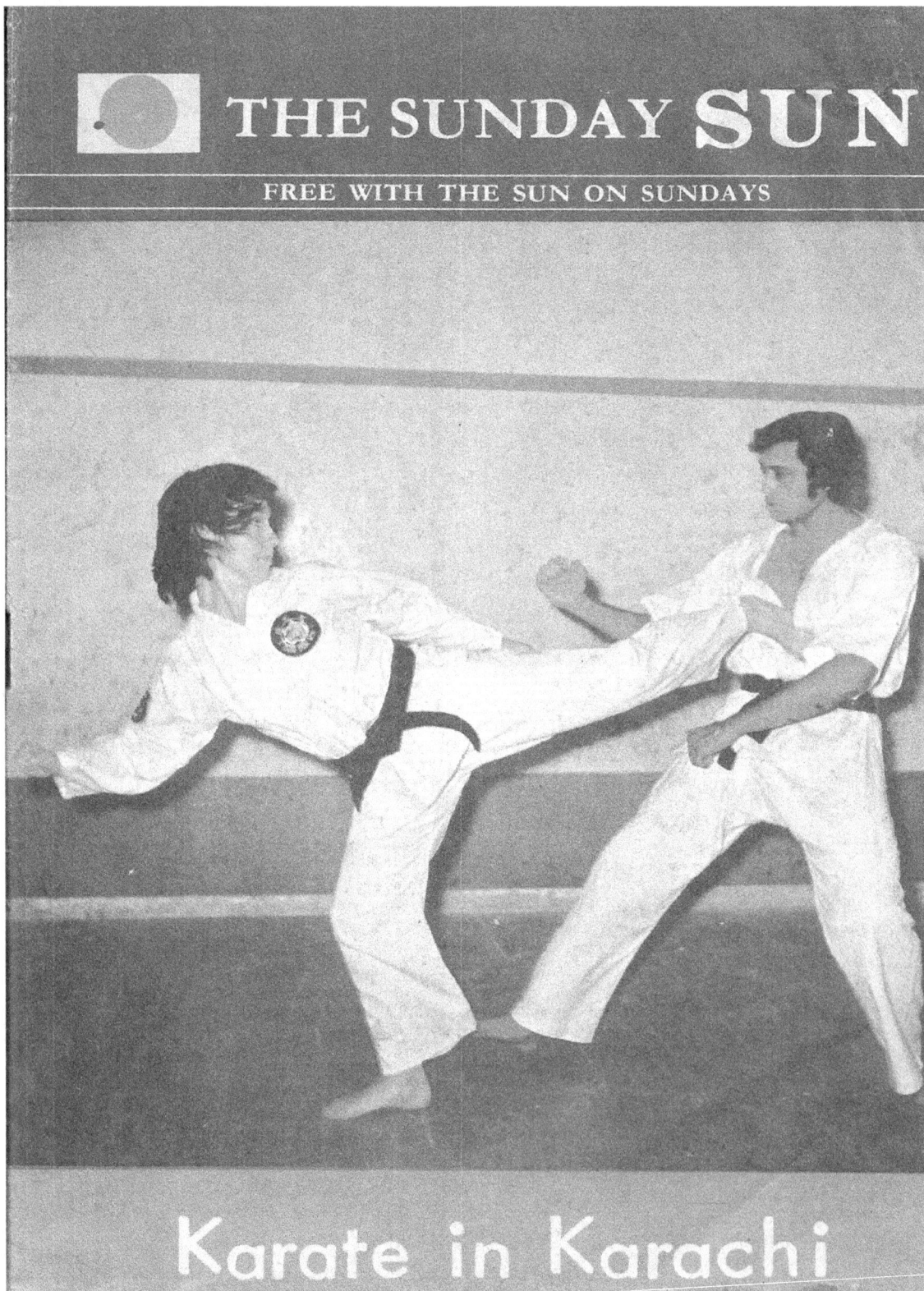

THE SUNDAY SUN

FREE WITH THE SUN ON SUNDAYS

Karate in Karachi

**Miss Jackie Adler with Mussarat Hussain on the cover
of The Sun magazine**

Karate in Karachi gets a

KARATEKA FROM CALIFORNIA

By Riaz Ahmad Mansuri

Cover :
Visiting Black Belt from
USA, Miss Jacqueline Adler,
at a coaching class.
Colour transparency
by Abdul Wahid.

Deadly by name, yes, but not deadly by nature---or in looks. That's Jacqueline Adler, one of the most genial American girls I have ever met.

Karate trainees at Karachi's National Sports Coaching Centre know well enough how deadly their attractive new instructor from California can be. Be it white belt or blue, or the whole range of belt colours in between—green, red or yellow—Black Belt Miss Adler, when she wants it, can leave her combined class of male and female students literally black and blue.

Relax just a bit and before you know it, you are flat on the floor because Miss Jacqueline has struck you with the speed of a panther.

An architect by profession, Jacqueline Adler came to Pakistan last month from the United States. She has been invited by the local Karate and Judo Association to coach young Pakistaniboys and girls in the art of Karate.

I met Jacqueline Adler during a coaching session at the National Sports and Coaching Centre. I asked her the following questions:

How did you get into Karate?

"I had a girl friend who was impressed by Mr. Chong who is recognised the world over as a leading exponent of Karate. Mr. Chong has been teaching Karate for a long time in the USA. She suggested that I should go and watch him at his coaching classes. I was immediately fascinated by him because Mr. Chong was so good. He would talk about what one could achieve and he had such a motivating philosophy of Karate. This is the kind of philosophy that is also followed in daily life. He told us that a person is always capable of having better things in life. He told us he believed that one should always work with one's potential. The system of theories on the nature of things and the rules for the conduct of life which Mr. Chong told me were strong enough for me to come under his influence and one

Jacqueline Adler leading training class.

day, rather abruptly, I decided to become a Karateka girl.

"I joined Mr. Chong's classes in 1970. Today I am a Black Belt—first dan. I think anyone else can achieve this because taking interest is the important thing. My ideal is to promote brotherhood and sisterhood between peoples. This is more important."

How do you feel about being a woman Karateka?

"I fell being constantly challenged. I discovered people think Karate is harmful. I will say it is nothing like that. It's only a system that promotes brotherhood. It's a very cool sport, a peace-maker and it is easily understadable."

"With me it was like this. I always wanted to learn how to fight, to take care of myself. I think everyone has a basic desire to be able to take care of one's self. A lot of people don't admit that they have this basic desire and they thus look at Karate as something dangerous. People learn Karate just because they want to beat people up. But I believe that every person, deep inside, wants to take care of himself and so do I."

If attacked by two strong men, could you defend yourself?

"Let me be frank about one thing here. I can fight men all right but it depends upon the circumstances. I have the self confidence and the concentration and I would not be afraid of getting hurt in fighting my way out of such a situation."

"What would you say to the kind of glamour that's given to Karate in films?

"I feel the kind of Karate commonly shown in movies is not real Karate. It's shown only for the sake of fun, to make people laugh mostly. A few of the one's who do Karate fights for films, like Bruce Lee, are good. Lee is a magnificent person, very talented and he is very beautiful to watch but the story lines in films are usually designed to make the Karate fights fit in."

Is Karate very popular in America?

"Karate is'nt winning many followers in the United States. Everything over there is Kung Fu and it's popular because television programmes have turned it into a craze. But there are lots of Karate Schools coming up too."

What do you feel about the standard of Karate in Pakistan from what you have seen of it in Karachi?

"In Pakistan Karate has a good standard, very good. All the students are dedicated and loyal. They have a strong beginning but they need more instruction. Anyway, they are very good for the facilities they have. Blue Belts who are far below Black Belts, are instructing the beginners. The fact is that there should be one Black Belt at least for the purpose of higher training. That's why I am here. I have met two or three boys in Karachi who are very good. For instance, Red Belt Syed Asif Hussain is an extraordinary karateka. The standard of Pakistani boys is definitely comparable to that of boys in America. The only thing is that I don't see any brown belts around here."

Do you think there is any potential for future development of Karate in Pakistan?

"Yes there is, but what it requires, initially, is development in other areas of physical fitness—like muscle and stamina training, weight training and running. Karate pupils over here should work out at least thrice a week. Six hours a week is the mimumum I would suggest."

What could be done to further popularise Karate in Pakistan?

"One way of doing it would be to show karate instruction films on TV. The art of karate contains some very good spiritual ideas that will surely be of interest to the people of Pakistan. Opening more clubs in different towns, especially at school level, is another way. I think Karate should also be introduced, like we have in our country, in such peace-keeping forces as the police and so on."

What would you say about the standard of female karatekas here as compared to the male?

"I find that there is very little interest for Karate over here among girls. But personally, I don't think girls should consider themselves as anything exceptional. Every girl should play some game. Karate teaches a special kind of self-confidence. It leads to mental well-being and gives you the sort of strength that cannot be got from anything else. It also teaches you to get what you want and to control aggressiveness. After all, one should only be aggressive when there is need for it, otherwise you have to learn how to control your aggressiveness."

Jacqueline Adler is in her early twenties. She was born in Santa Cruz, California and went to school there. Six years ago she shifted to Michigan to attend college and has been living there since then.

"Michigan has a nice community" she says, "and a lot of different cultures. It is a big cultural centre in fact. A lot of cultural groups come to Michigan and in this way one is exposed to a variety of things. Karate is one of them."

Agile and very alert looking, Jaqueline Adler does'nt love Karate all the time though it is her first love. She has been a good gymnast and a swimmer. Being single, she lives in an apartment of her own in Michigan. Her other interests include photography and music.

"I am a singer too but I love listening to eastern classical music," she says. The late Ustad Amanat Ali Khan and Ravi Shankar are her favourites. She was eager to meet Amanat Ali Khan but unfortunately the Ustad died just a few days before her arrival in Karachi. Jacqueline often listens to the raagas of Amanat Ali. She has them taped on a cassette."

Jacqueline says she has'nt decided about marrying yet.

"It's not necessary that my husband too will be a Karateka. What I am interested in is a man with a good heart and understanding."

Every evening after the coaching classes are over, Jacqueline sits with her students and discusses various things about Karate with them. She has also learned a bit of Urdu such as "Asalam-o-Alaikum, Shukria, Khuda Hafiz, Pani, etc. She

The spin kick to the solar plexus.
Jacqueline and Massarat.

tries to use these words often.

"I would love to learn more Urdu while I am here," she says. About her stay in Pakistan, says Jacqueline:

"I am being looked after so well, I often think it's a dream."

Jacqueline Adler

Miss Jacqueline Adler, from Michigan, U.S.A., is a moving ball of electrified strength and agility when dressed in a gi and practising — Karate.

Jacqueline Adler is on a four month coaching trip to Pakistan on the invitation of the Pakistan Tae Kwon Do and Judo Association. Since her arrival in Karachi in September, Jacqueline has been holding regular coaching classes at the National Sports Coaching Centre on Stadium Road. And her pupils, at all levels, have quite a fair idea of the extraordinary fighting and defence capabilities that she possesses.

Jacqueline is not a very old hand at Karate. Jacuqline started Karate just four years ago — in 1970. And today in 1974, she is already an established Black-belt holder of the First Dan.

What brought Jackie — as her pupils and friends call her—and Karate together?

In 1970, while she was attending college at Michigan, she happened to visit the Karate school of the renowned Mr. Chong with a friend. She was so fascinated by what she saw and heard that she developed an immediate liking for the art of Karate. Mr. Chong impressed her as a teacher. But what was more, the philosophy of life that Karate taught, clicked with Jackie's own philosophy of life. An so, it was from that day that Jackie fell for Karate. She is a architect by profession and single.

If there is any one person who has played any big part in bringing Jackie closer to Karate, it is Mr. Chong, the Karate master under whom she received her training and reached the standards of physical fitness and deftliness that she is at now.

She says she has been very impressed by what Mr. Chong has taught her not only about the techniques of the art but has also coached her in its philosophies. It was in fact the soundness of the thinking behind the art of Karate that initially attracted Jackie to this discipline of self-defence.

Jacqueline describes Mr. Chong's philosophy as "motivating" because it is also the philosophy that is followed in daily life. Jackie says, Mr. Chong told her, a person was always capable of having better things in life provided one utilised one's potentials to the full.

"The system of theories on the nature of things and the rules for the conduct of life which Mr. Chong told me, were strong enough for me to come under his influence," she says.

Jackie joined Mr. Chong's classes in Michigan in 1970. From then, onwards, it was no looking back for her, because she achieved one honour after another till she got the Black Belt and became one of the few American women to hold that honour.

The following will give some idea how Jackie progressively developed into a master Karateka.

November, 1970 — At Memphis,

The advanced Kata. Jacqueline Adler.

Tennessee, Jackie got 2nd place in the women's form.

February, 1971 — Trenton, Michigan — again 2nd place in the women's form.

June, 1971 — Lansing, Michigan — this time it was 1st place in the women's form.

December 1971 — An Arbor, Michigan, it was 1st place for Jackie for "Overall Best Performance" both in sparring and forms, in the combined "Men and Women's Section".

Nov, 1971 — at Lansing, Michigan, 1st place in women's sparring.

Jan, 1972 — at Memphis, Tennesee, it was 3rd place for Jackie in the women's form and 4th place in women's sparring.

April, 1972 — at Baltimore, Maryland, — Jackie got 2nd place in the forms section and second place in fighting (sparring).

Feb, 1973 — again at Baltimore, Maryland, Jackie scored firsts in both forms and fighting.

Nov, 1973 — at Toronto, Canada, Jackie managed second places in both forms and fighting.

Jan, 1974 — at Detroit, Michigan — Jackie got 1st place in the women's form.

Feb, 1974 — at Ann Arbor Michigan, Jackie stood first both in women's and men's fighting.

March 1974 — again at Ann Arbor, Michigan, — she got 1st place in women's form and 2nd place in sparring.

Then came the great moment.

Right after this, Jackie was declared

GRAND CHAMPION FOR FORMS which meant that she had achieved First place amongst all 1st place form winners including men Black Belts. That's when Jackie received her own Black Belt.

Apart from Canada, Jackie had not been to any other country outside the United States on a Karate assignment.

Jacqueline demonstrating a technique with Asif and Yahya.

When Pakistani Black Belt, Saleem Jehangir met her in Michigan, he was immediately impressed by her capabilities. He invited her to visit Pakistan, to coach boys and girls at the training school that the local Tae Kwon Do and Judo Association was running in Karachi.

Jackie was quick in accepting the offer and in a few months, time, she found herself in Karachi. This is her first visit to the Eastern part of the world in her own words, "it has been exhilirating."

کراٹے کا فن

جیکولین سے سیکھئے

انیس ہارون

خواتین شوہر سے لڑنے کی بجائے کراٹے کی مشق کریں: ایک ماہرانہ مشورہ

"اگر زندگی کی تیز رفتاری آپ پر جھلاہٹ طاری کر دیتی ہے تو اپنے غصّہ کا شکار گھر والوں کو نہ بنائیں۔ میرا مشورہ ہے کہ اس صورت میں شوہر سے لڑنے یا بچوں کو مارنے پیٹنے کے بجائے کراٹے سیکھیے۔ اس طرح گھر کا ماحول بدمزگی سے بچا رہے گا۔ اور آپ کی ذہنی اور جسمانی صحت بھی ٹھیک رہے گی۔ اکثر گھریلو خواتین اپنے احساس محرومی اور غصّہ کے اظہار کی کوئی راہ نہیں پاتیں۔ کراٹے کی مشق ایسی خواتین کی جارحانہ جبلّت کی تسکین کا بہترین ذریعہ ہے۔"

خواتین کو یہ مشورہ دینے والی کراٹے کی ماہر مس جیکولین ایڈلر ہیں۔ جو آج کل پاکستان آئی ہوئی ہیں۔ یہاں کراٹے اینڈ جوڈو ایسوسی ایشن قائم ہے۔ جس نے اپنے ارکان کو تربیت دینے کے لئے جیکولین کو امریکہ سے بلوایا ہے۔ جیکولین یہاں مسٹر سلیم جہانگیر کی مہمان ہیں جو ایسوسی ایشن کے صدر ہیں اور اس کے بانی ارکان میں شامل ہیں۔ سلیم جہانگیر آج کل امریکہ میں ہیں۔ وہیں ان کی ملاقات جیکولین ایڈلر سے ہوئی۔ جیکولین امریکہ کی ان معدودے چند خواتین میں شامل ہیں۔ جنہیں کراٹے کے فن میں "بلیک بیلٹ" حاصل کرنے کا موقع ملا ہے۔ کراٹے کے فن میں جیکولین کی مہارت کو دیکھتے ہوئے سلیم جہانگیر صاحب نے انہیں پاکستانی لڑکوں اور لڑکیوں کو تربیت دینے کی دعوت دی۔ جسے جیکولین نے قبول کر لیا اور ۹ ستمبر کو کراچی پہنچ گئیں۔

جیکولین ایڈلر کی شہرت کے چرچے سن کر ہم نے ان سے انٹرویو کرنا چاہا۔ وقتِ مقررہ پر جب وہ اخبارِ خواتین کے دفتر پہنچیں تو میں انہیں دیکھ کر حیران رہ گئی۔ نرم و نازک اور شگفتہ سی جیکولین کو دیکھ کر مشکل ہی سے یقین آتا تھا کہ وہ کراٹے کی ماہر ہیں۔ ہم تو سمجھ رہے تھے کہ وہ ضرور کوئی لحیم شحیم پہلوان نما خاتون ہوں گی۔ لیکن جیکی ہماری توقعات کے برعکس نکلیں۔

"یہ بتائیے کہ کراٹے کی شوقین ہونے کے باوجود آپ نے اپنی نسوانی نزاکت کو کس طرح برقرار رکھا ہے۔"

یہ میرا پہلا سوال تھا۔

"یہی تو غلط تاثر ہے" جیکولین مسکراتے ہوئے کہنے لگیں "خواتین کا خیال ہے کہ وہ کراٹے سیکھ کر اپنی نسوانی نزاکت کھو بیٹھیں گی۔ جبکہ معاملہ اس کے برعکس ہے۔ کراٹے ایک ورزش کی طرح ہے۔ یہ ورزش جسم کو سڈول اور متناسب بناتی ہے۔ اس سے بدن میں پھرتی پیدا ہوتی ہے اور ذہنی بھی صحت مند رہتا ہے۔"

"آپ کو کراٹے سیکھنے کا شوق کیونکر پیدا ہوا۔"

"میں بچپن ہی سے کھیلوں میں دلچسپی رکھتی تھی۔ میری شدید خواہش تھی کہ کسی ایسے کھیل سے منسلک ہو جاؤں جو میرا مشغلہ بھی بن سکے اور مجھے تمام عمر صحت مند رکھے۔ کراٹے کو میں نے ہر اعتبار سے بہترین کھیل پایا۔ چنانچہ اس کھیل میں میری دلچسپی بڑھتی گئی اور میں نے باقاعدہ تربیت حاصل کرنے کا فیصلہ کر لیا۔ جیکولین چار سال سے کراٹے کی تربیت حاصل کر رہی ہیں۔ اور اب تو وہ "بلیک بیلٹ" بھی لے چکی ہیں۔

کراٹے کی تربیت کی ابتدا سفید بیلٹ سے ہوتی ہے۔ جوں جوں زیرِ تربیت افراد اپنے فن میں مہارت حاصل کرتے جاتے ہیں انہیں مختلف درجے دیئے جاتے ہیں، جس کی ترتیب یہ ہے یلو بیلٹ، گرین بیلٹ، بلیو بیلٹ، ریڈ بیلٹ، براؤن بیلٹ اور آخر میں بلیک بیلٹ۔ بلیک بیلٹ میں بھی نو ڈگریاں ہوتی ہیں۔ جیکولین سات ڈگری تک بلیک بیلٹ ہیں۔ اگر وہ باقی دو مدارج بھی طے کر لیں تو کراٹے کے اعلیٰ ترین اعزاز تک پہنچ جائیں گی۔

جیکولین نے منگھم یونیورسٹی کے کراٹے کلب میں تربیت حاصل کی ہے۔ ان کے استاد کوریا کے مسٹر چنگ وا تھے۔ جیکولین کے ساتھ ابتدا میں دو اور خواتین اس فن کی تربیت حاصل کر رہی تھیں، لیکن کچھ عرصے بعد ان کی ہمت جواب دے گئی اور یہ تنہا رہ گئیں۔ "لڑکیوں میں یہی تو خامی ہے" جیکولین کہنے لگیں۔ "وہ کوئی کام شروع کرتی ہیں تو اس کو پایہ تکمیل تک نہیں پہنچاتیں۔ حالانکہ ان کی صلاحیتیں مردوں سے کسی طرح کم نہیں ہوتیں۔"

جیکولین نے بتایا کہ امریکی لڑکیوں میں کراٹے بہت مقبول ہوتا جا رہا ہے۔ یونیورسٹیوں کے علاوہ پرائیویٹ کراٹے کلب بھی اچھی خاصی تعداد میں ہیں۔ ان کے درمیان مقابلے بھی ہوتے ہیں جنہیں لوگ بڑی دلچسپی سے دیکھتے ہیں۔

امریکی لڑکیوں میں کراٹے کی مقبولیت کی وجوہ پر روشنی ڈالتے ہوئے جیکولین نے کہا "دراصل امریکی لڑکے اور لڑکیاں ہر نئے رجحان کو بہت جلد قبول کر لیتے ہیں۔ نئی چیزوں میں دلچسپی لینا ان کی فطرت میں شامل ہے۔ لڑکیاں

باقی اگلے صفحے پر ملاحظہ فرمائیں

اپنے مخالف کو زیر کرنے کا ایک انداز

اونچی کک اور مکّہ بازی مدافعت میں بڑی مدد دیتے ہیں

غو خوشند ہیں لیکن انہیں اپنے والدین سے اجازت نہیں ملتی۔
وہ سمجھتی ہیں کہ اس سکول کی لڑکیاں مروانہ روش اختیار
کرتی ہیں جس کی ساخت محض بگڑ جاتی ہے۔ یہ خیال غلط
ہے۔ پاکستانی لڑکیوں کو تو اپنے تحفظ کی شدید ضرورت ہے
اور خود اعتمادی تو ہر قدم پر کام آتی ہے۔

کراٹے جاننے والی خواتین، گھریلو زندگی میں جارحانہ رویّہ اختیار نہیں کرتیں

مدافعت کا یہ فن لڑکیوں کے لیے بہت مُفید ہے

صفحہ ۹ سے آگے

Miss **JACQUELINE ADLER**, a charming young American who is a Korean Karate Black Belt has been in Karachi for some time training Pakistani boys and girls in Karate at the National Youth Centre.

In an interview with **THE HERALD**, she described Karate as a martial art, a means of self-defence, and a moral and spiritual discipline with peace as its main theme. Karate, she maintains, is not for killing but to gain confidence and to belong to a Karate brotherhood and sisterhood based on the essential theme of peace and to enter into warm human relationships among people belonging to different countries and different cultures

…"A Karate expert can be a lethal person but only because you can kill does not mean that you should kill. You are still an ordinary person in your own special way. My Korean instructor tells us" 'if you want to kill go out get a gun, go out and get a good knife…

THE HERALD. What is Karate?

JACQUELINE ADLER: Karate is many different things to different people. It's a philosophy and a way of life. It's a way of making our bodies physically healthy and physically fit so that eventually it thinks fit. We want to coordinate our mental power with the physical power, and to produce a better person. So it starts at a very small level to encourage people to reach out and improve our cities and our culture. It is a universal philosophy.

Q. In other words, it's a physical as well as a moral discipline?

A. Right! Many times in Karate the mental and the spiritual aspects are left out so during my stay here I'll repeatedly emphasise this other side. Karate is a sport, a martial art and a means of defence but it is also connected with mental growth.

Q. Where did Karate originate?

A. Karate originated in China and it can be traced back to its early origins even back to India. But Chinese were actually first to come up with different schools and teaching methods. India has lost this art.

Q. How many kinds of Karate there are?

A. You have Chinese Karate, that is, Con fu, you've Japanese Karate, and Korean Karate. There is also the Okinhawa Karate.

Q.How is one Karate different from any other Karate? How does, for example, the Chinese Karate differ from the rest.

A. Con fu is like a discipline, a hard style to master. It's based largely on animal styles. They have seven major Schools of Con fu and they are all based on animal motion and the way animals like tigers, dragons, etc. fight among themselves. So Con fu is very spiritual and it's taught in monastories and the religious aspect is very strong. Over the ages as Con fu spread in other countries they modified it and consequently, the spiritual aspect was left behind. When the Koreans started working with Karate they studied in depth all these, and so a lot of changes are taking place. I think Korean Karate is more practical. It takes something like 20 years to master Con fu. It is so difficult, so complex. By simplifying it, taking out the best part of it, a lot of Koreans have come up with a style that is best; more effective; a lot better; you can learn much faster. In five years, you could become pretty proficient in Korean Karate with the same efficiency and effectiveness as Con fu would take 15 to 20 years.

Q. And Japanese Karate?

A. In Japanese Karate they use less kicks, Korean Karate is known for its very beautiful kicks, high kicks, spinning kicks turning kicks, and flying kicks. It is known for the strong use of feet and equally strong use of hands. Japanese Karate also uses kicks but not with the same variation as the Korean, and they are perhaps more limited. But it should be remembered that a good master of Karate, no matter what style, should be very beautiful. If you take all the styles — Chinese, Japanese, Korean, Okinhawa — try to attain the same goal to strive to attain the same pure ideals: Not to do anyone any harm but to use the strength and knowledge you have developed for the betterment of mankind.

Q. What about the spiritual aspect?

A. The spiritual aspect is getting lost. Our style however strives to save as much of the spiritual aspect as possible. The style of Kang Duk Won means "home of pride and virtue". So, we try and maintain a very virtuous attitude and a balance between the physical and the mental.

Q. Does it have anything to do with religion?

A. In some ways it can have a religious aspect, for example, meditation: the Buddhist Concept in India, Buddhist Concept in Japan, the Buddhist Concept in China. The idea of oneness of the universe, the search for inner peace and harmony within ourselves.

Q. What is Okinhawa Karate?

A. The distinguishing feature of Okinhawa Karate is the use of weapons. Centuries ago, they used what we now call Van Chukka, a rice beater. They would take a stick with a chain or rope wrapped on it and another stick and beat the husk with it. This virtually is a weapon. In a fight they swing it around with the twist of the arm. It can be used to grasp a person by the wrist and flick a person around. So the Okinhawa is a lot more weapon.

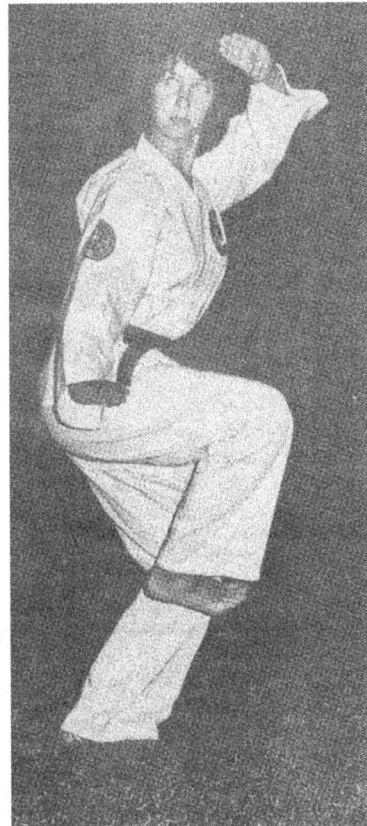

Q. How do you practice Karate? How do you start?

A. You usually start by just being very aware of your own body, to discover how much your body is capable of taking on a very personal level. When you know what you can do, then you start working up to reach your goal. So, let us say you start by gentle exercise, by limbering up, by learning to stretch your arms and legs, and, once you gain strength, you can do push-ups and sit-ups. It's like gentle exercise. Then you start learning techniques like kicks, punches and different sorts of Sudos, which are comically called Karate chops, and eventually you grow yourself. If in the beginning you can't do any push-ups, you keep working and maybe in a couple of months you do ten push-ups, and, all the time, you are aware of the idea for personal growth. You should never compare yourself with any other person. This is very individual.

Q. Is a Karate punch like a boxing punch?

A. No. A Karate punch is much different. It uses your full body power. A lot of power comes from the low stances, so the punch weighs down to the back and even to the rib cage. When you stand up with a twist, the twist at the end will have a lot more drive force and power than a boxer's job. A Karate punch must also have a lot of speed, much more than

23

chopping your way to peace

BY THE HERALD STAFF

in boxing.

Q. Are there any particular targets?

A. The body has several target areas. One is the solar plexus which is where the rib cage meets and makes a tender spot. The other target area is the floating ribs around the kidneys. In Korean Karate we only aim above the belt, so nothing below the belt is a target. We use the **FRONT** of the face. So you are very limited. If you are fighting an opponent you must observe control. If you are using the techniques to the face, you should not cause bleeding or bruises. It must be just a contact, the idea being to drive in with a lot of force and a lot of power but to have the control to pull back. To know that you could go on and do damage but have the control not to do that. A glance, just a light touch.

Now, to the body, we generally use more contact. It might be rough. Sometimes there would be soft contacts, sometimes hard depending on the person's development and rank. The higher the rank the harder the contact.

Q. How do you use "Sudo"?

A. Sudo is used at a person's neck.

Q. What's more important; the punch or the Sudo?

A. Punch is just another technique. A round kick, a front kick, a spinning kick, a side kick, a flying kick, a punch, or a Sudo are just different techniques to gain your point, to defeat your opponent. Equal emphasis is placed on different techniques. Some people may be better at a particular technique or a combination of techniques

Q. Where and how did you learn Karate?

A. I started Karate in January 1970 when I was a student at the University of Michigan. And I was very interested in Judo but the Judo training camp folded up and my room-mate told me there was a very good Karate instructor in Michigan. This man was a champion, a Korean champion, and he was an excellent instructor. His philosophy gave us moral strength; he was encouraging. His primary belief was that everyone was really capable of more than one thought one was. So, his desire was to encourage us to do more and to become better — and through constant practice one could always be better — that one should always reach for the stars. And this is very important in order to gain confidence. Karate gives you a lot of confidence. If you want to do well at school gain confidence. You should always be conscious of that. If you sincerely work for something, — whatever — in a very honest way, then you would eventually achieve it. He gave us a lot of beautiful, spiritual ideas which were very helpful. Confidence, patience, confidence that you could achieve your goal.

Everyone is very special. And the feeling associated with Karate training are very, very special because the people they train with become very friendly and close. A brotherhood and a sisterhood comes out of this hard physical training which makes you clean and clear in your thoughts. I came to Pakistan on a plane, all alone and I met a lot of people who are all our friends, although they all come from different cultures, different countries. This should be brought out. It is the goodwill and harmony that they are striving for.

Q. How long did you train?

A. I started in Jan. 1970. I had a slight injury, I hurt my leg, so I was out for a while. This injury had nothing to do with Karate. And then I attained a brown belt in December 1971. I had my black belt in Jan 1971 and I started teaching in Jan 1972, and, since then, I have been an instructor and I have taught at the university of Michigan. I worked very closely with the chief instructor, Mr. Salim Jehangir. He is unable to be in Pakistan this time because of his job in the United States. Now I was going on a vacation, so it is nice to take a vacation here and help the club.

Q. Are there any qualified instructors in Karachi?

A. Oh, yes! There are qualified instructors here at the Youth Centre. The training will continue after I have left (in early December)

Q. Is the age factor important?

A. We generally have a student start at not younger than 10. After that anyone can join. The important thing is how serious a person wants to be. Sometimes a person at 11 is much more serious than a person at 22. So how far one can go and what one can achieve depends upon an individual and not on one's age.

Q. How many students do you have now?

A. We estimate right now about 200 in Karachi at various schools and at the Youth Centre.

Q. Is it necessary to take lessons every day?

A. In the beginning, we have two to three sessions a week. These classes last about two hours. So, in total we spend 6 hours a week. One must attend at least two sessions a week, otherwise the development would be so slow that it would not be worth the trouble. After six months if a person wants to achieve his goal he should consider training four to five times a week. My own training was six days a week, and if I was travelling throughout the United States and if I had a tight schedule oftentimes I was trained three weeks in a row without a day off. That is training every day. So, the better you want to be the more time you must spend. **END**

Black Belt Jackie Adler Brings Bodhidharma's Ancient Art To K.A.S.

by Jawed Syed

The word Karate is the English equivalent of two Japanese characters, "Kra" meaning empty, and "Te" meaning hand. As nearly as can be determined, a form of this modern art of self-defense began several thousand years ago in India. It was brought to China by the Indian Budhist Monk, Bodhidharma, who on foot, alone and unarmed, successfully completed his journey across the Himalayan Mountains. Drawing upon the knowledge and experience gained from his journey. Bodhidharma developed a physical, mental and spiritual discipline which came to be known as Zen Buddhism. He knew that if properly developed, the human body could be a far more diversified and effective weapon than any instrument. Bodhidharma got his knowledge from observing animals, especially the breathing and relaxation techniques of the big cat. He invented striking techniques from watching insects, reptiles, bears, and dogs. The manpower weapon which Bodhidharma introduced to his followers came into this modern world as Karate.

In different countries, Karate has different names, such as Kung Fu in China, and Burmese Burendo in Burma. The most famous method practised throughout the the world is Korean Karate, generally known as "Tae Kwando", the syllables literally meaning foot, fist, and martial art.

Tae Kwondo has existed in Korea for over twenty centuries. It has become the most practiced form of self-defense because the Koreans were the first to realize that a human body has more power in its legs than in its fists. Thus the Koreans combined Karate with their famous Korean foot fighting called "Tae Kwon", which

Miss Jaqueline Adler poses for our Nomad photographer after a training session with K.A.S. students in the gym.

was developed over 1000 years ago, forming "Tae Kwondo".

In Tae Kwondo, mainly defensive moves are studied and practiced. The entire body is thought of as a weapon .One defends against an aggressor by using feet, open hands, fists, elbows, knees, and any other part of the body. Because of its tremendous power, Tae Kwondo is often misunderstood and thought to be a dangerous and violent sport. But its purpose is purely defensive.

Tae Kwondo is now becoming popular in Pakistan, through the efforts of Mr. Saleem Jehangir, a second Dan Black Belt, and chief instructor of the Tae Kwondo Club in Karachi.

KAS boasts its own Tae Kwondo enthusiasts. If one goes to the KAS gym on Tuesday afternoon or Saturday morning, he will find 13 sweating, tired, but happy bodies practicing Tae Kwondo. The class is instructed by Miss Jacqueline Adlow a female Tae Kwondo Black Belt from Michigan. Miss Adler, who is studying Archi-

tecture at the University of Michigan, and is the University's Tae Kwondo instructor, has won the "Best Performance of Form" Grand Championship trophy in 1974, at the first "University of Michigan Inter-Collegiate and Open Tae Kwondo Tournament". She placed first on women's form and second in sparring. Miss Adler is temporarily in Karachi as the guest of Mr. Jehangir.

Mansoora Rashid, a junior at KAS, holds the highest rating (Green Belt) of the KAS students in Miss Adler's class. Mansoora also has trained under Mr. Jehangir at the National Coaching Center. KAS students taking Tae Kwondo are also happy to have Mr. and Mrs. Dillon joining them.

Importance of Tae Kwon Do Training in Pakistan

Teach them Philosophy and Martial Arts in schools when they are young. Socrates

After all that I have written in this book, it should become evident that this is one way we can shape up our youth, mentally, physically, and spiritually. When our youth has embarked on such a rigorous training, it is they who will bring about the required change in our society. In fact the society will change automatically because they will be its only habitants, we will be long gone. I read a quote at the entrance to the Disney World in Florida, it said:

> We have not inherited this world from our ancestors, we have borrowed it from our future generations.

When I started the training of TKD in Pakistan, it was only one person, me. Now there are thousands practicing it, and hopefully their lives have changed for the better. If you want to change a whole nation, you change just one generation, and the change becomes permanent.

Pakistan is a country that has been fighting for its survival since its birth. Unfortunately, it is still in the infirmary, in infant critical care. There are forces, both domestic and international, working to destroy it. Every accomplishment to date has been like a castle built on sand, destroyed by the next wave that came in. Every institution existent in the country has been corrupted and facing an unthinkable end. The American threat to send Pakistan back to the Stone Age is coming true, day by day. And we will continue to be in this state till we eliminate the forces, internal and external, hazardous to its survival. Although we may be economically poor compared to the developed nations, we are rich enough to sustain ourselves, only if our riches can be recovered from the plunderers and looters of the nation's wealth.

Our National Character has been reduced to one of a beggar, a looter, a thief, a corrupt, a sick, unhealthy, illiterate, and at best complacent. You name it, and every one of us will fall in one category or the other.

We need to build the nation's character all over again, with a renewed approach. And we need to concentrate on our youth, starting from the youngest first. We need to nurture their characters with moral and ethical strength, with sound bodies and sound minds, disciplined in all phases of life, so they can become The Warriors of tomorrow, whose goals would be to do the Supreme Good. We need to build martial spirit in our nation, so they can stand their ground and fight for Right. At the same time we need to teach them to be calm and patient, so they don't destroy their own national assets and achievements. They need to be those who will not only save themselves from destruction, but help save others, and ultimately the nation. They need to be the ones who will stand firm with confidence to root out the evil from our society, and who will give others the strength to make themselves secure and safe from evil. They need to be the ones who are humble and approachable by all, who are a source of strength to others, who are disciplined and can lead by example, leading our communities into brotherhood and stability.

In doing so, they will build a better society, free of rampant evil and corruption, free of fear and insecurities, a society that will be confident, at peace, and constructive.

Such good can come if we only put our minds to it. It can come through the training of martial arts in our schools and colleges. There have been many nations in the past who have done this, so can we.

Coming Soon

Volume II

- Philosophy of Tae Kwon Do

- Philosophy gives you direction. The philosophy of Tae Kwon Do is to make you a perfect human being, one who is perfect in all phases of life. It is extremely vital to understand this philosophy, if you want to learn the real art of Tae Kwon Do. This chapter is dedicated to help the student in understanding the subject, and give a direction in life on which to concentrate all energies.

- Basics of training

- A building is as strong as the foundation it stands on. In any martial art, the real power comes from these basics. Learn how to develop that strong foundation on which you will construct the building of Tae Kwon Do.

- Self defense and offense techniques

- Learn how to effectively defend yourself and counter attack in real life situations.

- Sparring

- Learn the differences between sport Tae Kwon Do and the real art, the effective from the ineffective, the real life combat from the sport.

- Sport Tae Kwon Do rules and regulations

- Since the new generation is following sport Tae Kwon Do and competing on international levels, this chapter has been included for their benefit.

- Good health and eating habits

- You cannot be a perfect human being without having perfect health. Learn how to choose the right dietary habits.

- Character building and reformation of society

- This is perhaps the most needed theme for our nation. Korea's national achievements were due to the character building of their society in which Tae Kwon Do played a major role across the nation in every field, from military to government, from education to business. Tae Kwon Do developed the character of the entire Korean nation. Every nation can use its philosophy and training to do the same.

Volume III

- Basic and Advance Forms (Hyungs) in Tae Kwon Do

- Forms are the heart of Tae Kwon Do. Unfortunately, new forms have replaced old forms. This book brings back the old classic traditional forms that were developed by the original masters of the art who not only understood the philosophy of Tae Kwon Do but also borrowed from nature the themes from its elements to devise these forms. These forms are key to developing power, coordination, focus, rhythm, and flow. This volume includes the major forms taught in the past from the white belt to the advanced black belt levels, forms that may never be taught again, but which hold the secrets of the power that once used to be Tae Kwon Do.